TAKING A STAND

TAKING A STAND

Moving Beyond Partisan Politics to Unite America

RAND PAUL

New York • Boston • Nashville

Center Street
Hachette Book Group
1290 Avenue of the Americas
New York, NY 10104

www.CenterStreet.com

Printed in the United States of America

RRD-C

Originally published in hardcover by Hachette Book Group.

First trade edition: January 2016
10 9 8 7 6 5 4 3 2

Library of Congress Control Number: 2015936247

ISBN 978-1-4555-4957-3 (pbk.)

For Kelley

if i weren't so much in love with you
i'd paint lilacs and lilies
and stills of fruit languishing in bowls
insanely my love for you commands
run headlong into the first volley
cast caution to the wind
the bulls run only once
be fleet
and flaunt a brazen portrait
for you know
love lasts only when the passion bleeds
and gurgles and rattles as if it might be
the last gasp

Contents

1.	The Long Stand	1
2.	A Medical History	11
3.	Health Care: A Doctor's Opinion	29
4.	Getting to Work	51
5.	A New Kind of Republican	63
6.	Can You Hear Me Now?	79
7.	On the Road	105
8.	Waiting for Superman	123
9.	Government Overreach	133
10.	Economic Freedom	151
11.	The War on Liberty	171
12.	The War on Christians	189
13.	Defending America	207
14.	Peace Through Diplomacy, Trade, and Financial Solvency	233
15.	Libya: A Jihadist's Wonderland	243
16.	Tree Hugger	259
17.	A Look Forward	277
	Appendix	287
	Notes	294
	Acknowledgments	301
	Index	303

1

★ ★ ★

The Long Stand

I will speak until I can no longer speak. I will speak as long as it takes, until the alarm is sounded from coast to coast that our Constitution is important.

★ ★ ★

11:47 A.M. March 5 to 12:39 A.M. March 6, 2013

I was about seven hours into my filibuster when I saw Senator Mark Kirk coming down the senate chamber's stairs. Mark had suffered a major stroke a little more than a year before, so it took some effort for him to manage the descent. Along with his cane and the smile on his face, he held a thermos and an apple.

It had been a while since I watched the classic movie, so at first I didn't understand the significance of what Senator Kirk carried. In the filibuster scene in *Mr. Smith Goes to Washington,* Jimmy Stewart's character, Jefferson Smith, puts an apple and a thermos of tea on his Senate desk.

To be honest, I didn't think I was going to get to stand at all, let alone for thirteen hours, which was the full length of the time I held the Senate floor to block the nomination of John O. Brennan as CIA director. I was sure Harry Reid, the Senate Majority Leader, wouldn't allow the filibuster. But to my surprise he did.

Had I known, I would have been better prepared.

When people ask me what I would do differently the next time I stage a filibuster of that length, my answer is simple. "Tennis shoes," I tell them. "The next time I'll wear tennis shoes."

At the time of the filibuster, I'd been a senator for a little over two years. I'd won my seat by a considerable margin and in doing so took the establishment by surprise. I also came into the Senate carrying a mandate for smaller, more responsible government spurred by a movement that had taken the whole country by surprise. The idea of smaller and more responsible government, however, was nothing new to me. I've believed in those values long before there was a Tea Party.

I was eleven when I first campaigned for my father. Our whole family would stump with him at Texas barbecues and parades. With my brothers, sisters, and cousins, we knocked on literally thousands of doors, handed out campaign literature, and rode around in a van featuring a fat Uncle Sam on the side and the slogan "Put Big Government on a Diet!" You could say I grew up with politics. My father was in Congress for more than twenty years. His first term was back in 1976 when I was just thirteen. As kids, my brother and I would go for paddleboat rides in the Tidal Basin in front of the Jefferson Memorial. In high school, I spent summers in Washington, D.C., working as an unpaid intern in my dad's office. Later, while attending Baylor University, I was president of Young Conservatives of Texas (YCT). After a year, I was elected to the YCT's state board. It was there I got to know Stephen Munisteri, who had volunteered for my dad at age seventeen, went on to be a five-year Texas GOP State Chair, and recently became a senior adviser to my presidential campaign.

While I was completing my ophthalmology residency at the Duke University School of Medicine, my wife, Kelley, and I founded and chaired a watchdog group called North Carolina Taxpayers Union (NCTU), which kept track of state politicians' spending and pork. Each year we published ratings.

We were twenty-seven-year-old newlyweds working long and crazy hours—me as a first-year resident in ophthalmology at Duke and Kelley working in marketing communications for Nortel Networks in Research Triangle Park.

I drove to the legislative library in Raleigh whenever I had free time, pored through massive logs of the legislative votes taken, and created a ratings system based on how each representative had voted on the major spending and tax bills for each session. This was long before any of this information was available on the Internet, so it was tedious and time-consuming work.

I talked Kelley into writing our pamphlet copy and creating a layout for the ratings—not an easy feat since she was already working long hours and traveling across the country for Nortel.

We held meetings in our home and persuaded all of our friends—most of whom were other young Duke resident physician couples—to join our group, also not an easy feat since most of them were too busy and frazzled to even think about politics. But we usually included pizza, beer, and Duke basketball on the TV, which enticed plenty of new converts. Walter Jones was a state representative then and an adviser to the group. Walter would go on to win a seat in Congress and become one of my father's best friends.

At the end of the state legislative sessions, Kelley and I would go up to the state capitol in Raleigh and hand out report cards to the state lawmakers. Last year, when I was campaigning for Thom Tillis, the newly minted senator from North Carolina, a man came up with an NCTU scorecard from 1992 and asked me to sign it.

NCTU was my first foray into politics on my own, and even I was surprised by its success and the attention we were able to draw. We made contacts with concerned people from all over the state; one particularly active group was strongly opposed to the idea of a food tax. Within six months after I formed NCTU, both the local nightly news and the Raleigh and Durham papers had covered us. Across North Carolina, candidates used our ratings to run against big-spending incumbents. In a photo from the Raleigh papers, we are standing on the capitol steps with a rented podium and microphone, Kelley in her black Ray-Ban Wayfarers. We look like kids. We were.

Looking back, I think that our accomplishments with NCTU taught us both an important lesson: that a single person with an idea—and the passion, drive, and energy to put it into action—can make a difference.

When I finished my ophthalmology training at Duke, Kelley and I moved to Bowling Green, Kentucky, about thirty miles from Russellville, where Kelley's parents live. There we formed a new taxpayer group called Kentucky Taxpayers United and produced a "taxpayer's scorecard" with which we rated state legislators once again. By then, however, most of my attention was focused on my young family and the beginning of my career as a physician.

Physicians have a unique way of looking at life. In medicine, we first diagnose the problem and then go about implementing the remedy based on facts, not preconceptions. I came to find that such linear thinking doesn't happen all that often in the halls of Congress. We pass thousand-page bills no one has read. I work in a city where logic is the exception. We can't even pass things we agree on. I couldn't even get a vote on a bill that I cosponsored with Harry Reid. When I think of how screwed up Washington is, I think of a Groucho Marx quote. "The art of politics," he said, "is looking for problems everywhere, finding them, misdiagnosing them, and applying the wrong remedies."

While members of Congress spend their time blowing hot air at one another across the aisle, the president and his administration make a mockery of the separation of branches as defined in the Constitution. There is likely no greater problem we face than the executive branch usurping power that was assigned to the legislative branch. In some ways Congress is to blame, as Congress leaves the power it's supposed to assume lying around on the ground for the president to just vacuum up.

Still, this president has gone further to collapse the separation of powers than any of his predecessors. If the executive branch can initiate war, if it can detain citizens without a trial, if it can amend legislation, if it can declare Congress to be in recess, then government unrestrained by law becomes nothing short of tyranny. The president is blunt about it. He opines that Congress won't act, so he must. He has "his pen and his phone" and he will simply ignore Congress, never mind the Constitution. First he amended Obamacare without congressional action, then he amended immigration law without Congress's approval, and then he proceeded to fight another war in the Middle East without congressional authority. He has broken his own promises—those he ran on as a presidential candidate—by expanding warrantless NSA surveillance of cell phone records, and he has ignored due process of law by ordering extrajudicial drone strikes that kill suspected terrorists, including American citizens. I worry that, as the separation of powers collapses, the law will become unrestrained, arbitrary, and will eat away at our freedoms. We already live in a time when unelected bureaucrats write most of the laws. Tens of thousands of pages of laws are written by officials from an alphabet soup of agencies: OSHA, EPA, IRS, USDA, and the list goes on. Meanwhile, one truth remains: Congress never voted on any of these laws, nor did the president sign them.

I began my filibuster in the hope of sounding an alarm from coast to coast. The administration had already killed an American citizen with a drone without first charging him and, worse, was ambiguous over whether it would conduct such an egregious act against the Constitution on American soil. I asked that question at the beginning of my filibuster, but it took the White House nearly thirteen hours to answer it. As the minutes, then hours, of my filibuster went by, I was fueled by the thought of an outraged citizenry and I knew my filibuster meant much more than just blocking Brennan's nomination.

Yes, I was standing for due process of law. Yes, I was standing for the right to a trial by a jury. But I also stood for a United States that doesn't spy on its own citizens, a United States where a person's home and records are private, where law enforcement needs a warrant to enter a home or search your records. I stood for a United States that despises the idea of encroachment on personal liberty.

I stood for a United States that requires its president to obey the Constitution.

That America doesn't allow the bipartisan looting of the Treasury, the bipartisan destruction of our currency, and the bipartisan sprint away from a republic limited by a constitution to a democracy limited only by majority rule. In that America, Congress decides when to go to war.

In that America, the Bill of Rights isn't so much for the *American Idol* winner, the prom queen, or the high school quarterback as it is for the least popular among us, especially for minorities—whether that person belongs to a minority by virtue of skin color or a shade of ideology. You can be a minority because you live in a poor neighborhood or because you choose to teach your children at home.

That's the America I stood for.

I had no idea what was going on outside the Senate chamber during my filibuster. I was allowed only to talk and listen to questions. If I stopped speaking for more than thirty seconds or sat down, I would lose the floor. I could only monopolize the floor as long as I kept standing. I wasn't even allowed to keep the thermos and apple. Unlike what is depicted in the filibuster scene in *Mr. Smith Goes to Washington*, food and drink are prohibited in the real Senate chamber.

When I started to walk around to loosen up my legs, Senator Ted Cruz arrived at the chamber and read some of the tweets that were coming in, the first time such an occurrence had happened on the Senate floor, where cell phones are not allowed. From those tweets I discovered that I wasn't alone, that the Bill of Rights was not a lost cause, and that millions of Americans—Republicans, Democrats, and Independents—were excited to have someone stand up for the right of every American of whatever origin, black or brown, Arab or Jew or Christian, to be tried by a jury of his or her peers. To the surprise of official Washington, the Twitterverse exploded in agreement.

Not until the next day did I find out the extent to which my filibuster had influenced social media: there had been something like a million tweets with the hashtag #StandWithRand.

America's sense of justice was awakened, and millions of citizens—from all political viewpoints—were suddenly demanding answers. Finally, after thirteen hours and a million tweets, Eric Holder responded to the simple question I had posed at the beginning: "Does the president have the authority to kill an American citizen not engaged in combat, on American soil, with a drone?"

His answer: "No."

In the chapters that follow, you will learn some things about me that might surprise you. I'm not, for instance, the carbon-copy conservative of your grandfather's GOP. I want a New GOP that resonates with America, that looks like America—white and black, rich and poor, with tattoos and without. I want the New GOP to, once again, be the champion of individual rights. I believe that the reason the Republican Party hasn't connected with minorities is because we haven't tried hard enough, and I'm going to fight to change that.

I believe the GOP brand is broken, that many young people and many people of color simply won't even consider voting for or becoming a Republican. It's time for change, and the first part of changing is admitting your mistakes. Remember when Domino's Pizza finally admitted that it had bad crust? They got rid of the old crust and made a better pizza. I'm all for getting rid of the old crust in the Republican Party.

In the pages ahead, you'll find out about my journey to becoming a physician and how being a doctor defines me as a politician. You'll find I'm a tree hugger, literally—just ask my neighbors who watched me trying to grow a variety of trees, including giant sequoias, in my yard. I'm a Republican who wants clean air, clean water, and the life-extending miracle of electricity. I compost. In fact, I built my composting bins from the remnants of an old tree fort I built for our kids. None of this is at odds with wanting our government to be smaller, with wanting our regulatory bodies to protect both our land and water—and our ability to create jobs and provide affordable power to our citizens. Too often this balance is portrayed as an either/or proposition.

If you get to know me, you'll find I am as independent of petty partisanship as you'll find in Washington. I don't care if you're a Republican, a Democrat, or a Lilliputian. If you've got a good idea, I consider it. If I were president, I would analyze our problems and seek solutions regardless of party politics. I've sided with Democrats on civil liberties, and I've sided with Republicans on economic liberties. I've sided with Independents on reforming our criminal justice system. It took four years of lobbying, but I finally persuaded the Senate to sit down for a bipartisan lunch to be held regularly. Harry Reid even stood up at the first one last February and thanked me for not giving up on the idea. I'm predictably unbiased, and I consider that to be an asset.

I'm also a man of peace through strength. I believe the defense of our country is a president's first priority. I grew up as a Reagan Republican and believe that an unparalleled national defense is the greatest deterrent to war. Woe to those who would attack America or Americans on my watch—no matter where that happens in the world. But I also know there are too many of my colleagues who are far too eager for war. The decision to put boots on the ground always needs to be weighed against the enormous price that our soldiers have paid in life and limb during the long war in the Middle East and Afghanistan.

Every decision must consider first the cost in human lives. Because, for me, far deeper than my political conviction is my faith and my belief that we are all creatures of God, that human life is unique and should be protected, and that with life comes liberty—the two are indivisible. I believe that defense of personal liberty is the primary function of government. These beliefs provide an unshakable foundation that forms me as an American and as a man.

My belief in God is as much a part of me as my love for my family. I know that people across this great country share this level of faith. It's our secret weapon. When the president says we're clinging to our guns and our religion, that's my family and me. The elites may fly over us, but we still vote and we still believe in our God-given rights.

Not for a minute do I believe that America's best days are behind her. The challenges that we now face also provide an opportunity. I look to the horizon and see a future that is filled with hope and a people confident in their beliefs.

Imagine a time when liberty is again spread from coast to coast.

Imagine a time when our great country is again ruled by law.

Imagine a time when our country is once again led by lovers of liberty.

I see an America that is again innovative, self-reliant, and bold. I see an America worth taking a stand for.

2

★ ★ ★

A Medical History

Sometimes the best discoveries are not only what you find, but what finds you.

★ ★ ★

I was a sophomore in high school when I decided that I wanted to be a physician, like my father. As any other kid, up until that point I had other priorities, not all of which were helpful. But once I found my calling, I began to pay more attention to my studies. I decided to read books outside and beyond what was required of me in school, and I asked my father if I could go with him into surgery at the hospital.

I was fascinated by the technical skill and the confidence it took to open someone up, repair the problem, and put them back together again.

I knew, however, that my goal would only occur with great perseverance, some skill, and a little luck. I knew it wouldn't be easy. I went to college knowing that I would have to get good grades and not let up for a moment. Looking back, it's tempting to say my path was smooth and easy, but that would ignore the day-in and day-out work that it took to make it through college, medical school, and residency. The only way you get through it is to look only a few feet in front of you and not contemplate the whole.

Halfway through my third year in college, when I was twenty-one, I took a semester off to help my father in his 1984 U.S. Senate campaign. He lost, but the highlight for me was getting to debate Phil Gramm and Rob Mosbacher at the Pink Elephant Ball in San Antonio in front of 300 people. I remember being very nervous appearing alongside a sitting congressman and a wealthy businessman. Not so nervous, however, to resist informing the crowd of primarily establishment Republicans that the Gramm-Latta budget had nearly three times more debt than Jimmy Carter's most recent budget. I wasn't sure if Gramm remembered the night, but twenty-six years later he commented, "I listened to him pretty closely," he said, "and I remember the young man did quite well."[1]

I took the medical school entrance exam in the fall of my third year at Baylor, and Duke University School of Medicine accepted me early. I studied nonstop the entire previous summer in my carrel in the honors library at Baylor and achieved my best standardized test score ever—scoring higher than 90 percent of all premed students taking the test. Duke is my father's alma mater, and it gave me great satisfaction to follow in his footsteps. I worried some about the expense of going to a private medical school rather than a state school in Texas, but my dad told me not to worry. He wanted the best for me, he said.

On my first day in medical school, I rode my bike to class and sat down in the back left-hand corner of the Duke amphitheater. Little did I know that some of the young men and women around me would become lifelong friends. Three of them would be groomsmen in my wedding. Together, we would become physicians, overcoming the natural human inclination to avoid pain, blood, and suffering in the process. Together, we would go through the rite of passage that two thousand years ago Hippocrates understood to be knowledge that was not always easy to cope with and was not for general consumption.

While studying at Duke, I lived in the basement of a brick ranch house belonging to a widow named Mrs. Deal, and I would mow her lawn and do other yard work in exchange for rent. When the mower wouldn't start, I used the trick of dipping the spark plug in a little gas and trying again. I'd ride my bike to school in good weather, with an old station wagon that belonged to my parents as backup transportation. My friends gave me a hard time about the old station wagon. The lining of its roof hung down in the back, and since it appeared to be a dump my friends treated it as such and left their trash behind whenever they rode with me.

Often the station wagon wouldn't start, and I'd have to use a variation of the lawn mower trick. This maneuver, however, took two people to perform: one to sit in the driver's seat and turn on the ignition, and one very brave person to toss a little gas onto the carburetor just as the key was being turned. Though a small explosion would occur, more times than not the old station wagon would rumble to life.

Years later, when I returned to Duke for my ophthalmology residency, Kelley and I went back to visit Mrs. Deal. She made us dinner, and Kelley got to see my med student living quarters. Mrs. Deal also hosted families who had relatives at Duke University Medical Center for prolonged cancer treatment. Living under the roof of this kind woman had brought me some of the comforts of home.

I needed them. My first year at Duke was a flood of information. I relied on the work ethic I've had all my life and kept my head above water. As a medical student, I worked in three different Veterans Administration hospitals in North Carolina, one in Fayetteville, one in Durham, and another in Asheville. The VAs operated under a single-payer system, like the Canadian health-care system. What that means of course is that the government pays the tab—as it should for veterans. But it also means that the health care is rationed. I'm not breaking any news here by telling you there are long waiting lines at VA hospitals. When I was working at them, medical students went home only after we did the workup of our last patient. I often wasn't seeing my last patient until ten o'clock at night, so I had to get creative. I started asking the vets how long they'd been waiting. Some would say, "Since noon." So I started going down to the waiting room to find my patient. Sometimes the vet would be outside smoking a cigarette, and I'd say, "Look, the system around here is not good. It can take you ten hours, but we can speed things up if we do the workup now." I would do the workup before they were even checked in, drawing their blood and getting an EKG done. I knew somebody in X-ray, so I'd also get the X-ray done. In those days, med students had to learn about the disease and come up with a diagnosis and treatment for each case. I'd research the disease while the vets were waiting to check in. Once they were checked in, I'd stick the labels on the file and the vials, and both the patient and I would cut several hours off our day.

I thought of my days at the VA recently when the scandal erupted over veterans dying while waiting for care and VA administrators using fake waiting lists to hide the problem.

When liberals are aghast at waiting lists and lines for care at the VA, I remind them that the VA is the single-payer system they all covet.

The care wasn't bad in the VA hospitals of my time. Yes, there were young surgeons in training at the hospitals I worked in, but we were working under established doctors and surgeons. Nor do I believe the quality of care is bad today. What's bad is the distribution of veterans' health care. It's not the quality of the doctors and nurses working in the VA system that is the problem, but the economics of distribution, or, in the case of the VA, the poor distribution due to the lack of a pricing mechanism. Today, the problems are likely worse, as we have hundreds of thousands of disabled veterans from the two-decade-long war in the Middle East. Frankly, there are only so many doctors and surgeons to go around in VA hospitals. Under this system, the only way to distribute veterans' health care is to ration it. Everyone eventually gets care—that is, if they survive the wait time. It's the same principle on which Obamacare is based. Just like the VA system, Obamacare inflates demand through subsidies and tax credits. Demand then overwhelms supply, which causes rationing through mandates and waiting.

As I moved toward graduation from medical school, I began considering a specialty. I'd become fascinated by the idea of curing diabetes by transplanting insulin-making cells into "privileged" areas, locations where the body protects itself from immune responses. Two of those locations are the brain and the eye.

I spent my third year of medical school researching the immune status of the eye. My thought was that since the cornea and, to a certain degree, the entire eye is in somewhat less contact with the immune system during development, perhaps the eye's relative privilege might hold the answer for finding a place that wouldn't reject transplants of insulin-making cells. At the time, researchers were using similar logic to inject insulin-making cells into the fluid around the brain. Was a cure for diabetes to be found in this world of relative "privilege"? I was young and, like many med students, I believed that we could one day find a cure for most diseases. I spent plenty of late nights transplanting corneas into rats that had graciously volunteered. Even before I earned my MD, I published a solo-authored paper in the prestigious *American Journal of Ophthalmology*—an achievement of which I am very proud. It was a great honor, as very few medical students are sole authors of a peer-reviewed paper. My research was one of the reasons I began to pursue a career in ophthalmology.

The other reasons were my grandmother's eyes and a jar of pennies.

The story of the pennies begins in Pittsburgh, first in my father's childhood home and later mine in Texas.

My father had watched the pennies accumulate in a jar in his parents' kitchen. At the time, the country was just coming out of the

Depression, and his parents collected the pennies as savings, not as a hobby. Some of the coins were Indian Heads that dated back to the early 1900s. The pennies intrigued my father, and he offered to buy them from his father, who agreed, but only if his son paid above the market price—$25 for about 900 pennies. In those days $25 was a significant sum for a kid to have saved. My grandfather was both a practical man and a father who refused to favor any one of his five sons over the others. The surcharge would ensure that he wasn't making an exception for my dad. My father, though, having sorted through the pennies, knew that one of them was a 1909 S, which was rare. He gladly paid the premium.

My dad has always had a knack for successful investing, and he still looks at every penny he gets.

In about second or third grade, I became interested in collecting coins. My maternal grandmother, Carol Creed Wells, or Gram, as we called her, had taken over and added to my father's collection. I remember as a kid, when we'd go to visit, climbing four flights of stairs to her attic to see the coin collection. I knew the coins must be valuable to be hidden so deeply amid the rafters.

Gram would buy unsorted "wheat" pennies for me to look through. Wheat referred to the reverse side of the penny, which had two strands of wheat. The penny was minted from 1909 till 1959, and so by the 1970s the wheat penny was somewhat of a rarity.

There is a framed photo of Gram in the foyer of our house in Bowling Green that never fails to attract comments from guests. In it, she sits sighting a rifle in the crook of her shoulder. A row of carbines is seen in the background. The picture was taken in the 1930s at a shooting range at Ohio University, where Gram was a member of the rifle team. A stand for women's rights and the Second Amendment all in one photograph—I love it!

As a child, I spent hours with Gram. I've always felt very comfortable with older people, and my relationship with my maternal grandmother is one of the reasons why. Together, we'd pore through piles of change looking for mint marks while she told me stories. One of my favorites was of my maternal grandfather, who climbed in an open window of her dormitory one night at college when he was her beau.

As the months and years went on, however, Gram's sight began to dim. Soon we were spending our time together at the ophthalmologist's office instead of sorting coins. First she had her cataracts removed, then her corneas replaced, and finally she received the sad news that macular degeneration had irreparably damaged her retinas.

The study of corneal transplant research at Duke led me to my specialty, but it was the memory of Gram's dimming sight that cemented my decision to become an ophthalmologist.

Love Story

It's funny, but when you start looking back at life, the events that seemed so disconnected while you were experiencing them suddenly fall into perfect order. After I graduated from Duke Medical School in 1988, I took six months off to help my father campaign for the presidency. I traveled the country, mainly speaking to college crowds. Then, in January 1989, I began my general surgery internship at Georgia Baptist Hospital in Atlanta.

One Saturday afternoon, in April of 1989, I went to an oyster roast at a friend's house. When I walked out to the sunny backyard filled with twentysomethings eating, drinking, and socializing, I never imagined that I would meet my future wife that day. While I'm not always the most outgoing person, that spring afternoon something was in the air. Life is full of serendipity; you just need to recognize it when you come upon it. Sometimes the best discoveries are not only what you find, but what finds you.

The day I met Kelley, she had come to the oyster roast to meet a guy she was seeing on and off. To my good fortune, the soon-to-be ex-boyfriend was called away from the party—a friend of his was involved in some type of fender bender, I think. I was standing by the keg pouring myself a beer when Kelley and I first spoke. It was a brief encounter. Kelley didn't seem overly interested in me, much to my disappointment.

She later told me she thought I looked so young she figured I was still in college and, at twenty-five, she had no desire to meet an undergrad.

That evening, standing in the noisy, crowded kitchen, I found another chance to speak with her. Kelley told me she was working as a marketing communications manager for Sprint, the telecommunications company. A few years before, she had graduated from Rhodes College in Tennessee, where she'd majored in English. I'd taken many English classes in college and am a great fan of literature. I love the novels of Dostoyevsky and the short stories of Hemingway.

I tried my best to woo her with literature and wit, anything I could possibly think of to keep that dramatic, smart, and beautiful girl in the blue striped sundress from walking away again. We talked for a couple of hours and then I surprised myself with my boldness. I leaned over and gave her a brief kiss. We still laugh about it sometimes, since it was so out of character for me. What else can I say? I was already in love.

I asked for her phone number but didn't have a pen to write it down. I promised that I would remember it. Kelley half rolled her eyes. What were the odds that I would remember, her expression read. But I wasn't about to forget that number. I called her the very next day.

The following May, I invited Kelley to take a trip with me to Roan Mountain, North Carolina. We packed a picnic lunch and found a beautiful spot surrounded by rhododendrons, with a view of mountains all around. At the time, I was finishing up my surgery internship in Atlanta and was about to begin my ophthalmology residency back at Duke. I would be moving back to Durham in a month. I knew Kelley wouldn't move from Atlanta to Durham unless I showed her I was serious, especially since she quickly changed the subject whenever I tried to "casually" mention all the great companies in Research Triangle Park that she might want to look into.

I had hidden an engagement ring in the picnic backet. I'd purchased it just the week before with the money I earned working as a locum tenems (the Latin term means placeholder) doctor in various small hospitals on weekends. I was praying hard she'd say yes, and it was one of the very best moments of my life when she did.

We were married in Trinity Episcopal Church the following October in Kelley's hometown. Tiny Russellville, Kentucky, which was named in honor of Revolutionary War general William Russell in 1798, has a colorful history. Jesse James once robbed a bank in the town, an event that is re-created every year on horseback during the annual Tobacco Festival. Homes in Russellville date back to the early 1800s, and four Kentucky governors have lived there.

We were married in the evening and when our wedding party and guests stepped out from the storybook brick church, glowing paper lanterns illuminated the entire downtown street leading to the beautiful, historic Bibb House, where our reception was held. Once owned by Major Richard Bibb, a Revolutionary War officer and early abolitionist, the home was built in 1817 and is steeped in the Southern tradition. The white reception tent and lanterns, beneath a canopy of crimson maple trees, lit up the lawn in front of the grand home.

Kelley's bridesmaids included her college friends Brigid, Blair, and Meg, my sisters Joy and Lori, and Lally, Kelley's childhood friend. My brothers Ronnie and Robert and Kelley's brothers David and Jeff were groomsmen, along with my medical school friends George Ibrahim, Keith Ozaki, and Mark Goldberg. My dad was my best man.

We lived in Durham for three years while I finished my ophthalmology residency. Kelley took a job with Nortel Networks in Research Triangle Park, North Carolina. We had a blast those three years. Most of our friends from the residency program were newly married as well, and we all had a lot in common. We'd go out to dinner in Chapel Hill, go on deep-sea fishing trips, and spend weekends in the mountains in Asheville. We were especially close to Phil Ferrone, a fellow ophthalmology resident, and his wife, Jeanine. The Duke men's basketball team won back-to-back national championships during this time, and Phil, Jeanine, George and Stacey Ibrahim, Kelley and I, and others of our ophthalmology gang watched just about every game on television together, and often went to campus afterward to celebrate the big wins.

We were in our house in Durham with friends watching Duke vs. Kentucky in the 1992 NCAA men's finals. With 1.4 seconds to go, Kentucky sank a two pointer to go ahead by one. At the time we were Duke fans (after twenty years in Kentucky and with two boys at UK, our allegiances have shifted), so we were all pretty dejected. We were sitting there silently on the couch during the timeout and suddenly the phone began to ring. This was before everyone had a cell phone, and Kelley walked into the kitchen to answer it, thinking there was nothing more to see in the game.

Precisely at that moment Christian Laettner made his inconceivable basket, sealing Duke's come-from-behind victory. Because of the phone call, my wife missed one of the most famous shots in college basketball history—maybe *the* most famous. To make matters worse, whoever was on the phone hung up without saying a word. A year later Kelley's brother Jeff admitted he was the caller. A Wildcat fan, he had called a bit prematurely to razz us about Kentucky's victory.

During my residency, Kelley and I played on an ophthalmologist softball team called the Sy-Clops, named for fellow ophthalmology resident and team organizer Sy Maroi. Our uniform shirts featured a baseball mitt with a single large eyeball in the middle—gotta love that ophthalmologist humor! We had a great time and at the season's-end cookout Kelley was awarded a kitschy baseball figurine for being the most improved player. She says it's her only athletic trophy.

Our newlywed years in North Carolina were very happy, and we made many friends who have stayed in our lives through the decades. Kelley comes from a military family, and she likened our experience to hers growing up—people linked together in a common cause.

In 1993, as I came close to finishing my three-year residency, I began looking at ophthalmology practices. I looked at some in North Carolina and one in my hometown in Texas where there was an opening at a large practice. By then, Kelley was pregnant with William, our first son. To be honest, I thought we were going to go to Texas, but I came home one night and saw a look on my wife's face that told me otherwise. Kelley had talked on the phone that day with her mother, Lillian, and by the time their conversation had concluded, Kelley decided she wanted to go home. Including college, she'd been away for thirteen years. She is very close to her parents and wanted our children to grow up knowing them, especially since they had no other grandchildren nearby.

Mimi and Papa have been a big part of their lives and ours. I mentioned life's serendipity earlier, and I can't think of a better example than what occurred at this time. Had I gone to work in a practice in Texas or North Carolina I can't imagine where my life would be right now. I'm sure we would have been happy. I'm sure we would have been together as a family. But I'm just as certain I wouldn't be the United States senator from Kentucky.

We moved to Bowling Green that summer, just six months after William was born. Kelley's mom helped find us a brick ranch house that we rented there, only a short drive from Russellville. I loved my work and began to form professional relationships and friendships that have lasted until today. Although I interviewed for a few jobs in larger cities, my desire was always to practice in a small town. I grew up in a small town in Texas just like the one John Cougar Mellencamp sings about.

Setting up practice in Bowling Green, I knew I could fulfill my small-town dreams. There I would see my patients at church or in the grocery store. I loved being part of a community small enough that most people knew one another.

I performed cataract surgery but prided myself on doing a variety of operations, from straightening the eyes of children to examining the eyes of premature babies, to plastic surgery around the eyes, to corneal transplants. In a small town, with few subspecialists, I was able to practice many different types of surgeries.

After a year or so of establishing my medical practice, I became eligible for board certification. I passed both the written and oral portions of the American Board of Ophthalmology exam on the first try, in the summer of 1994. In fact, in each of my three years as an ophthalmology resident, I had passed the written board exams. So when some critics say I'm "self-certified" they often don't understand the full history of my experience both as a decade-long member of the American Board of Ophthalmology and my subsequent decision not to recertify with them.

Shortly before I passed my boards and was certified by the American Board of Ophthalmology, the organization's governing directors voted in a rules change requiring a new recertification exam after ten years—but only for younger ophthalmologists. Even though we had passed the same tests the older ophthalmologists had taken, the new rules exempted them from recertification requirements. The recertification demanded travel to a testing site (I took my initial board exam in Chicago) and payment of test fees every ten years. All older ophthalmologists, or those certified before 1993, were not required to do so to maintain their full certification.

I organized a protest, along with several hundred other ophthalmologists, against this unequal policy. As a newly minted member of the ABO, I thought it unfair that it was requiring recertification for younger members but not older ones. As you can imagine, the older doctors didn't quite see it that way and voted to be "grandfathered in"—so as not to be bound under the new rules.

If anything, it was the older members who were more distant from their training and potentially needed recertification. For example, I worked with surgeons at the time who had taken their boards once, as far back as the 1960s, and were still considered fully board-certified for life, but my certification from 1994 was suddenly only valid for ten-year increments.

I consider the nationwide protest I led to have been a noble fight. Our protest was met with deaf ears, and so a group of younger ophthalmologists and I formed our own board, the National Board of Ophthalmology (NBO), to compete with the ABO.

I have always believed that competition raises the level of quality in nearly every aspect of life, and medicine should be no different. After all, the ABO is a private certification group, which has absolutely nothing to do with a doctor's medical licensure, which is overseen and governed by the state medical boards. This is another point that is often left out by those seeking to deliberately misrepresent the issue. Our group was an attempt to create competition among *private* specialty certification boards, and had no bearing on state medical licensure or oversight in any way.

Political opponents and a few of their journalistic allies made accusations that our competing board was comprised of my wife and father-in-law because their names were on the incorporation papers required by the state, but the truth is entirely different. The new board was comprised of talented young ophthalmologists from Boston to North Carolina to Kentucky who weren't looking for a way to avoid recertification but seeking to have the rules apply to everyone equally, regardless of age.

For more than a decade, I fought this battle, finally shaming the ABO into requiring that at least the test givers be required to recertify. I took no financial gain from my efforts. The NBO ultimately netted about $20,000, which I donated to the international Orbis Flying Eye Hospital.

Only in politics could an effort like this be distorted and sullied by opponents with an agenda.

Another organization that I formed during my nearly twenty years as an eye surgeon in Kentucky was the Southern Kentucky Lions Eye Clinic. A month after I arrived in Bowling Green, I joined the Noon Lions Club, and I worked with them to create a clinic to treat uninsured patients. For nearly fifteen years, I performed eye exams on more than a hundred patients a year, and the Noon Lions Club would help the patients buy eyeglasses. I also performed free eye surgery on patients who came to me through the Lions Eye Clinic. We joined forces with the Children of the Americas foundation to provide surgery for kids from Central America.

Through Children of the Americas, I operated on several Guatemalan children. Their visits were arranged by Judy Schwank, a friend, attorney, and longtime advocate for adoption. One was a little girl named Juli who was severely cross-eyed. I was able to straighten her eyes. On my recent medical mission trip to Guatemala, I reconnected with Juli. She has grown up to be a beautiful young woman.

I kept working as an eye surgeon right through my senate campaign and would have kept my practice as a senator too had it been possible. It is against Senate regulations. But I am allowed to perform pro bono surgery, which I do several times a year.

Long before I took my oath of office for the Senate, I took the Hippocratic Oath, part of which, to my mind, is an obligation to treat the poor. I do believe we are our brother's keeper, and while government can and should have a role, too much government creates more problems than it solves.

As my practice grew, so did my family. Three years after William came Duncan, and then, three years later, Robert arrived. Our time became our children's time. Often it took a logistical miracle for Kelley and me to get three different boys to three different games. We enjoyed countless hours at Kereiakes Park and the Lovers Lane Sports Complex. I coached Bowling Green Little League, soccer league, and basketball. I laughingly say there is only one question I won't answer about my coaching career, and that's my win/loss record. Through the years, even before I ran for office, I'd seen much of Kentucky with our oldest, William, who played on various traveling baseball teams. Any part of Kentucky we might have missed we likely saw traveling to soccer games with our middle son, Duncan.

By the time Duncan was in high school, Kelley was a seasoned soccer mom and team chauffeur. Duncan played four years of soccer at Bowling Green High School, and often Kelley's car would be filled with Duncan's travel club and high school teammates. You might not think that a town like Bowling Green would be diverse, but it is. Many boys on the soccer team were immigrants from Bosnia, Africa, Poland, and Mexico.

A teammate from Liberia who was only about five feet five could do a bicycle kick over his head and jump as high as a player six feet tall. His name is Exodus, and the story of his name is worth telling. Nine months pregnant and fleeing from the Liberian civil war, his mother walked alone for miles to a camp. On her back she carried the one-month-old baby of a relative. When she gave birth, medical caretakers thought her newborn was dead and put him aside. Hours later, someone discovered Exodus was still warm and breathing where they had laid him—in a pile of other dead children and infants. In a quote to the *Bowling Green Daily News* about his mother's decision to give him his distinctive name, Exodus said, "It was basically like saying 'Let's get the freedom.' I guess she thought it was the right name for me."

Exodus came to America with his parents from a refugee camp when he was eight years old. When I think about the immigration debate we are having in our country today, I never want to forget that most of us, at one time or another, came to America seeking freedom and prosperity. I think of Exodus and how we need to be a country that is exceedingly proud of immigrants. All of us came from immigrant roots. It's what makes us the country that we are.

When I look back at my life—med school, meeting Kelley, starting a family, and establishing a medical practice—I realize what is most important to me. As I travel the nation, spreading a message of freedom and commerce and prosperity, the long hours in airports and on planes and trains can be a draining experience. But the thought of my wife and family always gives me strength. One night on a plane bound for home, I sent this message to Kelley:

> Home is an elusive notion. Its location is not latitudinal but emotional. A GPS will not guide me there but I will definitely know when I am there. I know after a time away, a very short time, I want to be there. As places replace places I have an anchor, a place I know is home. And that promises something nothing can best.

Home is not just an emotional refuge. Home and family are a civilizing force that binds us together and allows us to succeed. Often people come up to me and lament the loss of family and the brokenness of home and want me to somehow recommend a fix for that. I remind them that some things are outside the realm of government. No amount of government will ever create a home or help mend a broken family. We must turn our gaze from government and look to our families, our ethics and values, our pastors and spiritual leaders.

3

★ ★ ★

Health Care: A Doctor's Opinion

It is a noble aspiration and a moral obligation
to make sure our fellow man is provided for,
that medical treatment is available to all.
But compassion cannot be delivered in
the form of coercion.

* * *

In August 2014, I accompanied a group of some of the best eye surgeons in the United States to Salamá, Guatemala, to perform much-needed eye surgery for that country's poor.

To say Salamá is off the beaten track doesn't capture the experience. Don't expect to see a lot of Americans in cargo shorts and Disney World T-shirts if you're planning a trip there. The tiny village lies in a lush valley eighty-five miles north of Guatemala City, and the road winds treacherously through the mountains. I get motion sickness, so I sat up front, but that vantage didn't help. Heights are not my cup of tea, so it was less than comforting to be the first to see the areas where the road had collapsed and guardrails were absent. Often just a few stones marked the cliff's edge. Because of the tortuous nature of the road the trip took nearly three hours.

Halfway to Salamá we stopped on the top of a mountain at a roadside rest stop. I took a pass on the nachos. My intrepid staff tried them, though, much to their chagrin later that night. The hotel in Salamá was decent and clean but without air-conditioning, and the choice of running water was limited to cold.

Once we reached Salamá, my courage and appetite improved, and we enjoyed great Guatemalan dishes. Corn is omnipresent. The Maya grow it on the steepest of hillsides, and corn is inextricably linked to their daily life. In the Guatemala creation story the first humans were made of yellow and white corn. It is their sacred staple.

In Salamá, the operating room was a small, cramped space where we set up tables and equipment. In Spanish, the eye clinic is called the Hospital de Ojos Club de Leones Internationale, which makes it sound far more impressive than the facility actually is. Though immaculately clean, the operating room was tiny and crowded due to the fact that we set up three operating tables where there would typically be only one.

The Lions Club International has run a sight program for the world's poor for almost a hundred years, and the tiny clinic in Salamá is part of that program. For me, a longtime Lions Club member, it was like meeting an old friend when the Lions president greeted us wearing the familiar patch-covered vest.

I was excited to be back performing surgery. I trained for many years to be an eye surgeon, and not only was I returning to my passion, I would be operating with some of the most talented eye surgeons in the United States. It was an opportunity not only to reinforce my skills but to learn new techniques from masters.

Among those masters was Dr. Alan Crandall, who organized the trip to bring free eye surgery to an area in Guatemala in desperate need of it—there are only two ophthalmologists for every 800,000 people there. Dr. Crandall is the director of the international outreach division at John A. Moran Eye Center of the University of Utah Health Care System, and one of the best eye surgeons in the world. He's also one of the most giving: he spends two months each year on the road with members of his team performing surgeries in third world countries.

I would also be operating alongside David Chang from the University of California, San Francisco, a past president of the American Society of Cataract and Refractive Surgery, and Drs. Jeffrey Pettey, Susan McDonald, Roger Furlong, John Downing, and Charles Barr, each of whom occupy a spot at the top of our field.

The news of our arrival spread quickly. Outside the clinic that first morning the line stretched all the way around the building. Folks had taken hours-long winding bus rides from the hills that surround the

Salamá Valley. Sergio Gor, one of my staffers, said the line looked like Black Friday outside a Target store. Few of the Guatemalans, however, could afford such a luxury. The men were dressed in plaid shirts and worn straw cowboy hats, and the women wore simple floral dresses or jeans. Most were farmers, scratching out a living growing corn, beans, and peanuts. Some of them made as little as a dollar a day. The faces of most of those in line were old and weathered, but there were children, too. Both young and old were filled with hope that they would be able to see again.

The Maya people are very small. Some of the older patients were unable to see or walk and were carried by their children. Most of these patients were blind from cataracts. Cataracts are the most common ailment of the eye—the World Health Organization estimates that some 18 million people around the globe are blind from cataracts. In poor countries, cataracts can mean the difference between surviving and not surviving. The condition is mostly age-related or sun-related, or both. A cataract occurs when the lens of the eye becomes opaque or clouded. Functionally, the eye is still capable of seeing, but the opaque lens prevents light from passing through the eye to the retina in the back. Anyone who lives in Guatemala has accumulated a lot of sun over time. Probably half of the folks who came to the clinic couldn't see the big *E* on the eye chart, or a hand moving in front of their faces, or even light. Essentially, many of them were blind.

Cataract surgery begins by creating a small incision in the outer layer of the eye and then carefully making your way through the dilated pupil to the area just behind the iris. Access to the cloudy lens, or cataract, is achieved by tearing a circular opening in the extremely thin capsule. The cataract is then dissolved or removed in one piece. Finally, a plastic lens is placed inside the capsule and the wound is closed, often with no stitches.

In two and a half days in Salamá, I performed twenty-two surgeries, and our team performed more than two hundred. There were many emotional and tearful smiles as patches came off and patients discovered their newly regained sight.

One patient was unforgettable. A truck driver named Hermenaldo had been blind for more than three years because of cataracts. During that sightless time, he'd lost his job, fifty pounds, and his family. When his patch came off, with tears running down his face, he showed us a photograph of his wife and told us in Spanish how she'd left him when he could no longer work and how he hoped to win her back. He got on his knees and thanked God for the miracle that had restored his vision.

On our second day in surgery, a man showed up without an appointment and said that I had operated on his wife the day before, and that she was now able to see clearly for the first time in years. He wanted to know if I would help him also. I examined him and found that his cataracts were significant. We operated on him the next morning, and his wife was there to help unveil the patch. It was a powerful, emotional moment for me to see them looking at each other clearly for the first time in years. I remember hoping that their lives would be easier now. In remote Guatemala, if you are unable to see, there is little chance of work and not always food to eat.

The wonderful thing about cataract surgery is that the results can be dramatic—not only can vision be restored to the blind, the results are often nearly immediate. For those whose surgery is successful, the moment the bandages are taken off is one of pure joy. It's a truly awesome, unforgettable moment to witness.

In the developing world, there are not enough surgeons to keep up with the demand. In Guatemala, and other countries closer to the equator, cataracts are not only more common but more severe. Most of the cataracts we removed in the clinic were mature, with the appearance of a small pebble, densely brown, black, and white. While we were able to help hundreds, the ultimate answer is more surgeons. The John Moran Eye Institute understands this plight and has scheduled time to bring the local eye surgeons to Utah for more training.

I felt privileged to be with Dr. Crandall and his team, who had organized and completed more than sixty medical missions. His wife, Julie, was an integral part of the leadership that made the examination, measurement, and surgery of over two hundred patients go like clockwork.

I was grateful to be able to put on my scrubs, peer into the oculars of the microscope, and focus on the task at hand. I was excited to be back in my element. Since being sworn in to the Senate in 2011, I have operated on uninsured patients throughout Kentucky, but those occasions are limited to one day at a time. In Guatemala I was able to do what I love for several days in a row.

Familiar Faces

My connection to Guatemala goes back nearly fifteen years. When the idea of going on a medical mission during the August recess first occurred to me, Guatemala was my first choice, mostly because of my memories of children I had operated on in Bowling Green many years before. In the late 1990s, I'd treated the Hernandez brothers, Juan and Andres, and Juli Estrada. They were children when I saw them then: Juan was eight, Andres was fourteen, and Juli was ten or eleven.

I met them because of the humanitarian work of Bill and Judy Schwank. Bill was born in Guatemala and came to the United States to practice neurosurgery. As I've mentioned, Judy is an advocate for adoption.

The Hernandez brothers are from Jalapa, a tiny town in the mountains of Guatemala. Judy Schwank tells me it's beautiful, with a view of the lush green valleys below. Once when she went to visit them she saw a quetzal, the national bird of Guatemala. The quetzal is red and aqua green, with long green tail feathers that follow the bird like the tail of a kite. Sightings are rare. Judy has been going to Guatemala for many years and lives there part-time, and it was the first time she saw one. It's said that they die in captivity. They need to be free to live.

I admire the bird's values along with its beauty.

Though the setting is breathtaking, the boys' house is primitive, literally a stick shack with dirt floors and no electricity. When they arrived in Bowling Green, both the Hernandez boys had mature cataracts. Juan could see only hand motion, and Andres just light perception. Judy told me that Juan and Andres would hold hands and count the number of steps to a river that was eight city blocks away. There they would fill a bucket for their family and then count the steps back to their house. The story of the water buckets has stayed in my memory all these years not only because of its poignancy but because the boys caused something of a mini disaster for the foster family they stayed with in Bowling Green. The boys had never seen running water before, and somehow they stopped the drain in the upstairs bathroom and left the water running. The family realized it when they saw the water pouring through the downstairs ceiling.

Technically, the cataract surgery on the Hernandez boys was not that different from what we normally do for adults. The difference is in the expectations. In children, if vision is not normal in the first seven years of life, the vision center of the brain doesn't develop. Since the Hernandez boys were beyond age seven, I couldn't know in advance how much their vision center had developed or if removing their cataracts would restore much or any vision.

After the surgery we waited anxiously. As the patches were removed, big smiles beamed from each boy. I had a bowl of fruit in the office, and the sight of the bananas and oranges fascinated them. Outside, they were astounded to discover the color of the sky. Though their vision wasn't perfect because the vision center in their brains hadn't fully developed, the surgery did achieve what we call ambulatory vision. The boys could identify objects and find their way around their village. They would no longer have to hold hands and count steps to the river.

When they left, I didn't think I would ever see them again.

But here in Salamá, courtesy of Judy Schwank again, Andres and Juan stood in front of me.

"Hola, Dr. Pablo!" they said in unison. The trip had taken them almost twelve hours, stopping first at Bill and Judy Schwank's home on the other side of Guatemala City.

"*Mire la luz,*" I said to Juan as I pointed my pencil light into his eye.

Juli Estrada also came to the clinic in Salamá. When she came to see me in Bowling Green, her eyes were crossed inward, what we refer to as esotropia. As with the Hernandez boys, the vision center of her brain did not develop properly, and we could not restore the vision in the unused eye. But I was able to straighten her eyes and give her a normal appearance, and she'd grown into a beautiful young woman. The vision in her good eye could, however, be improved with glasses, which we were able to provide.

Fashion Statements

The trip went by quickly. There were some disappointments. Though the Hernandez brothers had desperately hoped for something that would further improve their vision, there was nothing more that could be done.

But there was laughter, too. The humanitarian organization the Hope Alliance brought suitcases filled with eyeglasses that had been collected by Lions Clubs, Rotary Clubs, and other organizations from across the United States, but especially from Utah. In total there were about eleven thousand pairs, with most coming from various lost-and-found boxes. Sorted and categorized according to power, they were piled on tables. By midmorning, elderly Guatemalan women were sorting through the stacks of eyeglasses, throwing back unwanted pairs, and looking for styles that suited them. Some things are universal.

Heading Home

My eighteen-year-old son, Duncan, also came on the trip, as did my niece Lisa Paul and her fiancé, Wes Kimbell. Lisa, a newly minted physician, was about to begin her training to become a pathologist, so the journey was of particular interest to her. While the medical team operated, Duncan, Wes, and my friend Rob Porter helped install a water purification system for a local school. One of the surgeons from Utah, Jeffrey Pettey, brought soccer balls to give out, and Duncan gave some of the soccer balls to kids at the school, which made him something of a hero.

We drove through the jungle toward Guatemala City and our flight home. Though the murder rate in Guatemala has dropped over the past three years, it can still be a very dangerous place. In the 2013 crime and safety report, the State Department's Bureau of Diplomatic Security calls the violent crime rate in Guatemala "critical."[1] The president of Guatemala, Otto Pérez Molina, was nice enough to loan us part of his security team.

As we wound through the mountains on the way back to Guatemala City, our security team proudly kept us safe from harm. Axel, a strong, quiet man, did his job professionally and without obvious emotion, but as he bid farewell to us in the airport, I think I saw a tear well up in his eye. He then sincerely thanked us for what we had done for his fellow countrymen.

"*De nada*," I responded, but it wasn't just nothing—the smiles on the faces of previously blind patients is a priceless reward that I will never forget.

A New Way to Look at America's Health Care

During the 111th Congress, the Congress passed and President Obama signed into law the Patient Protection and Affordable Care Act (PPACA), commonly known as Obamacare. I was not a member of the United States Senate during the 111th Congress, but had I been, I would have voted against Obamacare. The law expands government, inhibits the free market, and shuns individual responsibility. It also costs our economy 2.5 million jobs by forcing employers to take money from payroll to buy insurance.

Since the passage of Obamacare, states, businesses, and other institutions have filed constitutional challenges to many of the burdensome provisions of the law. While the Supreme Court has ruled on the provision of Obamacare that requires individuals to purchase approved health insurance or pay a penalty, dozens of lawsuits remain pending on various aspects of the law.

As a doctor, I have had firsthand experience with the vast problems of the health-care system in the United States. As in other areas of the economy in which the federal government wields its heavy hand, health care is overregulated and in need of serious market reforms.

Many years ago when my father first entered politics he wrote an essay on kwashiorkor. Caused by a lack of protein, the disorder creates the swollen bellies of starvation. I'm sure you've seen photos of African children with the disease.

As a medical student, my father dreamed of a cure for kwashiorkor. But the more he got to know about the disease, the more he realized that the answer was economic, not medical; it was more related to diet and poverty. In Guatemala, Alan Crandall gave me a book that explored the same theme as my father's essay.

The book, *Second Suns: Two Doctors and Their Amazing Quest to Restore Sight and Save Lives,* by David Oliver Relin, tells the story of two remarkable ophthalmologists and their ambitious goal of eliminating preventable blindness worldwide. One of the ophthalmologists is Dr. Sanduk Ruit, who was born in a poor village in Nepal. Three of his siblings died of diseases that are curable in the West. It was those sad events that convinced him to go into medicine. From the beginning of his schooling he showed brilliance. He could have practiced medicine anywhere in the world but decided to stay where he was needed the most—at home.

His partner has quite a different story. Dr. Geoffrey Tabin was a world-class mountain climber and repeatedly dropped out of Harvard Medical School to follow his passion of climbing the Earth's tallest peaks. Very few people drop out of Harvard Medical and are allowed back in, but Tabin was one. After becoming an ophthalmologist, he read of Dr. Ruit's work and traveled to Kathmandu to meet him.

By then, Dr. Ruit had discovered a surgical technique for cataracts that took about four minutes to perform at a cost of about $20. The procedure consisted of a small incision that didn't require sutures. The diseased lens of the eye was then removed, but the elastic capsule that covers the lens was left partially intact to allow an artificial or intraocular lens (IOL) to be implanted.

Though his medical accomplishment was substantial, the fact that he could manufacture intraocular lenses cheaply and locally in Nepal made his discovery a medical breakthrough with global ramifications. These types of lenses cost $150 or more in the West. In Nepal, they were making them for $4.

In all, Ruit's cataract surgery produced results similar to those in

America at a tenth of the cost. Ruit and Tabin, who are not only brilliant surgeons but also business dynamos, built cataract surgical clinics in seven countries and have trained thousands of doctors in the Ruit technique.

Ruit estimates his surgery has now been performed on over 3 million people.[2]

Though the debate over Obamacare may appear, at times, to be a debate over health care, it really should be a debate over what type of economic system distributes goods the most efficiently.

Since the collapse of the Soviet Union, most economists have acknowledged that only when the marketplace determines the price of goods and services can the goods and services be distributed efficiently.

What does that mean?

It means that the Soviet Union failed because a central planner, an office in the government, set the prices of goods. The Soviet Union failed because that office couldn't determine the price of bread. If it set the price too low, bread would fly from the shelves, and there would be shortages and scarcity. If it set the prices too high, the bread would spoil on the shelves, and again there would be a shortage.

Only in democratic capitalism, where millions of consumers vote daily, can the correct price of goods be determined. By definition, that price would afford the most goods to the most amount of people.

There is no moral price. There is no correct price that any one individual, or government, can discover and set for the rest of us. This has been true since the first item was sold. The eighteenth-century philosopher and economist Adam Smith coined the phrase "fatal conceit." In his book *Wealth of Nations* he wrote: "every individual, it is evident, can in his local situation judge much better than any statesman or lawgiver can do for him." A couple of centuries later Friedrich Hayek, the Nobel Prize–winning economist, titled a book *The Fatal Conceit* and wrote that individuals would be presumptuous to believe they had sufficient knowledge to discover a correct price for the marketplace.

The same can be said for the current governmental control of health care. Every time a Washington bureaucrat sets a price the consumer suffers.

"But health care is too precious to let consumers decide," the hand-wringers cry.

Health care is precious, but if you insist that it is somehow different from all other goods and services, you will suffer the consequences of economic fallacy. Our health-care situation is not a medical issue, it's an economic one, and only when we approach it as such can a fix be found.

For example: beginning in the 1990s, a trend of hospital mergers developed and, not surprisingly, patient costs began to rise because of the lack of competition. Hospitals have merged at an exploding rate over the past five years. According to a report in *Washington Monthly*, in 2009 there were fifty-two hospital mergers. In 2011 there were ninety. In 2012 there were 105. A report written by James C. Robinson, a health-care economist and professor at Berkeley, exposes the huge disparity in the prices these megahospitals charge compared to hospitals in competitive markets. For instance, a knee replacement in a competitive market will cost you or your insurance company a little over $18,000. In a market where hospitals have merged, the same procedure costs almost $27,000. In a competitive market, an angioplasty costs about $21,600; in a consolidated market, the cost balloons to around $32,400. In a competitive market, a pacemaker costs a little over $30,000, whereas a megahospital will charge you $47,500.[3] You get the idea.

I'll give you another example from my own experience. In the late 1990s, LASIK surgery experienced a price war. The cost of the eye surgery, which had been as high as $2,500 and more for one eye, dropped to as low as $500 because of chain competition and advertising. It was not at all uncommon to see "Introductory Offers!" and "Holiday Sale!" boldly displayed in the ads for the surgery.[4] Advertising a medical procedure was a relatively new phenomenon. Up until 1982, when the Supreme Court struck down the prohibition, the American Medical Association had banned the practice. Though some of the ads were cheesy, they were an indication of the free market at work.

There were those who railed at the idea of the market setting the price of eye surgery. In December 2000, Dr. David Kessler, former dean of the Yale Medical School and the former commissioner of the Food and Drug Administration, told the *New York Times* the trend was the "corporatization of medicine in the most extreme form."[5] Dr. Sandra Belmont, who served as the founding director of the laser vision center at Weill Cornell Medical Center in New York and a spokeswoman for the American Academy of Ophthalmology, said: "Patients should not choose their doctor based on price."

Yet look at what happened in both the LASIK marketplace and the contact lens marketplace. Prices fell and remained lower. Contact lenses, which were $15 or so when I started in practice, are now less than $3 and are available in abundance.

The problem with Obamacare, and even with the old system, is that when insurance or government pays for the first dollar of health care, the consumer doesn't care about the price and neither does the physician. Without a market, the price goes up. LASIK surgery is not covered by insurance. The average person will call multiple doctors to compare prices. I've never had one Medicaid patient call and ask about price. If you've got great Blue Cross with a $20 deductible are you going to call around and compare prices? I don't think so. If you don't shop for prices, you don't force prices down.

But emotions run high when we talk of health care. Only the government can distribute it fairly, some say. But that is the same thought process that caused Soviet shelves to be bereft of bread. Rationing, either by mandate or by waiting in line, is an inevitable side effect of government distribution of goods.

There is a better option than what we now have. Free up prices. Legalize and expand tax-free health savings accounts. Allow a marketplace of freely fluctuating prices for everyone. The consequences will startle you. The beauty of capitalism is that it distributes the greatest amount of goods at the cheapest price. Instead of socializing medicine, why not let the engine of capitalism distribute health care—it's what we do best. It's what made America great in the first place.

The economist Joseph Schumpeter once remarked, "The capitalist achievement does not typically consist in providing more silk stockings for queens but in bringing them within the reach of factory girls in return for steadily decreasing amounts of effort..."

But wouldn't capitalism leave some people behind?

Yes, but so does Obamacare, and so would any health-care system. If we put in place a structure that works efficiently for the vast majority, then it will be easier to address the needs of those left behind. Can we promise that every person in America will receive the best and most timely health care? Perhaps not, though that is always the goal.

When the indigent and uninsured are the exception and not the rule, it will be much easier for the government and charities to take care of those still in need. In the private sector, this happens all the time. The idea that the poor would not be taken care of discounts the elemental nature of doctors and others in the medical profession, and it discounts a fundamental character trait of Americans. Think back to this country's response to disasters both here and abroad.

Take the example of Dr. Barbara Bowers from Paducah, Kentucky.

Dr. Bowers has been a practicing ophthalmologist for twenty years and has always donated part of her time for surgery on people without insurance. I've been teaming up with her on my time off from the Senate. Working with Dr. Bowers gives me a chance to keep my skills sharp, so to speak, and updated on the latest equipment. Last year, Dr. Bowers introduced me to a LenSx® femtosecond laser, an amazing machine that emulsifies a cataract without a blade and makes the aspiration of it much easier.

With Dr. Bowers, I operated on a grandfather who would see his grandchildren and a red berry bush outside of his house for the first time in years. I operated on a middle-aged woman who couldn't afford health insurance. After the surgery she wrote: "Thank You Sen. Paul" on the rear window of her car with white shoe polish as they do with "Just Married" and rode around like that for a week. Dr. Bowers told me that she then added "Thank You Dr. Bowers" on the window, after Barbara performed a second surgery, a week later.

Of all the surgeries we performed, maybe the most poignant story belonged to a vet who Barbara Bowers told me was living in a homeless shelter. This was in May 2014, right when the VA scandal broke and Eric Shinseki resigned. An internal review had found misconduct in nearly two-thirds of VA facilities, and thousands of veterans across the country have been impacted by long wait times that were covered up by Veterans' Hospital Administration officials.

The people who think that the government can efficiently distribute medicine need to explain why the VA, a much smaller system, has been struggling for decade after decade.

In order for this veteran to get treatment for his cataracts, he would have had to wait for months, and then travel a few hundred miles to a VA hospital in St. Louis for the operation. He was homeless. How could he afford to get there? Even if he could find a way, he'd either have to live for weeks in a shelter in St. Louis or on the streets of a city he didn't know in order to make the appointments and follow-up for both eyes. Instead, he was resigned to going blind.

Which, for all intents and purposes, he was when he walked into Dr. Bowers's office. The surgeries restored his vision to almost 20/20. The last I heard, he was no longer living in the shelter. Dr. Bowers tells me he now has a car, a job, and his own roof over his head. I believe we have a lifelong commitment to our vets. As president, it would be a top priority of mine to fix the wait lines at VA hospitals. I think, however, that can only be done when we overhaul the whole health-care system. It's my belief that a free market health-care system would take care of our veterans and the indigent too.

Doctors from the United States like Barbara Bowers have been performing charity work since Benjamin Franklin's day. As soon as doctors are granted hospital privileges they have to agree to cover the emergency room for people who don't have insurance. There are doctors who give much more than I have. As of this writing, some two thousand medical professionals in the States have signed on to volunteer in Liberia and other Ebola-stricken African countries.[6]

But there is also plenty of medical help given right here in America, and it's given in a quiet, unpretentious way. In 1925, Helen Keller addressed the Lions Club International convention, a moment that began nearly a century of the Lions Club helping the world's blind. A quote from that speech hangs in my Senate office: "It is because my teacher learned about me and broke through the dark, silent imprisonment which held me that I am able to work for myself and for others," she said. "It is the caring we want more than money. The gift without the sympathy and interest of the giver is empty. If you care, if we can make the people of this great country care, the blind will indeed triumph over blindness."

America has a big, generous heart, and that heart beats because of a free market. Let's get government out of health care and allow what we do best to distribute health care to the greatest number of people. Government-controlled health care drives us toward bankruptcy. The freedom of the marketplace ensures solvency.

A New Approach

How would that look? Well, the first priority would be to get government out of the business of setting prices. The Sustainable Growth Rate, or SGR, is a policy created by Congress in 1997 that was supposed to tie Medicare payments to physicians to the country's economic growth—sort of like cost-of-living increases. But Medicare payments far outpaced the economy, so every year, and sometimes more than once a year, Congress has to pass something called a "doc fix" to free up enough money to cover the shortfall. The policy was flawed from the start, and yet here we are seventeen years later still putting plugs in a bucket that has more leaks than the NSA. It's time for a new bucket. End the SGR, the government system that sets fees.

The disappointing truth is that wasteful spending in Washington has drained the Medicare trust funds. The combination of massive debt, fewer active workers, and more retirees is pushing Medicare into bankruptcy. Medicare is unfunded by nearly $40 trillion. Simply put, this is an unsustainable path, and Obamacare is not the answer. In fact, Obamacare has borrowed money from Medicare to cover its cost. Washington cannot continue to promise everything to everyone without a plan to pay for it.

My plan is simple. We could still have a federal Medicare system to pay for our seniors' health care. Every senior would be covered. No one could be turned down, and it would deliver top care without some of the frustrations people have with the current system. In the current system, there are two problems. Government is the only "insurance" you can get, and the system is estimated to be $35 trillion in the hole over the next few decades.

It is simply not sustainable. Not just our children, but possibly those of us who are in our fifties may see a broken, unreliable, costly, and ineffective program if we don't look for a new path.

Doctors are already dropping off the Medicare payment rolls. More will follow. Seniors will be left with bigger bills and fewer options.

Instead, I want to put some competition back into the system, and I want to make sure seniors can choose from the best health-care plans in the country.

Before Obamacare, the best plans in the world were the ones your congressmen and senators received. These plans are still available to many federal employees, including the president and his staff.

Why not let every senior have these plans? Federal employees choose from more than 250 different insurance plans.

The federal health-care plan is less expensive than the current Medicare plan because it is not administered by government bureaucrats. My plan would save taxpayers $1 trillion over the next ten years and reduce Medicare's unfunded liabilities by almost $16 trillion. Individual seniors will save thousands of dollars from their personal health-care budgets each year while receiving more generous benefits.

The Federal Employees Health Benefits Program (FEHB) describes an array of insurance options available to 4 million federal employees and their dependents, roughly 10 million people. The government pays about three-quarters of the total costs of insurance plans chosen by beneficiaries based on their individual needs and preferences.

Like Medicare, FEHB is a regulated marketplace where plans cannot deny coverage to anyone for any reason. Everyone within the plan will pay the same premium regardless of health status or preexisting conditions.

This program also makes it easier for insurance plans to enter the market to compete for seniors' business—including allowing employers to continue covering seniors through retirement.

With my plan, all Medicare-eligible patients could enroll in FEHB as if they were federal employees, and willing employers can give eligible patients the option of staying on their current plans and still receive the government's contribution.

To make this fiscally possible, the initial eligibility age for seniors will be increased gradually from sixty-five to seventy over a period of twenty years, and the benefits will be means-tested. However, no current or near-term enrollees would have their eligibility delayed. If you are near retirement, this will not apply to you.

Medicare as we know it is broken and in desperate need of reform. It simply cannot survive without a careful fix that helps both the patients and the taxpayers.

My plan fixes the Medicare system and gives seniors access to the best health-care plans—those that used to be offered to members of Congress—and does so without breaking the bank. Seniors deserve to have a world-class health-care system, and U.S. taxpayers deserve to have their dollars put to better use in a system that will not eventually bankrupt the country.

Giving seniors the same plan that top-level federal employees have is fair, and it saves $1 trillion over ten years. This commonsense reform is the solution to putting Medicare on a sustainable path for our kids and grandkids.

Next, for non-Medicare citizens, my plan would let consumers decide what kind of insurance they want and where they want to purchase it. The idea of choice should be given back to the American people. It is ridiculous to require everyone, from single twentysomethings to sixty-year-old empty-nesters, to purchase federally mandated insurance plans that cover care they do not need or want, such as pediatric dental coverage for children they don't have. True freedom of choice would let patients buy any type of insurance they want, including inexpensive catastrophic care insurance.

When we were young, this was the type of insurance my wife and I purchased for our family and ourselves. We did the math and paid for our routine care out of pocket, which for us, as it is for most young people, was minimal. Our health insurance was true "insurance" against an accident or major illness, not prepaid medical care. We saved tens of thousands of dollars over the years by doing this. Shouldn't every American get to decide how much they want to spend on insurance? Why should the government determine that?

We need to keep our eye on the ball. What we have isn't working. It's important for Republicans, myself included, to not just oppose Obamacare but to present compelling ideas for replacement.

My health-care plan would bring a real marketplace to health-care delivery. Tax-free savings accounts are a big part of this. I have long supported making all medical expenses tax deductible, allowing insurance to be bought across state lines, state-level tort reform, and empowering all citizens to save for health expenses by removing the high-deductible insurance policy requirement for access to health savings accounts.

Allow the marketplace to work in health care; allow the purchase of insurance with lifelong tax-free savings accounts. Health savings accounts, started at birth, could accumulate to such remarkable levels that health insurance costs would plummet. It could be similar to the cost of term life insurance policies.

My plan wouldn't forget the poor: I know there are people who can't afford health insurance, and some who are in desperate need of care right now. It's not my intention to ignore the needs of those individuals. Besides having taken the Hippocratic Oath, I'm a Christian, and I have a deeply held belief that we help those less fortunate than ourselves. If we don't try to fix the problem in the system, then the less fortunate will always be less fortunate. If we properly reform the system, we will have more funds left over for those who truly need help.

For the exceptions to the rule, for those who live in poverty or are afflicted with expensive chronic medical conditions, helping them would fall both on charities and the government.

"The proper conservative reaction is not to imagine a government stripped of public obligations when it comes to the health of citizens," Michael Gerson and Peter Wehner wrote in an article in *National Affairs*. "It is to propose an alternative health-care plan that doesn't centralize all power in Washington and that keeps costs down, solves the problem of insuring those with pre-existing conditions, and reduces the number of uninsured."

My health-care plan would do just that. It would also bring something very special back to the American people, something that Obamacare stole from them—the freedom of choice. That's the health-care platform on which I stand.

4

★ ★ ★

Getting to Work

In Washington, they can't conceive of reducing the annual deficit, much less attacking the debt, and at home the people are ready and eager to attack both deficit and debt.

★ ★ ★

After I was elected to the Senate in November 2010, I lived part-time in my father's Virginia condominium. Like most adult children, I hadn't lived with my parents for a long time—more than twenty-five years. My dad was still a congressman and weighing the decision of running for president again, and I was the freshman senator-elect from Kentucky, trying to get the feel of how things worked in the Senate. In one of our joint interviews, my dad, invoking the long-held rivalry between the upper and lower chambers, joked, "Yeah, if he behaves himself and works hard maybe someday he could serve in the House, too."

My time living with Dad was fun for both of us, I think. I'm pretty sure it was the first time in history that a son served in the Senate and a father served simultaneously in the House. Of course, the press made all sorts of comparisons. I remember one political cartoon in particular that poked fun at Dad's economic philosophy.

The first frame showed my father and me in the kitchen. "Dad, let me write you a check for rent," I said in the cartoon balloon. "Son, we only accept gold and silver around here," Dad replied. The next frame had me telling my dad I was going to the store and asking if he had anything to add to my grocery list. "Son, we don't believe in central planning around here," Dad said.

Perhaps the sharpest comparison was made on the baseball field. Every year, Congress plays a charity game that pits Democrats against Republicans. Dad is a great athlete. In high school, he was the Pennsylvania state track champ in the 220. I grew up playing most sports and was pretty good at several, but a standout at none.

The Congressional Baseball Game is now held in Nationals Park but it used to be played on a Triple-A field in Virginia. It was there that my father hit a home run out of the stadium, the only member of Congress to ever do so. The feat landed him in the Congressional Baseball Hall of Fame. He was inducted in 2012 in a pregame ceremony. Dad threw out the first pitch and I caught it.

In the annual game, players wear uniforms representing their home states. My dad was wearing his old 1970s Houston Astros uniform and I was wearing the uniform of Western Kentucky University, which is in my hometown. I must admit my colleagues were a little disappointed. "How come you're not as good as your dad?" was a common razzing I heard that night.

Not that I'm being defensive about it, mind you, but the Democrats have a ringer—Cedric Richmond, the congressman from New Orleans who pitched varsity for Morehouse College (okay, maybe I am being a little defensive about it). I struck out my first year against the Democrat ace but got a single the next year—not that anyone's counting. The game benefits the Boys and Girls Club of D.C., and is one of the best bipartisan events in Washington. My dad always joked that if we played more baseball and did less legislating, the country would be in better shape. He might have a point.

I lived with Dad for a just a couple of months. I just couldn't take the traffic on the 14th Street Bridge. I imagined all of those lost hours commuting. I decided to rent a small apartment on Capitol Hill. I wanted to be within walking distance of my office. I was eager to get to work.

I will never forget seeing the Senate Chamber for the first time and learning the history of the desks, including those of Daniel Webster and Jefferson Davis. The desk Davis sat at still shows a mark from a Union soldier's bayonet after the senator from Mississippi left it to lead the Confederacy. In the desk drawers are hand-etched signatures of those who have occupied the Senate through the ages—though some are said to be forgeries.[1]

I was given Henry Clay's desk. Traditionally, the Clay desk was passed down through the years to the senior senator from Kentucky. Since Mitch McConnell was then, and is again, the Senate leader, the Clay desk came to me. When Joe Biden swore me in, he told me that Clay was only twenty-nine when he became a senator, which was under the minimum age of thirty set by the Constitution.

The age minimum for the House is twenty-five, and you can read into that if you want. Perhaps the Framers thought the additional five years would afford the senators more worldly experience and knowledge. Whether that's held true is anyone's guess. Perhaps Edward Everett Hale, the chaplain of the Senate in the early 1900s, summed up the collective knowledge of the Upper Chamber best. He was once asked if he prayed for the senators. "I look at the senators," he purportedly answered, "and pray for the country."

There is likely no legislator from Kentucky more famous than Henry Clay. He served as both the Speaker of the House and president of the Senate. He ran for president of the United States four times and, in 1844, nearly bested James Polk. He was Secretary of State for John Quincy Adams. After his death in 1852, he lay in state in the Capitol Rotunda, the first person on whom that honor was bestowed.

Henry Clay was called the Great Compromiser. During my orientation, one of my Senate colleagues asked me with a touch of irony and a twinkle in his eye, "Will you be a great compromiser?"

It was a question I would often wrestle with.

To me, Henry Clay's life story is, at best, a mixed message. His supporters argue that he rose above sectional strife to carve out compromise after compromise trying to ward off civil war. In their book, *Henry Clay: The Essential American*, David and Jeanne Heidler write that Abraham Lincoln admired Clay "more than he did any other man on the American political scene."

Clay's detractors contend that his compromises were morally wrong and may have even encouraged war. They say that during fifty years of public life, he not only embraced slavery—he owned forty-eight slaves—but supported the Fugitive Slave Law until his death. Henry Clay also compromised on the extension of slavery into new states. He was the deciding vote in the House to extend slavery into Arkansas.

In lionizing legislators like Henry Clay, writers sometimes attempt to mitigate their subject's faults by arguing that they were simply men of their time. That doesn't make it right.

Though a towering figure of American history, Henry is not my favorite Clay. That distinction goes to his cousin Cassius Marcellus Clay, the nineteenth-century abolitionist. Cassius Clay had a falling out with his more prominent cousin when he released a private letter that Henry had written to him that seemed to support the end of slavery. Henry denied having written it, and he never spoke to Cassius again.

For his part, Cassius was unapologetic. In Lexington, Kentucky, two brass cannons and a collection of friends stood guard over his abolitionist press, *True American*. He is known to have fought and won at least six duels in his life. In the Heidler biography, Cassius is described as a man whose weapons of choice were his pen and his Bowie knife. He was so adept with the first, the biographers write, that he often had to resort to the latter. He prepared for speeches by placing his Bible on one side of the lectern and his Bowie knife on the other.

One night, Cassius was ambushed by a slave trader named Squire Turner and his sons, and his big Bowie knife saved his life. According to *Blacks in Appalachia*, edited by Appalachian historians William

H. Turner and Edward J. Cabbell, the event boiled over after both men began targeting each other with invectives and derisive remarks. When Turner's boys approached Clay, the abolitionist tried to draw his knife but was clubbed on the head and the Bowie was pulled from his hand. Squire Turner's son Thomas then aimed a six-shot pistol point-blank at Cassius Clay's face and pulled the trigger three times. The gun misfired on each attempt. Clay wrested the Bowie knife from one of Thomas's brothers but almost cut his own fingers "to the bone," according to the biographers. During the struggle for the knife, Clay was stabbed just above his heart.[2] Blind with fury, he managed to wrest free the Bowie and retaliated by "burying the knife to the hilt" into the abdomen of Thomas Turner's brother Cyrus, killing him.[3]

In 1866, Cassius donated land and money to found Berea College in Kentucky, the first school of higher education that was open to African Americans. Berea, the town, is nestled in the hills of Appalachia and was founded by abolitionists. It takes its name from the Bible, a place where St. Paul went to escape persecution. The Bible tells us that the people of Berea were truth seekers and welcomed Paul's teaching of Christ. In its first academic year, Berea College's enrollment totaled 187 students, 96 of whom were African American.

As I sat at Henry Clay's desk in my early days in the Senate, I was mindful that compromise may be necessary to govern. Compromise can and should occur when policy is headed in the right direction. Though I might have been mindful of Henry Clay, I must admit there is a place in my heart for his cousin Cassius, for the steadfastness of his principles, and the courage to fight for what he believed in.

In my first 100 days, I was eager to get started, but the powers that be told me to keep my head down, my mouth shut, and put in my time to learn the way things were done in the Upper Chamber. After all, Hillary Clinton had done that, they said, and it had worked out fine for her, right? It has worked well for every new senator since time immemorial, they told me. Perhaps, but it seemed to me the Senate hadn't been working well at all for the people it was supposed to serve.

When I was sworn in to the Senate in 2011, unemployment had been hovering between 9 and 10 percent for nearly two years, lives had been ruined, and hundreds of thousands of jobs lost. Standard & Poor's was just about to downgrade our country's credit for the first time in history.

The federal budget had been operating at a $1 trillion yearly deficit or more for three years running. In addition, we'd spent over $3 trillion in stimulus by the government through the Federal Reserve, and we were adding to our $17 trillion debt at the rate of more than a million a minute.

But as I raised my voice in protest I could hear it echo through the Senate chamber. Don't cause a ruckus, now, I was advised.

These things take time, they said.

It was time for these things to change, I replied.

My first order of business was a plan that addressed out-of-control federal spending and the budget.

First, my proposal sought to roll back discretionary spending and then initiate reductions at various levels nearly across the board. So what does that mean? Well, specifically, it meant big cuts to agency bureaucracies that had become so bloated they nearly blot out the sun. Cuts to the Departments of Agriculture and Transportation would create over $42 billion in savings each, while cuts to the Departments of Energy and Housing and Urban Development would save about $50 billion each. Rescuing education from the federal government's jurisdiction and giving it to state and local governance would not only improve the system, but would create almost $80 billion in savings alone.

I also proposed reductions in other federal agencies and policies. Some worried about the loss of government jobs, but the money doesn't disappear. It's redirected into the private sector, creating more jobs—jobs not funded by the taxpayer. These cuts also expand individual freedom by removing unnecessary government controls.

The cuts totaled $500 billion.

Not surprisingly, my proposal was greeted skeptically even by my own party. Some were shocked. "What temerity!" they said. But back home, when I told the folks who had voted me into office, they said: "Well, that's all well and good, but what do you intend to do about the $17 trillion debt?" I love it. In Washington, they can't conceive of reducing the annual deficit, much less attacking the debt, and at home the people are ready and eager to attack both deficit and debt.

Like any senator worth his license plate, I listened to the voices from home and not the ones that hushed me on the Hill. I went about setting my sights on the big bloated elephants that the rest of Washington tiptoes around. In an op-ed I wrote at the time for the *Wall Street Journal*, I used the Commerce Department as an example. It has been consistently labeled for elimination, specifically by House Republicans during the 1990s. One of Commerce's main functions is delivering corporate welfare to American firms that can compete without it. Corporate welfare is a pet peeve of mine. More than a hundred billion dollars has been handed over to rich companies that don't need it. Think of it like this: imagine the richest person you know. Now imagine giving that person your rent or mortgage money for no discernibly good reason. When you boil it down, that's exactly what the government is doing with corporate welfare.

My proposal would have scaled back the Commerce Department's spending by 54 percent and would have eliminated corporate welfare altogether. Spending is out of control, and dramatic moves are necessary if only to drown out the nonsense that takes up so much of the discussion.

People who say there is nowhere to cut in government, or that we should only be arguing about how much or how little the government should grow per year, simply aren't getting the problem.

Yes, we should be able to help people. Yes, we need a strong national defense and to preserve Social Security and Medicare. Yes, we should make sure our children have outstanding educations.

Government right now does too much and exists to serve special interests in far too many cases. It operates inefficiently or with too much cronyism. Spending on programs such as corporate welfare and the Commerce Department are prime examples, but we have to make their elimination a priority, even a cause.

When the media, the other side of the aisle, and even my own party accused me of being extreme I responded, "What's extreme is trillion-dollar annual deficits and a nearly $18 trillion total debt."

How extreme?

In his first address to a joint session of Congress, Ronald Reagan said a trillion dollars of debt would be "a stack of thousand-dollar bills 67 miles high."[4] Can you guess how high that would be in today's debt dollars? Seventeen times 67 miles is 1,139 miles, or the altitude of some of our satellites.[5] In thousand-dollar bills!

Back here on Earth, the world is getting awfully crowded with people to whom the United States owes money, including $1.26 trillion to China, $250 billion to Brazil, $160 billion to Russia, over a trillion to Japan, and assorted billions to Belgium, Luxembourg, and Switzerland.

Yet far too few of my colleagues seemed to be taking this looming catastrophe seriously.

So while some were using talking points, my staff and I sat down and wrote the second part of my plan: a seventy-page budget that sought three main objectives: to cut spending further, reduce bloated government bureaucracy further, and bring the budget into balance in five years—all without raising taxes.

In comparison, Paul Ryan's budget, which got a lot of attention, was going to take nearly forty years to reach solvency. Sure, it was slightly better than Barack Obama's budget, as the president's would probably never balance. But anything would be better than that, as is evidenced by the fact that he couldn't even get a single Democrat to vote for it in the Senate.

I saw it like this: we could go stumbling around in the darkness of the Senate Chamber for the rest of recorded time, or someone could light a candle.

Funny thing happened when I struck the match. Now, instead of the talk being about my temerity, I was beginning to gain some traction with my colleagues. Harry Truman once famously said: "If you can't convince them, confuse them." I confused them by doing my homework and producing a work of substance. My budget proposal got high marks from FreedomWorks, the Cato Institute, and even from the left's flagship magazine, *The Nation*, which said I was "one of the few members of Congress who is contributing anything more than hype and hypocrisy to the current budget debate."[6]

One thing my budget proposals have made clear: Washington needs a lot more change. Some of it can come through a leader calling for that change, even if he doesn't yet have enough people following to make it happen. While every Republican senator voted for a Constitutional amendment to balance the budget in five years, few were willing to actually vote for the specific cuts necessary to achieve that balance. Only a handful of my colleagues joined me, but our numbers are growing. As the debt keeps piling up, minds are starting to change. Each time I've introduced my budget, more Republicans have voted for it. So the debate is moving. The numbers are shifting.

Representatives are starting to hear the voices of the outraged voters who cannot run their homes the way our government runs this country. I have no desire to endorse the status quo. I came to Washington to take stands like this. Exactly this stand, as a matter of fact.

5

★ ★ ★

A New Kind of Republican

When I ran for office, my opponents claimed I wasn't qualified because I had never held public office before. I responded that not being a career politician was precisely my strength and that we needed more doctors, teachers, businesspeople, barbers, accountants, and maybe fewer lawyers.

★ ★ ★

One of the first calls I received after my election was from Al Franken congratulating me on my victory. Freshman senators are encouraged to ask one of their colleagues to be a mentor of sorts. So, I figured why not? I asked Senator Franken to be my mentor—how about that for a reach across the aisle? Al was gracious and truly helped me in my early days. In looking back, I should have taken his advice more to heart on at least one occasion. I was asked to appear on the David Letterman show after I published my first book, *The Tea Party Goes to Washington*.

I went to Al and asked him for some jokes. "Don't tell any jokes," he said. "You're not that funny."

My late night debut didn't turn out that bad. Letterman asked me if my jeans were standard senatorial garb. I told him my wife said I shouldn't wear them. He responded, "You should have listened to her." For the most part, though, David didn't get the memo that it was supposed to be late night comedy and insisted on engaging me in a debate. In the end he sort of just gave up and said, "I think he's wrong about some of these things, I just can't tell you why."

It was John McCain, though, who put the Senate in prospective for me during those early days. "For the first six months you're going to pinch yourself and wonder how you got here," he said. "For the rest of the time you're going to wonder how the hell everybody else got here."

In my first four years in the Senate I have authored more than 100 bills. I wasn't naming post offices, either. Right from the start, I set my sights on righting what is fundamentally wrong with the way our government works. I raised my share of eyebrows in the process.

Term Limits

Back in 1996, when my father was running for Congress again after a twelve-year hiatus spent practicing medicine, I attended a national medical meeting to see if I could find support for him with the medical PAC. Boy, was I naïve. When I approached a medical lobbyist with the idea, her response was direct, which is a nice way to categorize it. "We support people in power who can help us," she said. "Like incumbents and committee chairmen."

"That's exactly why we're in this mess with trillion-dollar debts," I responded. I brought up the name Rostenkowski. The longtime Democrat congressman from Chicago had just been sent to federal prison for, among other things, having at least fourteen people on his congressional payroll who did little or no official work. [1]

"Rostenkowski has always voted with us," she said coolly.

"That's the problem," I replied. Special interest groups support members of Congress who vote for their pet projects, to the detriment of the general welfare of the country. Rostenkowski always voted for higher fees for physicians, but he also voted for every deficit-spending package that came down the pike. Special interests were satisfied but the general interest of the nation was ignored.

The Dan Rostenkowskis of Congress are the reason I believe one of the most important reforms necessary to take our government back is term limits. When I ran for office, my opponents claimed I wasn't qualified because I had never held public office before. I responded that not being a career politician was precisely my strength and that we needed more doctors, teachers, businesspeople, barbers, accountants, and maybe fewer lawyers. I fully believe capable men and women who are not career politicians have the ability and insight to be legislators. In fact, what we really need in Congress is fresh perspective.

The very first piece of legislation I introduced as a U.S. senator was an amendment to the Constitution to limit congressional terms of office. My amendment sought to limit legislators in the House to six two-year terms and in the Senate to two six-year terms. I believed then, and do now, that term limits would fundamentally transform Washington, taking it from the stagnant status quo to a vibrant agent for change. The Twenty-second Amendment limits the president to two terms, so why wouldn't we want to limit legislative terms?

Needless to say, my support for term limits hasn't always helped me make friends in Washington. I remember that during my initial campaign the media would clamor and exclaim that my support of term limits was a direct affront to long-serving Mitch McConnell and Hal Rogers of Kentucky.

I reminded them that my dad served for over twenty years, albeit not consecutively. I'm sure there are politicians who remain in office for years and years who don't become jaded, sedentary, or abuse the power they've accrued. My father was one of them. I'll never forget one story where the leadership was beseeching a Republican Congress to vote for a bloated budget full of pork. In front of the entire caucus the leader opined, "There's something in this budget for every one of you and I expect a yea from every one of you—except Ron Paul, who votes no on principle."

Long terms of office increase the likelihood of apathy or the abuse of power for personal gain. The proof of this resides in a long and inglorious list: William Jefferson, Robert Nay, Randall "Duke" Cunningham, James Traficant, Austin John Murphy, and on and on. You don't have to be a criminologist to figure out that term limits would eliminate much of the opportunity for elected officials to use their position to commit a crime. Limits would also consistently refill the halls of Congress with energetic people and new ideas, people who would get things done simply because they had only a limited time to do so. They wouldn't be worn down by the steady drip of negativity that erodes character on Capitol Hill.

I'm not alone in this fight, at least from a popular perspective. According to a recent Gallup poll, fully 75 percent of the public supports term limits.[2] The grassroots group U.S. Term Limits has been fighting this battle for three decades now. According to their website, term limits have been placed on fifteen state legislatures, and eight of the ten largest cities in America have adopted term limits for their city councils and/or mayoral positions. Thirty-seven states place term limits on their constitutional officers. Several states even passed term limits on their representatives to the U.S. Congress. But the Supreme Court struck down those laws, arguing that eligibility for federal office must be uniform among the states.

Nevertheless, there has been absolutely no movement on the Hill toward term limits. Why? The answer is easy. In order for it to become law, Congress would have to pass it. You think some old barnacled congressmen who've been around since the Hoover administration are going to vote for a bill that removes them from office? Not likely.

If you don't believe me, just look at the dearth of cosponsors for my Term Limits Amendment. At last count we had twelve.

Does that mean that term limits are a dead issue? That Congress will never submit to the will of the people when it comes to term limits? Maybe not. There are a couple of other ways to enact term limits besides a straight congressional vote.

The first is a constitutional amendment. The Constitution allows for amendments in two ways. The first way is by a two-thirds majority vote in both the House and Senate. Then the amendment is sent to the state legislatures for ratification. This is the process that has been used for all twenty-seven amendments to date. The second way, which has never been used, is when two-thirds of the state legislatures call for an Article V convention, which deliberates and passes the amendment. It then must pass by a three-fourths majority of the state legislatures. I think if enough state legislatures called for an Article V convention, Congress would do anything it could to prevent such a spectacle from occurring, including doing the right thing and finally passing amendments to require limited terms in office—and a balanced budget.

The other way term limits can become a reality is if a president is elected with a mandate that includes them. As I begin my run for the presidency, one message that I will take from coast to coast is a call for a balanced budget amendment and term limits. I believe that if a candidate were to win the presidency on this platform we could finally get it done.

I am not aware of any candidate for president making term limits a leading cause in a national campaign. I aim to do just that in the coming year.

How About Reading the Bill?

People sometimes like to rail against Congress for not getting enough done, that not enough bills are passing. While I understand their point, after being here for four years I can tell you that's *not* the biggest problem in Congress. Not even close. The problem is in what they *do* pass, and that almost no one here has read the bill before it passes. Not all of Congress's reluctance to pass bills is bad, in my estimation. I'm against enacting laws that expand government, raise taxes, or impede personal liberty, but some of Congress's ineptitude is due to tribal righteousness, petulance, apathy, and plain old laziness. Early on, my staff and I began to put together legislation based on the novel idea of having senators read bills before they vote on them. I'm not joking.

I once received a 600-page highway bill on the morning of the vote. Six hundred pages to read and I was given a couple of hours to read it! On the way over to the vote, I passed two senators in the hallway of the Russell Senate Office Building who were heading back to their offices. They had been on their way to vote when they found things written into the bill that affected their states and were trying to figure out a last-minute way to get them out. This happens all the time. During the debate before the vote on Obamacare, Nancy Pelosi famously said, "We have to pass the bill so that you can find out what is in it." No wonder Congress has an 11 percent approval rating. We don't even know what we're voting on. So my Read the Bill legislation proposed that, before calling a vote, Congress had to wait one day for every twenty pages of legislation, which would provide plenty of time to read every bill before we vote on it. So, a 2,000-page bill like Obamacare would require a hundred days of reading time. That would keep us busy.

Maybe if we did a little less voting on bills we haven't seen, and a little more evaluating and debating the bills, the product up here would be better. It can't be much worse.

Along with term limits and the reading bills, another change that has to be made is redistricting. When districts are gerrymandered, people are often elected for life, and sometimes in spite of behavior that would get them fired in any private business. To hold on to power, state legislatures have drawn up congressional districts that look like sea creatures. A district in Illinois is shaped like an open clamshell. In North Carolina there is a district that connects the urban centers of several cities, runs over a hundred miles in length, and looks like an eel.

For the lengths state legislatures go to ensure "safe" seats for their prospective parties, they might as well be stuffing the ballot box.

What we need is computer software to design legislative districts fairly and without any connection at all to voting patterns. Currently, gerrymandering splits counties, cities, and communities, even individual streets.

Today, 80 percent of districts are unwinnable by a candidate of the opposite party. It takes a sea change, to continue the metaphor, of public opinion to affect the maps, and even then there is often a lag time of over ten years. For example, in the 1980s Texas turned Republican, culminating with George W. Bush receiving over 60 percent of the gubernatorial vote. But the congressional delegation continued to be 60 percent or more Democrat for ten years.

Above the Law

There is nothing more egregious that happens on Capital Hill than Congress passing laws that include exemptions for senators and representatives. In my opinion, it's the height of arrogance.

If it weren't for the book *Throw Them All Out* by Peter Schweizer and a *60 Minutes* interview of Schweizer that followed the book's publication, Congress might still be exempt from federal statutes guarding against insider trading. Here are some of the other laws Congress holds or held itself above: the Social Security Act of 1935 (up until the 1980s), the National Labor Relations Act of 1935, the Equal Pay Act of 1963, the Freedom of Information Act of 1966, the Privacy Act of 1974, and the Ethics in Government Act of 1978.[3]

In the Federalist Papers essay 57, James Madison warned us that we would remain free only as long as lawmakers live by the laws they pass. It's not asking much, is it?

How about a bill that says Congress shall pass no law that does not bind members of Congress as well? I have introduced just such a concept in a proposed amendment to the Constitution.

Of course, if my legislation came to a vote, the first thing Congress would do is exempt itself from it. As the late, great congressman Henry Hyde once said, "Congress would exempt itself from the law of gravity if it could."

I know the ideas above are bold, and it will take something of a political upheaval for them to be enacted. But I also know something about political upheavals, and I know the good that can come out of them. I've also seen what sticking to the status quo can do.

Much of this recalcitrance in Washington comes from the contentious relationship between the legislative and executive branches. Yes, some of it is politics. But much of it is leadership. Along with a new direction and new ideas and lawmakers, I believe we need a change of heart at the top. Rudderless, our great country struggles with core issues that divide us.

The Fed

One of the first bills I introduced was the Federal Reserve Transparency Act of 2011, also known as the Audit the Fed bill. My father championed this bill for more than a decade before finally getting it to pass the House with a huge bipartisan majority. Unfortunately, Harry Reid let it die in the Senate. I asked the then Senate Majority Leader time and again for a vote. On my Facebook page, I even posted Senator Reid's floor speeches from the 1990s in favor of auditing the Fed. He wouldn't budge, but I wouldn't give up. I scheduled appointments with him. We sat by the roaring fire in his office and I tried to convince him to give me a vote. He just sat there, listened, and wagged his head no. So, a bill that received more than 350 votes in the House was never allowed to see the light of day in the Senate.

There is something very wrong with not allowing a vote on a bill that passes the House with over three hundred votes and has the support of the overwhelming majority of the American people. It is a bipartisan bill. It is *exactly* the kind of legislation we should be moving in Washington, but we won't. Our system is broken. Too many career politicians. Too many people with partisan political scorecards in their pockets. Too many people who are themselves in some special interest's pocket.

It amazes me that anyone would oppose a simple call for transparency at the Federal Reserve. Why would they want the movement of America's money supply kept secret? Opponents argued that transparency would undermine the Fed's independence. It seems they've forgotten that Congress created the Fed, and that it's Congress's job to oversee the central bank. Many of these same opponents voted for a new agency called the Consumer Financial Protection Bureau that would also operate without congressional oversight and be funded by, get this, money printed up by the Fed! Talk about blind trust. Just let the fox watch the chickens, but make sure you close the door to the coop to give him some privacy.

All of this happens in utmost secrecy and without accountability. The only oversight of the Fed currently in place is a yearly audit by the Office of the Inspector General. Below is an exchange between former Florida congressman Alan Grayson and the then Federal Reserve inspector general Elisabeth A. Coleman. This illuminating Q and A occurred some months after the financial collapse of Lehman Brothers.

Rep. Grayson: What about Bloomberg's report that there are trillions of dollars in off-balance sheet transactions that the Federal Reserve has entered into since last September? Are you familiar with those off-balance sheet transactions?

I.G. Coleman: We do not have jurisdiction to directly go out and audit Reserve Bank activities specifically.

Don't let anyone tell you we already have an audit of the Fed. No meaningful audit of the Fed exists, and when the primary auditor and overseer of the Fed was asked about nine trillion dollars, she had no clue what had been purchased with nine trillion dollars.

Is there a chance that the Fed only has our best interests at heart? Sure. But when trillions of dollars change hands, wouldn't you want to know who gives and gets the money and if anyone enriched themselves in the process? We'll never know until we get a real audit of the Fed. The House has overwhelmingly and in a bipartisan vote passed Audit the Fed. With the Republican majority in the Senate, I will get a vote on Audit the Fed in 2015. That's a promise.

There's another promise concerning the Fed that I will make, and that is: I'll work to stop the revolving door from Wall Street to the Treasury to the Fed and back again. The Fed and its captains conduct crony capitalism at its worst. "The most powerful entity in the United States is riddled with conflicts of interest," writes Senator Bernie Sanders on his website. Senator Sanders goes on to explain that the Government Accounting Office detailed instance after instance of top executives of corporations and financial institutions using their influence as Federal Reserve directors to financially benefit their firms and, in at least one instance, themselves. "Clearly it is unacceptable for so few people to wield so much unchecked power," Sanders writes. "Not only do they run the banks, they run the institutions that regulate the banks."[4]

We have former secretaries of Treasury who go from government to Wall Street, pocketing hundreds of millions of dollars, and federal regulators on all levels who are prone to what's called "regulatory capture," the practice of going soft on companies they're supposed to be keeping an eye on to boost their prospects of a job down the road. It's hard to imagine that the Fed isn't rife with conflicts of interest.

Maybe you don't believe that there are conflicts of interest at the

Fed. But if you don't, then tell me how they decided to bail out Bear Stearns but not Lehman Brothers. Taxpayers deserve to know what kind of "distressed" assets the Fed is buying. We deserve to know if these "deals" involved friends or acquaintances. We deserve to know if there are liabilities from companies Fed employees once worked for.

I often hear people say that greed was the primary reason for the 2008 housing crisis. Greed is simply a pejorative term for self-interest. It wasn't a strange accumulation of greed that brought on this crisis. To explain how so many people acted in concert to cause a boom in housing you need to look at something systemic that permeated all decision making at the time, a cause that influenced every decision. Without question, the universal factor behind the collapse was government-fixed interest rates, which were fixed below the market rate and were not allowed to rise in such a manner that would have naturally curtailed the boom. Self-interest, or even greed, didn't begin the boom. Government manipulation of interest rates did.

By 2001, Federal Reserve chairman Alan Greenspan had lowered the interest rate to a measly 1 percent. We had just come out of a spending bubble in the late 1990s, and pressure from the Clinton administration and inflation worries influenced his decision. He then kept the interest rate at 1 percent for the next three years, and when he finally raised it in 2004, he did so only by .25 percent. So what effect did low interest rates have?

Interest rates are like insulin. In medicine, we have a concept we call homeostasis, which means maintenance of balance. When you eat a meal your blood glucose rises and insulin is stimulated to rise. As a consequence, your blood glucose falls. In a free market, as the demand for more money occurs the price of money (interest rates) should rise, which slows the economy. You get a gentle, cyclical nature to economic growth. What happens if interest rates are kept artificially low by government? The feedback loop breaks and the economy expands without any checks or balances, which is exactly what happened during the housing boom. The Fed fixed interest rates below the market rate, and with the feedback loop severed, housing prices soared. The crash came when it was finally revealed that there was nothing of substance backing the loans. It's like the Hans Christian Andersen story "The Emperor's New Clothes." When the public discovers that the emperor isn't wearing any clothes the whole belief system falls apart.

Congress encouraged and abetted the boom by legislating lenient lending practices. Large fines were levied on any bank that refused to go along with zero down-payment loans. Banks didn't complain because the government pledged to insure the loans.

Then, after the crash, the Fed's bailout of banks and brokerages like AIG was conducted in such secrecy no one really knows to this day how many trillions of dollars and zero-interest loans it doled out. We do know this: the bailout the Fed conducted made the Troubled Assets Relief Program (TARP) and its original $700 billion handout look like a weekly allowance from Dad. Some sources maintain that the Fed leveraged more than $7 trillion to banks. The Fed's balance sheet grew by over $4 trillion.

At first blush, you might say that having assets is good, right? Well, not if those assets are bad car and home loans and derivatives that no one else will buy, and especially not if the "assets" are purchased with an IOU by the Fed. Those who defend the Fed say there is no credit risk. No? How about the $4 trillion they spent on bad mortgages?

That vast sums of taxpayer money are used in such a hidden and fishy manner is inexcusable under any circumstance, but that it's done by an agency that can't keep its own fiscal house in order is preposterous. Estimates have the Fed overleveraged between 56:1 and 90:1.[5]

How bad is that? Well, consider that Lehman Brothers was overleveraged 30-1 on the day it shut its doors.

The noteworthy quote ascribed to Ludwig von Mises, the Austrian economist, can be applied to the Fed perfectly. "Government is the only agency that can take a valuable commodity like paper, slap some ink on it, and make it totally worthless."[6]

Guess who is adversely affected the most by this? You, the middle class. As the money the Fed controls changes hands, the moneyed class gets richer and the middle class gets shortchanged. President Obama plays the partisan game and speaks of income inequality and blames Republicans. Yet income inequality has gotten worse under his administration.

I believe in the free market. I believe it's the engine that will pull the middle class from its rut and return to it the promise this great class of American workers once held. That promise has been diminishing by the decade, one of the great travesties of our time.

I have no sympathy for the banker who made $100 million a year while his or her bank plunged into bankruptcy, only to be bailed out by the taxpayer and then, without missing a beat, goes back to making millions of dollars. I'm all for people profiting from success, but in a true free market they are also punished for their mistakes. Only in a world of crony capitalism would bankers whose faulty decisions caused bankruptcy be allowed to cash out as the middle class absorbs the losses. Capitalism isn't the problem. The problem arises when cronyism creates special playgrounds and safe niches for a few connected individuals.

Those bankers who made millions selling derivatives should have been the first to suffer the reversal. Anyone who committed financial crimes should be punished. No one should get a free pass. As in so many sagas, the connected rich didn't get a scratch. They convinced Congress to have the middle-class taxpayer bail them out and went on as if nothing had happened. It's infuriating. Not only are the cronies protected from suffering for their mistakes when they're at fault, no one bothers to examine the underlying causes of the collapse.

I entered politics and embraced the Tea Party movement primarily because I abhorred the idea of big government taking money from the middle class to bail out the big rich banks. During my Senate primary campaign, I wrote that federal bailouts reward inefficient and corrupt management, rob taxpayers, hurt smaller and more responsible private firms, exacerbate our budget problems, explode national debt, and destroy the U.S. dollar. Even more importantly, any bailout of private industry is in direct violation of the Constitution. It is a transfer of wealth from those who have earned it to those who have squandered it.

Millions of people lost their jobs because of the 2008 crisis. Millions of lives were irreparably changed for the worse, and millions of people suffer from fear that it will happen again. They insist on saying that the economy has rebounded. But don't tell that to the financially wounded middle class. People are still looking over their shoulders and, given the same policy and secrecy in place at the Fed, I don't blame them.

One of the things that baffles me about the so-called recovery we are having is the sheer brazenness of the Obama administration and the willing participation of the press in distorting the truth. The truth is that even though unemployment may appear to be declining a bit over the last year or two, it is simply not true that more people are working. The drop in those labeled "unemployed" is due only to them dropping out of the workforce—not because they are finding work.

What kind of leader claims victory in the fight to create new jobs by using the number of people who have been looking for one for so long that they have simply given up? This is symptomatic of the problem in Washington. Everyone is looking to take credit, even for something that hasn't actually happened. No one will tell the truth.

The truth is more people are out of work. Fewer new jobs are being created. They can't tell you that because then you'd ask why, and the answer is the government is taxing and regulating the job creators out of our country.

A generation of leaders has told these same lies regarding unemployment. They come from both parties. They share something in common, though: they believe the government can fix all problems, and they have to make up statistics to prove that point. If we don't understand history and if we don't correctly diagnose why the crisis occurred, we may well be doomed to repeat it. I, for one, will do everything I can to protect the middle class from another economic meltdown. Auditing the Fed and putting an end to crony capitalism should be an administration's priority. It certainly would be mine.

6

★ ★ ★

Can You Hear Me Now?

there comes a time
there comes a time in the history of nations
when a country passes the point of no return
when liberty recedes and tyranny ensues

that time approaches
the time draws near
but the question remains
will we be sunshine patriots
shrinking at the first shot
shrinking at the first sense of privation
or will we stand as men and women of courage
will we stand and fight for our freedoms?

* * *

In his wonderful biography of John Adams, David McCullough describes the moment that might have sparked the American Revolution. It was on a winter's night in 1761, and the Province House in Boston was filled with indignant colonists and merchants. Adams, then a twenty-five-year-old lawyer, had gone to the royal governor's mansion on Marlborough Street to hear his hero argue against the Crown's use of generalized warrants called writs of assistance.

His hero was the fiery and brilliant lawyer James Otis.

The year before, the British Parliament had reissued to soldiers and customs officials the power to enter any colonist's home at any time to search for smuggled goods. The warrants needed neither probable cause of wrongdoing nor the signature of a judge. This exercise of power had infuriated the colonists, especially Otis. He had been the Advocate General in Massachusetts for the British government but resigned his office in 1761 in protest over the writs. Adams expected a dramatic performance from his champion.

He wasn't disappointed.

The five judges in "scarlet English cloth, in their broad hats, and immense judicial wigs" sat by a blazing fireplace in the second-floor courtroom, Adams would recall.

But the brightest flame in the room that evening was Otis. During a five-hour oration, one in which he evoked a phrase that is perhaps the cornerstone of American freedoms—"A man's house is his castle"—the Boston lawyer mesmerized the courtroom. "I will to my dying day oppose, with all the powers and faculties God has given me, all such instruments of slavery on the one hand and villainy on the other as this Writ of Assistance is," Otis thundered. "It appears to me the worst instrument of arbitrary power, the most destructive of English liberty and the fundamental principles of law, that ever was found in an English law-book..."[1]

Otis brought the courtroom to a fever, Adams remembered. So much so, it seemed everyone there was willing to take up arms against the writs.

"Then and there was the first scene in the first act of opposition to the arbitrary claims of Great Britain," Adams would later write. "Then and there the child independence was born."

Two hundred and fifty-two years after James Otis's eloquent and emotional challenge of the writs of assistance, a thirty-year-old systems administrator on contract with the NSA sat in a hotel room in Hong Kong and hit the send button on his laptop. What followed was a torrent of classified documents that exposed the NSA's wholesale practice of warrantless spying on Americans—a revelation that no doubt made James Otis turn over in his grave.

Otis and his opposition to generalized warrants is the reason we have a Fourth Amendment, which promises Americans will "be secure in their persons, houses, papers, and effects, against unreasonable searches and seizures." In the United States, we don't have generalized warrants, which the NSA uses as grounds to intrude into hundreds of millions of Americans' phone and Internet records. The Fourth Amendment says you have to have a name on the warrant, that the warrant has to identify what the authorities are looking for, and the warrant has to say there is probable cause for them to look for it.

If a warrant with the name "Verizon" on it, seeking millions of individual customers' phone records, is not a general warrant, I don't know what is. James Otis wouldn't understand the technology of today. We no longer keep our records in our house only. We keep our records on our phone, on servers, even suspended in a "cloud." But he would certainly recognize that the principle remains the same.

The Fourth Amendment intended to protect privacy. The Fourth Amendment intended that government would have to present probable cause of a crime to a judge, who would then issue a warrant, and only then could an individual's private papers be accessed. One's records are no less private because we allow a third party to hold them. In fact, in our privacy contract with businesses that hold our records, we acknowledge and retain a privacy interest in those records. Our privacy contract forbids the business from sharing information about us without our permission.

When our Founders wrote the Fourth Amendment they guaranteed that the warrant would be deliberated upon and written by an independent judiciary, not a policeman, a soldier, or the NSA. Separating the power was a key element to protecting the privacy of the individual.

Big Brother

Digital technology has for the first time made the specter of George Orwell's *1984* a reality.

When I first read *1984*, I had trouble relating to it. The book made me profoundly sad, but I was just a teenager, and teenagers are full of angst for no good reason at all. I understood and was wary of Big Brother but took consolation in the fact that government did not have two-way televisions to monitor our every action. Government didn't have drone surveillance to monitor our every move.

When I read *1984* the first time, before I had ever been in love, I had trouble connecting with Winston, Orwell's everyman protagonist. The next time I read *1984* I was a forty-something. I had experienced love and could understand what it would be like to renounce the person you loved.

What would it take to renounce the ones you love? What would it take to renounce your rights as free men and women? We've fought for more than 800 years to restrain the state. From the Magna Carta on, our tradition has been to fight to limit the power of the state.

Would it take starvation and beatings to give up your right to property? Would it take rats pressed up against your face to get you to renounce your right to a trial by jury? Or will we let fear alone cause us to relinquish our guarantee to due process? Will we let fear of terrorism allow us to give up our most basic liberties?

The desire by humans to control fellow humans has always existed, as has the desire to resist being controlled.

We always had places to hide. We always had places to flee. One's thoughts, one's books, one's private actions were hard to control, discern, and disrupt.

Dystopian novels were just that—anti-utopias, but not practically possible. One could always sigh in relief that such surveillance, such invasion of privacy, was not technologically possible.

The individualist who feared 1984 in 1949 need now shout from the top of his or her lungs...for technology has now made the unthinkable thinkable.

Big Brother surrounds us not only in the form of the surveillance state; we now face a government that invades even our basic right of trial by jury.

In 2011, the defense authorization bill came up in the Senate, allowing American citizens to be imprisoned indefinitely without trial. Along with a coalition of civil libertarians, I tried to remove the language allowing for indefinite detention. The sides were drawn.

Proponents, filled with fear, believed that we must give up our liberties to be secure. Opponents believed, like Benjamin Franklin before us, that those who give up liberties for security will have neither.

It took hundreds of years to force monarchs to allow trial by jury, and now that basic right was taken away without so much as a whimper. Virtually all the Democrats and a handful of Republicans, including John McCain, voted to kill this assault on eight hundred years of jurisprudence.

Yet one particularly zealous senator wanted more. Not only did he want to dismiss the right of trial by jury, he wanted the bill to include the power to nullify a jury's verdict that had already been given. This senator sought an amendment that would allow indefinite detention of defendants found innocent by a jury of their peers.

As the Senate debate heated up, as the realization that the majority had allowed detention in America without a trial, a flicker of rebellion occurred.

Amendment sponsors wanted a voice vote, a process usually reserved for noncontroversial subjects. It was late by Senate standards, about nine o'clock. Everyone was tired and wanted to go home. I started for the door, but then I turned and came back. I asked the bill's sponsors again, "Shouldn't we stop this miscarriage of justice?"

The sponsors told me not to worry, that they would remove the amendment that allowed for indefinite detention in conference committee. The Democrat sponsor of the bill said the amendment only reiterated the current law. I responded incredulously, "Current law allows people found innocent to be held indefinitely? How can that be?"

It takes only one senator to force a roll call vote. I knew in my heart I had to try. The indefinite detention amendment would have passed a voice vote. I stood and addressed the chair: "Mr. President, I call for the yeas and nays."

I did not care how strong the tide was against those of us who believed in the Constitution. I had stood my ground. For a change, those who love liberty won. A majority of the Senate decided that a citizen found innocent by a jury of their peers could not be detained.

"If the evidence does not support conviction, it would be against everything we believe in and fight for in America to still allow the government to imprison you at their whim," I said that night. "Tonight, a blow was struck to fight back against those who would take our liberty."

We are becoming what George Orwell once feared. The state is increasingly, and frighteningly, less respectful of the individual and more certain of its own omnipotence. This authoritarian trend has been as rapid as it is dangerous. Today the breadth of government spying on citizens is without precedent in our history.

And that is saying something. Let me tell you why.

J. Edgar Hoover

On February 12, 2014, I had lunch with Attorney General Eric Holder. The lunch had been previously scheduled to discuss our common interest in giving nonviolent felons a second chance and a restoration of voting rights upon completion of their sentence. The attorney general greeted me in a conference room decorated with elaborate murals and included a portrait of Bobby Kennedy. He laughed as we shook hands. "I understand you're suing me," he said.

That morning, I stood with Matt Kibbe and Ken Cuccinelli, the president and lead counsel of FreedomWorks, to announce a class action lawsuit against the NSA for data collection of Americans' phone records. Along with the attorney general, named in the suit is President Barack Obama, Director of National Intelligence James Clapper, Director of National Security Agency Keith Alexander, and

FBI Director James Comey. It is the largest class action lawsuit in defense of the Bill of Rights ever filed. The class of the suit might conceivably include 300 million people. We didn't define the extent of the class, the government did, by collecting the phone records of virtually every American.

Holder and I had a cordial lunch nonetheless. As I was leaving, he mentioned that J. Edgar Hoover's office was just around the corner from where we stood. I asked, given veritable presence of Hoover's ghost, how Holder could condone the massive surveillance state erected by President Obama. I told him I was disappointed that our first African American president wasn't more sympathetic to the potential for abuse in domestic surveillance.

After all, I said, surveillance was used to try to cripple the civil rights movement. You would think this president above all others would be mindful of the potential for abuse in allowing so much power to gravitate to the NSA. Holder nodded his understanding but was noncommittal. We both knew of the outrageous and dangerous domestic surveillance that went on during the civil rights era.

In those pre-mega-data-collecting days, Hoover had spied on some half million Americans. During the early 1970s, FBI agents infiltrated college campuses across the country and conducted illegal surveillance of organizations as disparate as the women's liberation movement and the Black Liberation Army.

Americans had their mail opened, their phones bugged, and, in a precursor of the recent transgressions against the Tea Party, Hoover's FBI used the IRS and private tax returns to collect information and apply pressure on political enemies.[2]

What's more, just like the NSA does today, Hoover spied on Congress.[3] In the spring of 2014, it became apparent that the CIA was secretly searching Senator Dianne Feinstein's Intelligence Committee's computers and reading Senate work product. They surreptitiously removed a report that analyzed the CIA's torture of prisoners. Senator Feinstein, to her credit, called them out. "I have grave concerns that the CIA's search may well have violated the separation of powers principles embodied in the United States Constitution, including the speech and debate clause. It may have undermined the constitutional framework essential to effective congressional oversight of intelligence activities or any other government function."[4]

How could we have not learned from Hoover's abuses of civil liberty?

In her book *The Burglary: The Discovery of J. Edgar Hoover's Secret FBI*, Betty Medsger tells the story of Vietnam protestors in 1971 breaking into an FBI office in Pennsylvania. The files they stole showed the breadth of Hoover's criminal abuse of power and disregard of the Fourth Amendment.

In a magazine article about the break-in, Medsger wrote, "files revealed that African-Americans, Hoover's largest targeted group, didn't have to be perceived as having liberal, or even radical or subversive, ideas to merit being spied on. Nor was it necessary for them to engage in violent behavior to become a watched person. Being black was enough."

The most explosive piece of information that came out of the break-in was Hoover's investigation of Martin Luther King Jr. Hoover had Dr. King's bedroom bugged to record his extramarital affairs. Just a few weeks before King was to receive the Nobel Peace Prize, the FBI sent the damning tapes to both him and his wife. The package also included a letter suggesting to Dr. King that he consider suicide. "King, there is only one thing left for you to do. You know what it is. You have just 34 days in which to do it, this exact number has been selected for a specific reason. It has definite practical significance. You are done. There is but one way out for you."[5] The letter was mailed thirty-four days before Christmas.

Again, I was struck by the irony, and as I left I continued to express my disbelief to Holder. "How could our first African American president condone pervasive spying on Americans?" I asked.

"Let's just say the administration's position on the NSA is not monolithic," he said.

He left it at that, which only left me with more questions. Did the attorney general mean he was against the spying? If so, why was his voice falling on deaf ears?

As I walked away, I had an uneasy feeling and less faith than ever in the way the administration and the NSA were carrying out their surveillance program.

The Spooky History of the NSA

So just how did we get to a place where the Fourth Amendment is given no respect? Well, to answer that question you have to know a little about the National Security Agency.

If you wanted to, you could probably trace the beginnings of the NSA back to the Civil War, when telegraph cables were first intercepted. In more recent history, the NSA grew out of our involvement in World War II. In his famous Day of Infamy speech, Franklin Roosevelt promised America that we would not only defend ourselves to the utmost, but would "make very certain that this form of treachery shall never endanger us again."

FDR gave that speech to a joint session of Congress, asking for a declaration of war. It was, by the way, the last time we followed the Constitution in declaring war properly. Our Founding Fathers set up checks and balances for a reason: so that unchecked power did not accrue to one person, and certainly not the power to declare war. The president can't declare war, or is not supposed to. A declaration of war comes from Congress.

With FDR's declaration of war came his battle cry—"never again"—which became the de facto motto of the U.S. foreign intelligence agencies that kept FDR's promise until 9/11. In fact, many historians credit our proficiency at intercepting messages and breaking codes with turning the tide of World War II. The Battle of Midway and the D-day invasion certainly profited from intelligence, though our armed forces paid an extraordinary price in both. A strong nation requires such tools. Surveillance and deciphering are an integral part of our national defense.

It was after World War II, however, in 1952, that the modern NSA was born, though the event wasn't exactly announced in your local paper. For many years, the agency went about its business so stealthily that the joke was the initials stood for No Such Agency. A memorial plaque in the Maryland office reads: "They Served in Silence."[6] The agency grew from adolescence to adulthood during the Cold War. Working out of its headquarters in Fort Mead, Maryland, the NSA was never meant for domestic intelligence use. Its function was purely to spy on messages from foreign entities—mostly from the Soviet bloc. Which reminds me of what James Madison famously said. "If tyranny and oppression come to this land it will be in the guise of fighting a foreign enemy."

For the next couple of decades, the NSA ran silent and deep. It was during these years that technology, especially in computation and communication, developed rapidly. Although novelists and movie directors were enamored with the FBI and CIA, it was the NSA that owned perhaps the biggest advancement in spy craft. It was also during these years that the NSA began to spy on Americans.

James Bamford has written four books about the NSA. In his first, *The Puzzle Palace: Inside the National Security Agency, America's Most Secret Intelligence Organization*, published in 1982, he writes that, from its inception, the NSA was "free of legal restrictions" and holding "technological capabilities for eavesdropping beyond imagination." "Like an ever-widening sinkhole," he writes, "N.S.A.'s surveillance technology will continue to expand, quietly pulling in more and more communications and gradually eliminating more and more privacy."

That sinkhole began to widen just after World War II when Project SHAMROCK and its sister project MINARET[7] began collecting all the data from telegraph transmissions to and from the United States. The Armed Forces Security Agency (AFSA), the predecessor of the NSA, ran the projects. In the 1960s, with the maturation of the computer, the NSA upgraded the program and called it HARVEST. At its height, HARVEST analyzed 150,000 American messages a month.

As the Cato Institute's Julian Sanchez aptly writes, "The machine was built to fight communism—but it was reprogrammed to fight democracy."

The extent to which democracy was being pummeled was uncovered in the mid-1970s during the Church Committee hearings. The Senate investigation was formed after Watergate and headed by Frank Church, the Democrat Senator from Idaho. The public unraveling of Nixon and his presidency, combined with Hoover's wanton abuse of power, which was also investigated during the hearings, had America angry and suspicious of government—not a bad national mindset, if you ask me. Our Founders never intended for Americans to trust their government. Our entire Constitution was predicated on the notion that government was to be restrained and minimized as much as possible.

With the Church hearings, America got its first look inside the NSA. What they saw disturbed them.

"The United States Government has perfected a technological capability that enables us to monitor the messages that go through the air," Senator Church said on *Meet the Press*.[8] "At the same time, that capability at any time can be turned around on the American people. And no American would have any privacy left—such is the capability to monitor everything...There would be no place to hide."

Church's televised remarks weren't the only prescient moment of the hearings.

During the questioning of Air Force general and NSA director Lew Allen, Senator Walter Mondale wondered what NSA's future held. "What we have to deal with," the senator said, "is whether this incredibly powerful and impressive institution that you head could be used by President 'A' in the future to spy upon the American people."[9]

If my math is correct, our current president was a sophomore or junior in high school at the time. I assume (and I know you can get in trouble doing such, but I'll go out on a limb) that Barack Obama at the time didn't give the Church Committee hearings and Senator Mondale's warning a second thought. He might, however, want to go back and read the transcripts.

In 1978, as a result of the Church Committee and the exposure of domestic spying by the NSA,[10] Congress passed the Foreign Intelligence Surveillance Act, and President Jimmy Carter signed it into law. The bill was meant to safeguard the American people from the NSA by establishing the Foreign Intelligence Surveillance Act court, which was supposed to approve only legitimate surveillance requests. So far, so good, right? Except for one minor detail. The FISA court would conduct its business in secret. Not only was the public denied access to the court, only lawmakers in classified settings were apprised of its proceedings.

So what does the FISA court look like? Well, even my access is limited, but from what I know the court is physically housed in a windowless room in a secure area of the U.S. District Court on Constitution Avenue in Washington, D.C. Eleven federal district judges make up the court, and they sit for seven-year terms. They perform the FISA tasks in addition to their regular duties. The chief justice of the Supreme Court appoints the judges. Neither the executive nor the legislative branches of the government are included in the selection process.

The greater mission of the court is to issue permission or search warrants for the purpose of gathering foreign intelligence information, for example, on foreign spies, foreign terrorists, and other threats from abroad. Or at least that's what it was set up to do. The government has to demonstrate to a FISA judge that the information it wants to collect is relevant to an international terrorism investigation. Targeted individuals are not allowed legal representation.

Though the court was set up as a safeguard, without transparency there is no way of knowing if the American people are being protected from the spy agency. Advocates for the FISA court say the exceptions to privacy protections were narrow in those simpler days.

Then we were attacked on September 11, 2001. In the aftermath of that terrible tragedy the balance between liberty and security tipped precipitously toward security, without protections for freedom and privacy. Though I wasn't a senator at the time, it's easy for me to imagine how high emotions were running in Congress. But history has taught us that laws passed in the heat of battle can do more harm than good in the long run.

The wording of the Patriot Act allows the NSA to obtain any "tangible thing" that is "relevant to an authorized investigation."[11] So what does the NSA define as relevant? Everything and everybody. Every single American citizen could theoretically be a potential terror suspect and therefore can be spied upon without their knowledge, or so the government's logic now goes. This new definition is what inspired Patriot Act author Rep. James Sensenbrenner to speak out against the NSA and promote legislation to rein it in.[12] We literally have no idea how much information our government has on us, and by the government's loose rationale it can obtain as much as it likes for virtually any reason.

Since 2001, the FISA court has approved on average 1,800 warrants a year for wiretaps and searches. And for the first time since the writs of assistance, we allow warrants to be written by soldiers, or their modern-day equivalent, the police and the FBI. Calling them National Security Letters, FBI agents now write tens of thousands of warrants each year, with the total number reaching far into the hundreds of thousands.[13]

Most FBI agents are hardworking, honest, and would never think of abusing their power. I know wonderful men and women in law enforcement. I play golf on occasion with my local FBI agent, and we have discussions on this topic.

I believe he would do what is right, but our system is not set up so that I should have to believe that. We write rules to protect us against those who may not always do what is right. We separated police power from the judiciary for a reason: so the emotion of the chase, the adrenaline of pursuit, would not cloud the judgment of probable cause.

In the same way, I don't ascribe bad motives to the president. But it's not enough for the president to argue, "I am a good man and will never abuse this power." Power must always be circumscribed. Madison realized this when he wrote in the Federalist Papers that even if the government were comprised of angels, we would need Constitutional limitations on power.

President Obama fundamentally misunderstands the concept of the separation of power, especially when it comes to the National Security Agency and the way it tramples the Fourth Amendment. That doesn't make him a bad person. It just makes him a bad president.

The tendency of power is to corrupt. The historical examples of this are plentiful. Power needs to be reined in because we never know when a leader will arise who will use the power to target Jews, or blacks, or Evangelical Christians, or the Tea Party, or any other minority. Or as Senator Mondale warned us, when "President A" uses the agency to spy on ordinary Americans.

It's not just the executive branch that can be seduced by power. If the legislative body that makes laws also had the power to enforce them and to try them in court, it would lead to "tyranny," as James Madison said.

Supreme Court Justice Louis Brandeis once said, "The greatest dangers to liberty lurk in insidious encroachment by men of zeal, well meaning but without understanding."

After terrorists attacked our country, that well-meaning zeal Brandeis cautioned us about was in full force and brought about poor decisions. After 9/11 we gave the police the power to write warrants because we believed that it would help us stay free and safe. In 2001, George W. Bush issued an executive order that instituted a program called StellarWind, which allowed the NSA to look at the content of Americans' email and phone calls to overseas. StellarWind was the beginning of the post-9/11 assault on the Fourth Amendment. Because of President Bush's overreach, the Bill of Rights protection of our privacy began to fall apart.

During my first hundred days in Congress, the Patriot Act neared its sunset. Provisions were added to the act that required Congress to revisit the law outside of the "Climate of Crisis," as the *Christian Science Monitor* called the atmosphere in which it was conceived. I fought to let the law expire, or at the very least to have it amended, specifically its violation of two personal freedoms. One powerful senator looked at me with great concern and said, "But what will happen if the Patriot Act expires at midnight?" as if the country would immediately be overrun by extremists if it did. I cracked a little smile and replied, "Maybe we could rely on the Constitution for a few hours."

Bush's Patriot Act represented the opposite of the Constitution's mission. Based on fear, it depended on Americans forgetting or ignoring our rights, and allowing big government to be unleashed. The Patriot Act was about forgetting to protect privacy. The Patriot Act was conceived with the naïve notion that government will only act for good and will never abuse its power.

I pushed the Senate to the deadline on the Patriot Act vote—I was the only senator holding it up. The Senate ultimately allowed a vote on two amendments that I had fought to include. For a freshman senator to force such action is extremely rare, and my colleagues weren't too happy about it. Republicans and Democrats alike were in agreement—the war on terror trumped the Bill of Rights. One of my amendments would have ended the requirement that banks file suspicious activities reports on hundreds of thousands of innocent customers without a warrant and without probable cause. My other amendment would have forced the government to get a warrant before searching gun ownership records. Though I lost both votes, across the country gun owners and privacy advocates took notice. Although the Patriot Act extension ultimately passed overwhelmingly, I had put the Senate on notice. There was a Bill of Rights defender in their midst with whom they would have to tangle at every turn.

Over time, Congress has expanded this assault on the Fourth Amendment. A FISA amendment was passed for the purpose of allowing government to intercept foreign emails outside the United States that might be "relevant." We already know that the federal government's definition of relevant is at best hazy. We now also know that under these provisions, the NSA uses supercomputers through a program called Upstream to collect countless emails. It has already been shown that many of these emails were and are domestic, not foreign.

As the CATO Institute's Julian Sanchez wrote in his piece "Decoding the Summer of Snowden,"[14] the scale of the NSA's interception is so massive, it is likely that the agency is collecting upward of 56,000 "wholly" domestic emails annually. What that means is emails that don't travel outside the United States—it means Americans emailing other Americans in America! This is a practice that is in direct and, I would say, hostile disregard of FISA and the Constitution.

The NSA also has a program called PRISM in which the agency bullies Internet companies like Google, Apple, Microsoft, and others to monitor online communication. How much monitoring? We don't know exactly. We do know that the government's logic in what it thinks it can do is so broad that its scope is basically unlimited in seizing our online communications. Sanchez writes that the blanket surveillance orders "resemble nothing so much as a modern version of the 'general warrants'—or 'writs of assistance'—that outraged the American colonists and inspired the Fourth Amendment. They may 'target' information about foreigners, but they give the NSA—not neutral judges—the discretion to determine which particular 'places' and digital 'papers' will be searched or seized."

The war on terror provisions had morphed into an unrestrained, very expensive, and secret war on American citizens.

Secret, that is, until the then unknown systems analyst hit his send button.

The Leaker vs. the Liar

In January 2013, a documentary filmmaker named Laura Poitras received an anonymous email from someone claiming to have extraordinary access to explosive surveillance material.[15] Ms. Poitras was working on a film about surveillance at the time. At first skeptical, she eventually agreed to meet the mystery man in Hong Kong to see what he had. She brought along her writing partner, journalist Glenn Greenwald.

Mr. Greenwald worked as columnist for the American version of the British newspaper *The Guardian*. It was *The Guardian* that broke Edward Snowden's story.

In the video that accompanied the online news piece, Snowden told his interviewers that his reason for leaking the documents was that he didn't want to live in a world where there wasn't privacy, and therefore no room for intellectual exploration and creativity. He said he didn't do it for money or personal gain. He thought what the NSA was doing was "an existential threat to democracy."[16]

Snowden would also later say that he made his mind up to release the documents in March 2013 after seeing the director of National Intelligence, James Clapper, tell a Senate committee on intelligence that the NSA was not collecting data on any Americans. Snowden's leaks proved Clapper a liar and showed us that the NSA is a giant, indiscriminate vacuum cleaner of personal phone conversations. So why does this matter? There are some who say the NSA is keeping us safe, so leave them alone. Others say, as Obama told the press, that the NSA does not abuse its power, so why make a big deal about it? Still others say they are not listening in. If you are doing nothing wrong you have nothing to fear. It's only metadata! It doesn't matter.

I say it's a tragic retreat from a standard of innocent until proven guilty.

And metadata does matter.

Two Stanford students recently developed an app called Metaphone, which collects metadata just like the NSA. Some 500 people participated in the experiment. What they found was that metadata is easily distilled into personal information. By using ordinary phone books available on the Web, like Yelp and Google, they were able to identify 95 percent of the places and people to whom the calls were placed. So say you're dialing a suicide hotline or a doctor who specializes in diseases you don't want anyone to know about. Metadata gives them that information. Or say you're calling a divorce lawyer, or an unpopular political group, or a gun shop, or even just a boyfriend you don't want your other boyfriend to know about. All of that information is available through metadata. Those who have metadata can figure out what religion you practice, who you voted for, what diseases you have, your sexual identity, and the list goes on ad infinitum.

To those who argue that metadata's no big deal, consider that the former director of the NSA said, "We kill people based on metadata."[17]

The documents released by Edward Snowden revealed a secret FISA court order approving the collection of metadata from the phone companies AT&T and Verizon, and Internet giants Microsoft, Google, and Facebook.

I don't know about you, but when I first heard about metadata the first question that popped into my head was just how many people are there in a metadata? I have to tell you, I actually asked that question in a classified briefing. I asked how many Americans the government has spied on since 9/11 through the use of drones, legal search warrants, illegal search warrants, federal agent–written search warrants, and just plain government spying. Even if they did give me an answer, it's classified, so I can't share the number with you. Ah, the heck with it! There's enough secrecy surrounding the NSA as it is.

It was a gazillion. That's, of course, a made-up number—so I can't be accused of revealing secrets. But, the truth is, in the past decade the U.S. government has collected records on an unimaginable number of U.S. citizens.

We really have no idea how much our government is spying on us. Recent revelations exposed the United States Postal Service's massive surveillance program. The USPS approved nearly 50,000 law enforcement surveillance requests last year to track your mail.[18] What we have learned is disturbing enough. What we might learn in the future may very well reveal a government with absolutely no limitations on its ability to monitor citizens. The comparison of the modern United States to Orwell's Big Brother is not hyperbole. It is far closer to fact than even the NSA's most strident apologists are willing to admit.

It could very well be that every single American is under surveillance.

The NSA can also tap into email, contacts, and notes on your smartphone. It can tell where you are and where you've been.[19]

With the Banking Privacy Act of 1986, the government can also go back as far as it wants and read emails more than six months old on any device without a warrant. Senator Mike Lee and I have put forward a bill to end this practice.

Supposedly, the NSA is allowed to search only phone numbers that have a connection of "reasonable suspicion" to a foreign terrorist group. Those search parameters are not very restrictive, however. They include records of people three "hops" from a suspicious number, according to Cato's Julian Sanchez. "If you've ever called anybody who has called anybody who has called anybody who has called a suspect, your phone logs can be copied into a second database for analysis unencumbered by all those pesky restrictions," Sanchez wrote.

Since the Snowden revelations, there have been thousands of documented breaches of FISA rules by NSA analysts, including something they've dubbed LOVEINT, spy speak for "love intell."[20] Although the number of these transgressions was small, if you're either an ex-lover or prospective love interest of an NSA analyst, you might want to watch what you say when you're talking on your cell.

Out of all of the transgressions the government inflicted on the Fourth Amendment, maybe the worst was the NSA's intrusion into our cyber lives. Call me old-school, but there once existed an element of trust between Internet users. Yes, I know, there have been scam artists and other misuses of personal data since the invention of the Internet, but nothing close to the scale perpetrated by the NSA. If you read the tech blogs and columns today, there is a real sense of dissatisfaction not only with the government but with the Internet-based companies that once held themselves to be above reproach, the ones that shouted they were changing the world for the better. As with all of these transgressions, it's the average American who suffers.

American Internet companies are trying to restore confidence in their users.[21] Google is now helping users code their own email and is laying its own fiber-optic cable on ocean floors to give them better control over their customers' data. Apple phones now encrypt emails, photos, and contacts. Last year, when the iPhone 6 came out with this new technology, FBI director James B. Comey told the *New York Times*, "What concerns me about this is companies marketing something expressly to allow people to hold themselves beyond the law."[22]

Though Mr. Comey keeps the request for the Dr. King wiretap on his desk as a reminder, he heads an agency with an extensive history of holding itself above the Constitution. Meanwhile, those "people" Comey talked about wouldn't have felt it necessary if the Director of National Intelligence, James Clapper, hadn't lied to the American people and told us that the government wasn't collecting all of our data all of the time.

Meanwhile, the FBI and other federal agencies have already found ways to circumvent the encryption. One is the use of small planes equipped with "dirtboxes," a device that mimics cell-phone towers and is able to track a suspect within three yards and can intercept data and text even from the iPhone 6.[23]

We've arrived at a strange moment in American politics where the government asks the public to view anyone who challenges its authority as wrong or traitorous, while simultaneously asking the public to ignore or accept intrusive behavior that a strong majority views as wrong. Are we now really supposed to vilify all whistle-blowers and trust government in everything it does?

In the South, it was once a crime for African Americans to drink from "whites only" water fountains. Civil disobedience in pursuit of higher purpose has taken place often in our country. Martin Luther King Jr. once said that there comes a time when you have to stop being a thermometer and start being a thermostat.

I'm not comparing Edward Snowden to Martin Luther King Jr. There are different opinions of Edward Snowden, the "Leaker" of classified NSA information. Some call him a risk taker. Others call him a traitor. Snowden's "flight" to Russia didn't help his standing in many Americans' eyes. Though you have to question his destination, his actions are understandable. Years before there was an Edward Snowden, there was Diane Roark, a staffer for the House Intelligence Committee. It was Roark who was among the first to raise an alarm that the NSA was collecting data on Americans. But when she took her concerns to people she thought would be sympathetic—members of the intelligence committee, a Bush administration official, and even a FISA judge—she was stonewalled. The judge, in fact, reported her to the Justice Department. From that moment on, Roark lived the nightmare of being the target of the intelligence committee. She quit her job and moved to Oregon, where her home was subjected to both "sneak and peek" delayed warrant searches and warranted searches. She was grilled by the CIA and FBI and remained for years under their surveillance. Like many, she thought the election of Barack Obama meant a return to a constitutional rule of law, only to find out that the new administration was worse than its predecessor.[24] In fact, the Obama administration has prosecuted more government leakers than all other administrations combined.[25]

But the bigger point isn't whether Snowden was right or wrong. The bigger point is whether the NSA is.

The bigger point is the erosion of trust we have in government. James Clapper lied under oath to Congress. Yes, there need to be laws against leaking information that involve national security, but there are also laws against lying to and deliberately misleading the American people. Perhaps what makes Clapper's dishonesty more dangerous than Snowden's is that it comes within a series of lies and systematic lawlessness delivered by this administration: from the IRS scandal to Benghazi to the director of Intelligence and the NSA. Connect the dots and what appears on the page is frightening.

All those years ago, in the courtroom in Boston's Province House, James Otis would lose his argument. Obviously, there were no fiber-optic cables in those days and so it would take a year and a half for the decision by the judges to make its way back to the Crown and then return to the colonies to be handed down.

But Otis only lost in a legal sense.

His fiery words echoed through the colonies. He had enunciated what most colonists felt: that they had the right to privacy, that the British government was overstepping its bounds. By virtue of being human they held these rights, which were given to them by God.

The rumble of Otis's words wouldn't die out. Over the next fifteen years they were evoked time and again. And each time they were, the fervor grew. But so did the Crown's callous disregard of the colonists' rights: the Sugar Act, the Stamp Act, the Townshend Acts, and so on.

Then on a December evening in 1773 a group of Boston patriots took a stand. Dressed like Mohawk Indians, they boarded ships and threw chests of tea into the murky Boston Harbor.

It might not surprise you that the Boston Tea Party is one of my favorite moments in our fight for independence.

Nor should it surprise you that I consider James Otis and his burning defense of our right to privacy a fundamental moment in the forming of America's character.

That character is what is sorely missing from our current administration. Repairing this is one of my top priorities.

7

★ ★ ★

On the Road

We don't need new principles, we just need to stand by the ones we have.

★ ★ ★

When I spoke at Howard University here in D.C. in April 2013, I opened my talk at the traditionally black college by explaining that the Republican Party had historically been the party of civil and voting rights. Republicans were a driving force behind the civil rights bills of the Eisenhower and Kennedy eras, and Republicans had supported the 1964 Civil Rights Act at a much higher rate than Democrats in either chamber of Congress. In fact, the story of emancipation, voting rights, and citizenship from Frederick Douglass until the modern civil rights era is the history of the Republican Party.

My audience wasn't impressed, to say the least. Though I was well received that day in general, and have been so many other times at historically black colleges around the country since, the lesson from that day stayed with me. My audience didn't want or need a history lesson. They needed to know that I understood the problems of the community.

How was my party's past a remedy for the intractably high unemployment rate among African Americans, they wondered. How did it aid an educational system that continues to fail inner-city communities? How was it a cure for mandatory minimum sentencing and other racially biased outcomes of the war on drugs?

What did Republican ancient history have to do with the problems African Americans still face?

They had a point.

Luckily, I'd come to Howard, the first Republican to do so in quite a while, with more than just some dusty old references. I also came with a message and a plan. And I came to listen.

I believe at its root the Republican Party, at least the Republican

Party that I embrace, stands for self-reliance and individualism, both of which are the cornerstones of the proud tradition of African Americans. I also know my party has let the bond it once enjoyed with minorities fray to the point that it is nearly beyond repair.

I don't believe it's beyond repair.

What I believe is that the Republican Party needs to bring our civil rights agenda into the twenty-first century. We need to be the champions of voting rights restoration, sentencing reform, and school choice.

Voting rights are a good example of how a love of liberty and respect for the Constitution should work to reverse destructive policies from the past few decades. Currently, if you serve prison time for a felony—even a nonviolent one—you lose many of your rights, even after you have paid your debt and return to society. You often cannot vote, have a hard time getting a job, and encounter many obstacles to starting over as a good citizen.

We should take the opposite approach. When a person has served the time for their crime, they should be encouraged to become an active, productive member of society again. It's not only the morally right thing to do, but has the added benefit of preventing a return to crime and prison.

One way we let these individuals know that they are welcome back into society is to allow them to vote again. Denying a citizen his or her constitutional rights after they have served their prison sentence is unjust. I am proud to have championed this reform in both my home state of Kentucky and through federal law.

We must recognize that, for many people, issues such as voting rights, sentencing reform, and the inability to escape failing schools through school choice are not debates going on in a think tank. They are not committee hearings with scholars and talking points. This is real life for far too many Americans.

I was repeatedly reminded of this when I held school choice forums around the country, but especially in Louisville, Kentucky. I have attended school choice events and charter school functions in the West End of Louisville for years. The citizens who live in the West End are predominately black and low-income. Their schools face a host of challenges, which I wanted to better understand and help find solutions for.

Time after time, when I took questions after a school choice forum, the issue of the restoration of civil and voting rights for felons would arise. I was struck by how often the questions were raised, and how problematic this issue was for so many people.

One father told me that he could not go to watch his children perform in their school plays because of laws restricting felons from school property. This man, who has paid his debt to society, now wants nothing more than to be a supportive and involved father to his children. Obviously we need laws to protect our kids, but we must consider the unintended outcomes of some of these laws—and how they affect individuals, families, and communities.

That is why I've chosen to stand with those who want nothing more than a better school—and eventually a better life—for their kids. It's why I've chosen to stand, against most political advice, with those who want their voting and other rights back after they have served their debt to society. And it's why I've chosen to stand with those for whom our criminal justice system has forgotten the part about justice.

We need to address the inequity of the war on drugs and the contentious relationship that still exists between law enforcement and the black community.

These are among the issues that the audience at Howard University cares about. Our country—and the GOP—needs to better address these issues.

Right now, the Republican brand sucks. I promised Reince Priebus, the chairman of the Republican National Committee, that I would stop saying the GOP sucks, and I will (except for this last time). But both Reince and I know that the same old begets the same old. I believe the Republican Party and minorities have common ground. The Republican Party can rightly serve minority communities if we stay true to our core, be open to new ideas, and boldly profess what we believe.

People say that in order for the Republicans to win back the minority vote they have to be more like Democrats, maybe even "Democrat lite."

I vehemently disagree.

Not only do I know that Republicans share core beliefs with minority communities, I think our policies will succeed where the Democrat policies have failed. Democrats do a lot of talking about poverty and income inequality but, by nearly every measurement, poverty and income inequality are worse under Democrat rule.

Study after study[1] shows that federal assistance does not reduce poverty. Today, after six years of the Obama administration's policies, one in six Americans lives in poverty, more than at any other time in the past several decades. In fact, despite the uptick in the economy, the poor have only grown poorer in the past six years. Black unemployment is at 14 percent, nearly twice the national average.

The objective evidence shows that big government is not a friend to minorities. Big government relies on the Federal Reserve to print money out of thin air, which only leads to higher prices. When the cost of food, tuition, and home repair skyrocket, it's a direct result of our national debt, the million dollars we borrow each minute. Inflation hurts everyone, but particularly the poor and those who are struggling. If getting new brakes for your car causes personal financial collapse, something is very wrong.

I get it, though. What the Republicans offer is less tangible than a government check. The promise of equalizing opportunity through free markets, lower taxes, and fewer regulations doesn't arrive in a mailbox at the first of the month, but it does reside in a life-changing future, a future in which the disadvantaged have the opportunity to break the bonds of poverty.

I know it's not going to be easy for the Republican Party to win the trust of African Americans, Latinos, and other minorities. If you are struggling to get ahead, if you have school loans and personal debt, if you're sick and tired of living month to month, maybe you should think about voting for someone who wants to leave more money in the private sector so that when you look for a job, there just might be one there for you.

According to the NAACP, if current trends continue, one in three black men will spend some time in prison.[2] In Washington, D.C., 57 percent of high school students drop out. In Baltimore the rate is 62 percent, and in Detroit more than 78 percent of students don't graduate from high school. These statistics are staggering. But they are also part of an abysmal record of failure on the part of Democrat policies: the ten poorest major cities in America have been under exclusive Democrat control for decades, many since the sixties.[3]

I remember reading Dr. King's "Letter from Birmingham Jail" and learning of his nonviolent strategy of civil disobedience and realizing how he really understood the idea of just laws. "One has a moral responsibility to disobey unjust laws," he wrote.

Dr. King knew things wouldn't change by inches. To wait for policy and public opinion meant the slow, agonizing death of his cause. He knew that change had to be seismic, a tectonic shift in the plates of the Earth's mantle. He knew that only through civil disobedience would this occur. Rosa Parks, those brave men and women on the bridge in Selma, and the students who sat at the lunch counters were the silent soldiers in this assault on inequality.

But the assault on inequality continues, as evidenced by the color of the population of our jails, the hopelessness of the unemployed and dependent, and the heartbreaking failure of our inner-city schools. My message to the audience at Howard, and in Chicago, and Atlanta, and other venues where I speak to those of all races and backgrounds, is that my Republican Party, the Republican Party I hope to lead to the White House, is willing to change.

Saying you're going to change is one thing, but actually changing takes a lot more than words.

On the Road

From Howard, I set off to travel the country. I began my discovery tour in the West End of Louisville.

Like most inner-city neighborhoods, the West End has both a vibrant cultural history and one of racial strife. It was the boyhood home of Muhammad Ali—an avenue there bears his name. It's also the home of Shawnee Park, a two-hundred-acre oasis designed by Frederick Law Olmsted, who also designed Central Park in New York City. Samuel Plato, the renowned architect and graduate of Simmons College, designed and built many of the houses and churches in the historic section of the West End. He was the first African American architect to be given a government contract, and he went on to build thirty-eight post offices around the country.

But much of the vibrancy of the West End was drained as factories closed and jobs moved overseas. One of the major employers of the neighborhood, Philip Morris, closed its tobacco plant in 2000. The unemployment rate in this Louisville neighborhood is now 16.4 percent.

I started going to the West End during my senate campaign and then, after I was elected, visited in an official capacity. It was in those early trips that I first met Reverend Kevin Cosby, the longtime pastor of St. Stephen Baptist Church. He likes to say he's been at St. Stephen's "since the days when Abraham Lincoln was a precinct captain." Pastor Cosby is a brilliant public speaker. His sermons soar to legendary heights, but they come from a street-level perspective. From our meetings I learned of his passion for bringing higher education to the West End and his mission to reaccredit the historically black Simmons College. Reverend Cosby donates his time and salary to that wonderful institution of higher learning. In our conversations, I told him how I wanted to reform draconian drug sentencing policies that have filled our prisons with people of color. Over the course of our friendship he has said some very kind things about me, including this quote: "I have heard no national politician speak on the substantive issues that affect African Americans like Senator Rand Paul."[4] I carry those words as a badge of honor.

I came away from my talks with Reverend Cosby with a new understanding—a new resolve. It was in the West End that I first began to sense the unease that would later explode in Ferguson and on Staten Island.

Even before I was elected, I met Pastor Jerry Stephenson from the Midwest Church of Christ in the West End. Jerry was concerned about the dropout rate of the students in the West End and disillusioned with the policies of the Department of Education. It was from these early conversations, and talks with other city leaders, that I began to see firsthand just how dire the need for education reform was in poorer neighborhoods. Jerry shared my vision of school choice, and he lamented the fact that many students in the West End had to travel forty-five minutes by bus or car to get a decent education.

In the West End, I reached out to Markham French at the Plymouth Community Renewal Center, a nonprofit urban mission. Markham organized a roundtable of people from the community. From them,

I heard stories of how criminal records prevented people who had served their time and had reformed from getting good jobs; I learned how government confiscates homes for unpaid taxes; how it can shut down private businesses when an employee gets caught with drugs. I saw eyes fill with tears as people told stories of homes broken apart by a war on drugs that imposes excessive sentencing and carts too many fathers off to prison, from which they don't return. I met a woman who'd found Christianity, quit her drug habit, and wanted to care for her two kids but was under the threat of a mandatory minimum sentence of a decade for a drug charge.

In one of our discussions, I met Christopher 2X and learned about his weekly youth group called the War Zone that helps West End teenagers deal with violence that erupts too often in their neighborhood.

This is where I saw the hope and promise that the West End owns. I visited with Larry McDonald, the president of the Lincoln Foundation, which is dedicated to scholarships, mentorships, and after-school guidance for disadvantaged children. I met with the scholars, including one fifteen-year-old who told me he wanted to become a lawyer. I believe that young man can become whatever he wants to be. That's how it should be for all of the children of the West End, for all the children of both our impoverished inner cities and rural communities, for all American children.

From the time I decided to run for public office, my plan was always to champion issues such as school choice, sentencing reform, and employment empowerment that I believed were of particular concern to our country's poor. But it was in the West End that my plan solidified.

From Louisville, I traveled to Nashville, Philadelphia, Chicago, Milwaukee, Atlanta, Cincinnati, Detroit, and elsewhere. I visited charter schools, community centers, and local Urban Leagues. In each place, my resolve to change the policies and dismantle the overblown bureaucracy that has failed to serve poor communities for generations grew stronger. Today, it grows stronger still. During these travels I made a vow that I would work tirelessly to change how government disproportionately treats minorities unfairly. Here are some of my plans.

Mandatory Minimum Sentencing

Several years back there was a very popular HBO television series called *The Wire*. In March 2008, the writers and creators of the show wrote an op-ed that appeared in *Time* magazine.[5] It read in part:

> Since declaring war on drugs...we've been demonizing our most desperate citizens, isolating and incarcerating them and otherwise denying them a role in the American collective. All to no purpose. The prison population doubles and doubles again; the drugs remain.

Our criminal justice system as it pertains to the war on drugs went off track in the 1980s and '90s with the "broken windows" theory of policing. The theory espoused the idea that targeting smaller crimes like graffiti and other vandalism in urban areas, or, to use a more recent tragic example, the selling of loose cigarettes, will stop the escalation to more serious criminal behavior. The controversial stop and frisk tactic used by the New York City Police Department grew out of this theory. The broken windows approach to law enforcement wasn't limited to New York, however. It became a national mindset. From 2001 to 2010, marijuana arrests accounted for nearly half of all drug arrests. In fact, according to a recent FBI report, someone is arrested for a marijuana crime every forty-two seconds.[6] Nearly 90 percent of those arrests are for simple possession, and many of them occur in inner-city areas. Why? Because it's easier to arrest people who live close together and where there are more police patrols. It's easier to arrest people who live in poverty. People who are trapped in these crime-infested neighborhoods often have no means to escape, which exacerbates the cycle.

Federal incentives also drive arrests in minority areas. Departments across the country compete for anti-drug grants dispersed by the U.S. government. Federal money encourages police departments to overstep their power. According to a report by the Drug Policy Alliance (drugpolicy.org), between the years 1981 and 1995 New York City police made 33,775 marijuana arrests. Between 1996 and 2010 they made 536,322.

But, as the writers of *The Wire* eloquently stated, under our current federal policies, little has actually been accomplished to lessen drug use, while irreparable damage has been done to even the most casual drug users. If Bill Clinton, George W. Bush, and Barack Obama were caught and penalized for their alleged and/or acknowledged drug use, under our current laws, they would have been barely employable, let alone allowed to become presidents of the United States.

This is a conservative issue. We spend an enormous amount of money and resources on prisons. Right now, U.S. prisons hold more than 2.4 million people. That's more than the population of Houston, and just a little under the number of people who live in Chicago. Since 1980, the American prison population has quadrupled. Since 1998, the main reason people are in federal prison is because of mandatory and longer sentences for drug offenders. Recently George Will wrote that in California alone there are currently 2,000 inmates who didn't commit violent crimes serving twenty-year to life sentences because of the "three strikes and you're out" law of that state. The average inmate in federal prison costs the American taxpayer between $21,000 and $33,000 a year, and those costs are expected, by 2020, to jump to 30 percent of the Department of Justice's budget. In 2013, the DOJ's budget was more than $27 billion.[7] In 2015, I supported Proposition 47 in California, which reduces some nonviolent drug felonies to misdemeanors. Within months, enough space opened up in prisons to keep violent criminals for their entire sentence. Before Prop 47, violent criminals were sometimes released because of overcrowding, some serving only 20 percent of their sentences.

The money spent on prisons has no return. Inmates don't pay taxes, they don't buy goods or services, and they don't hire anyone. For all the good we supposedly do with rehabilitation, we might as well flush the money down the toilet. According to a Pew study, 40 percent of ex-cons commit crimes within three years of release from prison.[8]

How bad an investment is prison funding? A statistic used in the movie *Waiting for "Superman,"* a documentary about the ineptitude of our system of education, puts the cost of our prisons into perspective. In Pennsylvania, 68 percent of inmates are high school dropouts. The state spends $33,000 a year on each prisoner, making the total cost of the average prison term, which is about four years, $132,000.[9] The average private school costs $8,300 a year.[10]

So for the same amount we spend on the average inmate's time in prison, we could have sent that person to private school from kindergarten to twelfth grade and still had $24,000 left for college.

My views on these reforms mean much more to me than just numbers or the amount of money we can save. The supply and demand of illegal drugs is a rapacious creditor, but the punishment for its use is patently unfair. Nowhere is this inequity felt more deeply than in our minority communities. The majority of illegal drug users and dealers nationwide are white, but three-fourths of the people in prison for drug offenses are African American or Latino. Many with previous petty marijuana arrests receive long prison sentences, including life sentences. The injustice of these laws is impossible to ignore when you hear the stories of the victims.

For example, consider Atiba Parker. When he was twenty-nine, he was arrested for selling three grams of crack cocaine. Because of prior misdemeanor marijuana arrests, he was sentenced to forty-two years, according to the advocacy group Families Against Mandatory Minimums.

Then there's Weldon Angelos, a twenty-four-year-old Utah music entrepreneur who received a fifty-five-year sentence for a few small pot sales. According to Brett Tolman, a former U.S. Attorney for Utah, the DEA could have busted Angelos after the first undercover buy but instead waited until Angelos was carrying a gun, which he had strapped to an ankle holster. Angelos was a small-time pot dealer. He never brandished the gun, let alone shot it. Even the judge in the case thought the mandatory sentence he was forced to give Angelos was ridiculous.[11]

Then there's Timothy Tyler. Journalist Andrea Jones tells Tyler's story in the October 2014 issue of *Rolling Stone*. A Deadhead, like a generation of other kids, Tyler followed the Grateful Dead for years. He was well known on the Dead's tours, operating a popular fried dough stand. Like some other Deadheads, he also liked to drop acid. In 1992, he mailed 5.2 grams of blotter acid to a friend in Florida who had become a confidential informant, no doubt under pressure of pending charges. Then, while Tyler was tripping on acid, police picked him up—he thought he was building a dam in the middle of a road. He was hospitalized but arrested on his release for mailing the acid. The fact that it was blotter acid (LSD soaked into paper) increased the weight of the transaction. He was ultimately sentenced to a mandatory minimum of double life. He was just twenty-three years old when he was arrested; Tyler's jail time ends only when he dies.

In no way, shape, or form do these sentences have anything to do with justice.

We need drug sentencing that makes sense.

We need to get rid of the lopsided penalties of crack cocaine sentencing altogether. We should free those who are in jail under the old guidelines. Our prisons are bursting with young men—and women—who are poor or of color (usually both), and our communities are full of broken families because of it. Mandatory penalties came about in the 1980s. At the time, there were approximately 25,000 federal prisoners. Today, that number exceeds 218,000.[12]

Our criminal justice system continues to consume, confine, and define our young men. In the Senate, I've introduced the RESET Act, a bill that would reclassify simple possession of small amounts of controlled substances from a low-level felony charge to a misdemeanor. It also eliminates the crack cocaine disparity.

Along with Senator Patrick Leahy, the Democrat from Vermont, I've also introduced the Justice Safety Valve Act of 2013, which expands the so-called "safety valve" that allows judges to impose a sentence below the mandatory minimum in qualifying drug cases. This legislation is driven by common sense, something that's severely lacking in Washington. Mandatory minimums disproportionately target the poor and minorities. Getting rid of mandatory minimums simply means allowing judges to use discretion in sentencing, rather than being bound to draconian federal parameters that discount any mitigating circumstances or human factors.

Given greater flexibility, judges won't be forced to administer needlessly long sentences for certain offenders, which is a significant factor in the ever-increasing federal prison population and spiraling prison costs. Taxpayers would be better served by investing that money in programs that keep our communities safe and get those who have paid their debt to society back in society.

Across the Aisle

Pat Leahy isn't the only Democrat with whom I'm working on these issues. I've also teamed up with Senator Cory Booker from New Jersey. Though some in the press have dubbed us a "political Odd Couple," we're really not all that dissimilar. We're both freshmen senators. We both have big ideas and the energy to match, and we both try to get beyond petty partisanship.

Together, we introduced the REDEEM Act, a law that would give Americans convicted of nonviolent crimes a second chance at the American Dream. The legislation helps prevent youthful mistakes from turning into a lifetime of crime by setting up a process to expunge criminal records for people who stay clean. The bill also helps adults who commit nonviolent crimes become more self-reliant and less likely to commit future crimes.

The bill would expunge or seal the records of juveniles who commit nonviolent crimes before they turn fifteen and allow eligible nonviolent criminals to petition a court to ask that their criminal records be sealed. Sealing the records would keep them out of the FBI background checks often requested by employers and would likely make it easier for former offenders to secure a job.

Last but not at all least, the legislation would place limits on the solitary confinement of most juveniles. The idea of putting a teenager in solitary confinement for a marijuana arrest is outrageous, and yet the practice of locking youthful offenders away by themselves happens at an alarming rate. The results can be disastrous.

When he was just thirteen, Kevin DeMott tried to hold up a Little Caesar's pizza restaurant in Battle Creek, Michigan, with a toy gun.

He owed money to a local marijuana dealer. Kevin was arrested and two years later sentenced to prison for up to five years on four counts of attempted armed robbery. He spent four months in solitary confinement in Ionia Maximum Correctional Facility. Diagnosed with bipolar disorder when he was eleven, he was found in his solitary cell banging his head against a bloodied brick wall. He was pepper sprayed and locked in chains and leg irons.[13]

This is unconscionable. It must not be allowed to happen.

Our criminal justice system takes kids who make youthful mistakes and punishes them for a lifetime. I know a guy about my age who grew marijuana plants in his apartment in college. Thirty years later, he still can't vote, can't own a gun, and when he looks for work, he must check a box that basically says, "I'm a convicted felon, and I guess I'll always be one."

Even misdemeanor convictions erode the foundation of a good life. They can cause the suspension of driver's licenses, impacting the ability of the person to make a living or care for children, and they take away professional licenses that do the same.

Don't get me wrong. People who are in prison for harming other people should be kept in prison. But people who are in prison for harming themselves should be given a second chance. The biggest impediment to civil rights and employment in our country is a criminal record. Our current system is broken and has trapped tens of thousands of young men and women in a cycle of poverty and incarceration.

It has to stop. Given the chance, I will do all I can to stop it.

Voting Restoration

The Brennan Center for Justice here in Washington isn't exactly a bastion of conservatism, and especially when the American Civil Liberties Union sponsors an event there. Yet there I was, sharing the dais with several convicted felons and Senator Ben Cardin, the Democrat from Maryland. Just for the record, Ben is not a convicted felon (he has been described as a hard-core liberal, though)!

As one Beltway observer wrote, it was perhaps the last place you'd expect to find a Republican with higher political aspirations.

I took the remark as a compliment, because out of all the minority issues I've been fighting for, this might be the most important.

Lyndon Johnson once called the right to vote "the struggle for human rights."

Martin Luther King Jr. said, "So long as I do not firmly and irrevocably possess the right to vote, I do not possess myself."[14]

The face of the Republican Party should not be about suppressing the vote but about enhancing the vote. I'm sure you've heard that there has been some controversy about this topic recently. An unflattering light has been cast on my party. To be frank, I believe most of the rhetoric is by partisans who have tried to make voter ID into some sort of voter suppression movement, when most advocates are simply trying to promote honest elections.

To make matters worse, the media has thoroughly confused my position on voter ID. I've said it's dumb of my party to make it such a big issue. I've been showing my driver's license for twenty years in Kentucky. Nevertheless, many folks in the minority community think that the intent is voter suppression and that it's up to us—the Republican Party—to change that perception. To help people understand that Republicans aren't for suppressing voting, I have taken a prominent role in trying to restore voting rights for nonviolent felons who have served their time.

According to the Sentencing Project,[15] 8 percent of the black voting-age population of the United States isn't allowed to vote because they've been convicted of a felony. For whites, it's 1.8 percent. The total number of people who are not allowed to vote because of felony convictions is 5.85 million.[16]

Testifying in front of the state legislature in Frankfurt, Kentucky, I urged my home state to restore voting rights to some nonviolent felons. I spoke about the racial disparity of drug incarceration rates, about unfair sentencing, about how doors to jobs are closed to these men and women who have served their time—a third of all non-working men between ages twenty-five and fifty-four have a criminal record, according to a *New York Times*/CBS News/Kaiser Family Foundation poll.[17] Here's the cycle many are trapped in: they start out in poverty, make a youthful mistake, go to jail, sometimes have child support payments that build up to thousands of dollars while they're in jail, get out of jail, can't pay their child support, can't get work, and then go back to jail for either not paying their child support or going back to a life of crime. Then, on top of this cycle of hopelessness, they're not allowed to vote.

In the U.S. Senate, I have introduced a bill called the Civil Rights Voting Restoration Act. The bill would allow people with nonviolent criminal records to vote in federal elections. States that don't go along with it would not be eligible for certain federal prison funding.

My cosponsor on the bill is Harry Reid.

I will give you a second to digest that last sentence. While Senator Reid and I don't agree on many issues, I'm happy to partner with any senator, even the Democrat leader.

Voting rights is an issue that transcends party lines. The Constitution says that no person shall be kept from voting because of his race or his color. We have all sworn an oath before God to support and to defend the Constitution. We must now act in obedience to that oath.

8

★ ★ ★

Waiting for Superman

I challenge you to see the faces of the children who are the victims of this strangling bureaucracy (the Department of Education) and not be moved and angered.

I have and I am.

★ ★ ★

In the opening moments of *Waiting for "Superman"*, the award-winning documentary about the state of our educational system, the educator Geoffrey Canada tells the story from which the film takes its title. Mr. Canada grew up in the South Bronx and was a fan of comic books, especially *Superman*. When he was eleven or so his mother told him that Superman did not exist. The news crushed young Geoffrey. "She thought I was crying because it's like Santa Claus is not real," Mr. Canada said. "I was crying because there was no one coming with enough power to save us."

Mr. Canada was talking about life growing up in the ghetto, and specifically about his experience as a kid trapped in a school system for which the word "dysfunctional" is grossly inadequate. Mr. Canada was speaking of the Bronx, but he could have been speaking of Detroit or Los Angeles or Louisville or any number of school systems across the country.

Our children walk through the doors of these schools and into a sinkhole from which they never emerge. Like the cycle of poverty, the lack of a good education becomes self-perpetuating and lasts for generations. If you don't finish school your children won't finish school, and their children won't, and on and on forever. Some say that failing neighborhoods are to blame for bad schools, but those who know say it's really the other way around. Bad schools lead to bad neighborhoods. You've all heard the numbers before, the embarrassing rankings of U.S. students: twenty-fifth in math and twenty-first in science out of the thirty top developed countries. Many of our schools have become dropout factories. I challenge you to see the faces of the children who are the victims of this strangling bureaucracy and not be moved and angered.

I have and I am.

The status quo is unacceptable. But here's the thing: Washington has no clue how to fix this problem. Washington has no idea why schools are failing. Washington doesn't know whether you're a good teacher or a bad teacher. All Washington knows how to do is spend money—your money. And they spend it badly. The basic structure of our educational system is flawed. Public schools are funded by property taxes. Tax revenue is higher in the suburbs and in wealthy areas, so those places get the best schools. But where education is needed most, tax revenue is minimal, and so is the level of the education. Title I funding was supposed to even the playing field. Federal dollars were allocated to public schools serving low-income students. The funding comes from No Child Left Behind (NCLB), a piece of legislation that has only left children behind. Here are the goals NCLB hoped to meet by 2014:

1. All students will achieve high academic standards by attaining proficiency or better in reading and mathematics by the 2013–2014 school year.
2. Highly qualified teachers will teach all students.
3. All students will be educated in schools and classrooms that are safe, drug free, and conducive to learning.
4. All limited English proficient students will become proficient in English.
5. All students will graduate from high school.

Pretty lofty goals, right? But big government initiatives always have great goals. They're good in theory. But in practice? Not so much.

Do you want to guess how NCLB did? It might be more depressing than you think.

As of this writing, only 33 percent of American fourth graders are reading at proficiency, and that number drops to 20 percent with low-income students.[1]

Right here, outside my office in Washington, D.C., only 56 percent of high school students graduate, only 18 percent of eighth graders read at level, and yet each student costs more than $18,000 a year in taxpayer money.

The further shame is that, while there is a general consensus that No Child Left Behind should be dramatically undone, Congress can't get its act together long enough to undo it. This has to change. It has to change for the sake of our children.

Today we have a system in which politicians and bureaucrats have too much control, parents have too little, and students' needs are not being met. Our children have much potential. On an equal playing field I would match them against any other country's children in the world, but their natural skills and talents are neglected in our education landscape. Their true potential is not being realized.

So is there nothing we can do?

There are indeed things we can do, but it will take bold ideas to stop the damage our schools do every day.

Here's one idea: how about instead of pouring money into failing schools, we send the Title I funds directly to the parents or guardians of school-age children to pay for the school of their choice. Voucher and charter school programs that allow public education dollars to follow the student greatly improve performance and give children opportunities they wouldn't otherwise have.

That's exactly what I had in mind when Lamar Alexander and I came up with our school choice amendment. The amendment would use the $14.5 billion in current Title I funds to go directly to 11 million students currently attending high poverty, low performing schools, at $1,300 per child. The money would follow a student to any accredited public or private school a family chooses.

Everywhere it's tried, school choice has allowed parents to give their children the education they deserve. The *Wall Street Journal* noted in 2010 that 2,000 of our nation's 20,000 high schools produce roughly 50 percent of all dropouts. Black children have a 50-50 chance of attending one of these schools. Compare these statistics to Washington, D.C., where a Stanford University study showed that 41 percent of students who attend charter schools learned the equivalent of 72 days more in reading and 101 days more in math each year than similar students attending district schools.

Today, government holds a virtual monopoly on education. A small percentage of kids who are rich or very bright can elect out of public schools, but most kids do not have that choice. I propose that we allow school choice for everyone, rich and poor. Innovation comes only when individuals are free to choose. Competition breeds excellence and encourages innovation. We need innovation. Don't get me wrong. There are excellent public schools across our country. My boys graduated from a great public high school, Bowling Green High, and I went to great public schools. The president's girls go to a great private school. There are a lot of choices out there.

I want to make it so that all Americans get the option of choosing the best schools for their children. Allowing school choice is a significant idea; education is the great equalizer, and lack of a good education is a lifetime albatross that for many prevents access to the American Dream. A pastor friend of mine in Kentucky has called school choice the civil rights issue of our day. He's right. Until we treat choice in education as a fundamental right, we won't be able to begin to understand and alleviate pervasive poverty.

Here's another idea. Let's start thinking twenty-first century when it comes to education.

I believe Silicon Valley is poised to lead an education revolution. Venture capital and equity financing firms are poised to pour billions into ed tech. I believe a revolution in education led by Silicon Valley would profoundly change the way our children and their children are taught.

For example:

Out of a home office that began in a closet with a $900 Best Buy computer and microphone, Salman Khan built an educational platform that offers free online courses in math, science, engineering, and technology that reaches 10 million students around the world. He calls it the Khan Academy, and Bill Gates is an investor.

Gates also discovered a college online course called Big History taught by a history teacher from Australia. David Christian's TED Talk "The History of Our World in 18 Minutes" has been viewed more than 4 million times. You should watch it. Gates thought it would be a great idea for Christian to teach in a high school with a user-friendly interface. So did Christian. The first year it was offered, 2011, only five schools received it. Last year, it was offered free to 1,200 schools from New York City to Seattle.[2]

Here's why it's a great idea: if you have one person in the country who is the best at explaining calculus, maybe that person should teach every calculus class in the country. Just imagine!

Imagine the top thousand teachers or experts in a field sharing their skill and understanding with 10 million children.

Educators have labored for decades to reduce class size so as to enhance learning. Little data exists to support any significant improvement in scores resulting from smaller classes—the Brookings Institution calls the results of such studies "tentative."[3] Instead of going smaller, I think we should consider the opposite. Perhaps class sizes should expand to a million students per teacher or beyond. With the Internet that's now possible.

Now imagine if this system evolves into a perpetually sustainable enterprise. In other words, imagine what would happen if it incorporated profit. After all, there are only so many billionaires like Gates in the world, and only a profitable enterprise is sustainable in the long run.

Can you imagine if our teachers were treated like those who are great in other professions? If we pay our best athletes millions of dollars a year, what would the market pay our best Internet teachers? We have no idea of the value of teachers because we've never really had a marketplace for education.

Would we still have local teachers? Of course. The personal dynamic between teacher and student can be one of the most powerful relationships in anyone's life. In addition, we should give our children access to truly extraordinary teachers, who could teach millions of kids in the classroom all at once, with local teachers reinforcing the lessons and providing personal guidance.

Here's the best part: the cost of education would tumble while its quality would increase. By making exceptional teachers available via the Internet to the entire country for pennies on the dollar, you would also multiply the number of potential geniuses logarithmically. Stay with me here. Remember, it was only about two hundred years ago that a monarchy prevented most ordinary citizens from getting an education and consequently from contributing to innovation and discovery.

The American Revolution opened access to the vast nonaristocratic classes of people. In all likelihood, America's independence quadrupled the number of individuals who became inventors and creators.

When women came into the workforce we again doubled our innovation. When all races came into the workforce human capital and ingenuity grew again.

The untapped revolution of the Internet has the potential to bring an online, personalized education to even the poorest kids in America. Companies like Amplify, Schoolnet, and Bookette are already bringing education to the remotest parts of the globe. We're only scratching the surface.

Here's the thing: do not, absolutely do not wait for government to understand this boldness, and do not count on them not to interfere or try to stifle it.

Remember that Congress established the Department of Education as a Cabinet level agency in 1980. In the thirty-five years since, American students' scores have stagnated while much of the world has leapt forward. The only thing, in fact, that has grown is the size of the bureaucracy and the budget, nearly doubling during the last ten years. More governmental control over our education system is not the answer. We would be wise to remember what the late Senator Daniel Patrick Moynihan once said: "The single most exciting thing you encounter in government is competence, because it's so rare." No one is educated by a D.C. bureaucrat, and nearly $100 billion a year that could be used in our local schools is instead passed through the sinkhole of Washington.

Which leads me to another bold idea: why don't we leave what doesn't work behind?

The standardized process of our educational system might have been fine for the 1950s, but it is severely outmoded now. A child in kindergarten today who is lucky enough to stay in school all the way through college won't enter the workforce until 2029. How can we presume to know what the workforce will look like then? One of the more disturbing statistics that *Waiting for "Superman"* cites is that by 2020, Americans will be qualified to fill just a little over a third of the highly skilled, highly paid jobs.

Many Democrats, and even some Republicans, support a national curriculum such as Common Core. I think a national curriculum is a terrible idea. Having one central authority decide the curriculum means that if that curriculum contains errors, students all across the country will suffer. If a national curriculum contains political bias, all students will suffer. Leaving curriculum in the hands of local educators and school boards allows adjustments to occur more rapidly and allows for a quicker and more direct response to parents' wishes. This doesn't mean that we shouldn't have national tests, or even international tests, to compare our students' progress. It just means that local parents, leaders, and teachers should determine the tests and the frequency of testing.

By definition, core curriculum limits the education of our children. Why in the world would we think an idea as antiquated as core would be the model for the Internet age?

Recently, I spoke in Chicago at an event sponsored by the Illinois Policy Institute. The meeting was held at the Josephinum Academy, a small, all-female Catholic high school with mostly nonwhite students. It's in Cook County, which doesn't exactly count as a home game for me. But the county's alignment with the president did little in helping its woes in education. Twenty-seven percent of low-income students there don't make it through high school.[4]

The Democrat Party has opposed charter schools and vouchers pretty much steadfastly, and I would say the teachers unions have as well. I told my audience at Josephinum Academy that I call those opposed to school choice dead-enders. Dead-enders are people who don't believe in innovation. Dead-enders believe what we have now is the best we can do. Dead-enders throw money at the problem and then look the other way.

We've been trying the same thing in education for too many years. And all this time our education system, particularly in our big cities, has been in a downward spiral. In Louisville's West End, eighteen schools are failing, and the graduation rate is 40 percent.

Our children deserve better—they deserve a choice in education.

Geoffrey Canada's mother was right. Superman isn't real. But maybe we don't need Superman to save our schools. Maybe we just need to empower the people who can make a difference, people like Geoffrey Canada. His Harlem Children's Zone, a charter school network and nonprofit that currently serves more than 12,300 children, has a 95 percent college acceptance rate among its high school seniors.

I know the education system in our country presents a very complicated problem, and I don't want you to think that the little I've covered of it here is the complete answer. But one thing is for certain: we need new ideas. We can start by not telling parents how to educate their children. They want to be able to choose what is best for their families and their situation. This isn't rocket science. It's regular science, and good old math and American history. Parents know what is best for their children. The best thing government can do is get out of the way and let them decide. I really don't think anyone would even notice if the whole Department of Education was gone tomorrow anyhow. Now there's a bold idea.

9

★ ★ ★

Government Overreach

The primary purpose of offender-funded justice is simply revenue, and most of the time it's revenue that is collected from those who can least afford it.

* * *

When I was still an intern at Georgia Baptist Hospital in Atlanta, making $22,000 a year, I owned a convertible Volkswagen Rabbit (the station wagon had died an honorable death). I had a lot of fun in the car, but it was by no means a prize. My friends called it a dog runner. It was five years old, and the frame was bent such that the front two wheels were not aligned with the back two wheels. It looked like a dog running. If that wasn't embarrassing enough, the top didn't close without great effort. To close the convertible roof, I had to get under the car and attach a "come-along winch" to the frame and the roof. On my first formal date with Kelley, at a black-tie event hosted by the hospital, we came outside to find it raining and I'd left the top down. I had to get down under the car in my tuxedo to attach the winch to close the roof. Believe me, no girl ever dated me for my car.

The only thing worse than having a crummy car is having no car. One night I parked the Rabbit in front of Kelley's house and some punk kids decided to steal it.

Dog runner or not, I needed my Rabbit to get to work.

I called the police, expecting them to come and investigate. Instead, they kind of laughed and asked me to give them the vehicle identification number. "It will show up in a few days," the cop said nonchalantly. He was right, it did. They called me to retrieve it from the impound lot.

My relief turned to exasperation when the cops notified me that I would have to pay the fee for the tow to the pound. The car also had four flat tires, and I would have to pay another towing fee to take it to be fixed. I don't know which made me more frustrated—that my car had been stolen in the first place or that the authorities were making me pay coming and going. Actually I do know—it was the authorities making me pay. I wasn't about to fork over another $150 for the second towing, so I bought four "fix-a-flat" air canisters, injected them into each tire, and took off for the closest gas station. I arrived rolling more on rims than rubber.

Now, the story of a medical intern and his impounded Rabbit certainly doesn't compare to someone who goes to jail because they can't afford to pay a fine. But the memory of my experience got me thinking about people who are subjected to unreasonable civil fines that can mean the difference between eating or not, or the difference between sleeping in a bed or on the street—or in a jail cell. No one should be imprisoned for debt, especially debt to the government. But it happens; it happens all the time. Right here in America.

In recent years, Ferguson, Missouri, has been a suburban destination for African Americans longing to leave the grit of East St. Louis behind. Migration like this one is nothing new. For fifty years or more, families have moved from the big city to the suburbs looking for nicer neighborhoods, better schools, and outdoor space where their kids can play. Yes, I know that some cities have been getting more populated in recent years, in spite of the fact that rents have skyrocketed while the needle on middle-class wages hasn't moved at all. But most of that reverse trend is made up of younger people seeking better jobs, more excitement, and more young people.[1] Historically, however, a family's move to the suburbs from the city is as much a part of American culture as Thanksgiving dinner, senior proms, and outdoor barbecues. The black population in Ferguson increased from 25 percent to 67 percent in less than twenty years.

The distance between Ferguson, Missouri, and East St. Louis, Illinois, is only fourteen miles, but the two communities are worlds apart.

Ferguson offered sprawling apartment complexes along West Florissant Avenue, the section where Michael Brown lived with his grandmother. For inner-city residents, an apartment in the complexes in southeast Ferguson was like a dream come true—at least one apartment building even came with a swimming pool.

What made a move to Ferguson almost impossible to turn down, however, were not the amenities.

It was the federal subsidies.

Federal programs meant to help the poor more often than not chain people to poverty. FDR's Agricultural Adjustment Act (and other acts that followed it in the 1930s), which spawned the Great Migration, is one example. Federally subsidized housing projects of the 1950s and '60s, along with the welfare system, is another.

In Ferguson, in order to qualify for a federally subsidized apartment, you could earn no more than 60 percent of the median income of the area. The government would give you an affordable apartment, but you had to stay poor to live there.[2]

In the complexes, as unemployment and federal handouts proliferated, crime rose, and ultimately the apartments, once all gussied up with $12 million in federal funds, fell into disrepair. The pool was drained, doors to the apartments featured bullet holes, and people slept in beds below window level to keep out of the line of fire, according to the *St. Louis Post-Dispatch*.

In time, concrete barriers and fences were erected to cordon off access to the low-income apartments. Only one road was left open to get in and out. Essentially, what was created was a separate but not really equal black section of Ferguson.

Not only did residents of the apartments have trouble leaving their neighborhood, some of them feared just walking out of their homes. There are reported instances where some residents of Ferguson quit their jobs for fear of being arrested on the way to work because they had unpaid tickets.[3] According to municipal court data obtained by the *New York Times*, Ferguson issued more than 1,500 warrants per 1,000 people, the highest percentage in Missouri.[4]

Rabbit Redux

There is a moment in Tom Wolfe's novel *A Man in Full* that reminds me of the episode with my Rabbit and the people victimized by offender-funded justice. The real hero of Wolfe's book is Conrad Hensley, a young married man who works in a frozen food warehouse in Oakland. Though he's a hardworking guy, he struggles to get by. Then one day his car is towed for nonpayment of traffic tickets. He arrives five minutes before the impound lot closes, and there are five people ahead of him. At 5 P.M. the window is shut, with him still standing in line. Knowing he will lose his job if he isn't able to drive to work over the weekend, he makes the decision to climb the fence and attempt to steal back his car. When he's caught, he's sent to prison, where the story begins. If you haven't read it, I won't ruin the book for you (if you haven't read it, you really should; *A Man in Full* doesn't get nearly the respect it deserves). Only an act of God saves Conrad.

Many poor people in Ferguson and other neighborhoods like it live lives not much different than Conrad's. If you exist hand to mouth, a traffic ticket or fine can spiral your life out of control. Eighty-six percent of the traffic stops in Ferguson are of black motorists. A fine for a defective windshield wiper is $143. Twenty-two percent of the people in Ferguson live under the poverty line, and most of those live in the West Florissant neighborhood. For them, $143 is lot of money, and yet it's money from such fines that, according to Ferguson's financial statements, funds a fifth of the town's budget—that's $2.5 million in municipal court revenue.[5] According to the *New York Times*, a Ferguson city finance officer asked the police chief if he could "deliver" a 10 percent increase in revenue from tickets to cover an increase in court costs. The chief reportedly said that he would try.[6]

Most of us have run into offender-funded justice. Maybe it's the speeding ticket you received at the end of the month to fill some kind of quota or the penalty you pay for filing your taxes late. I once got a $770 speeding ticket in Atlanta. They doubled their normal extortion because construction was allegedly occurring, though no workers were within miles of my driving. For me $770 is a big deal, but I can't imagine what it must be like for someone struggling to make ends meet. For many of the people reading this book, offender-funded justice doesn't materially affect their life, but for some, fines can make the difference between living on the edge or being pushed to a point of no return.

The primary purpose of offender-funded justice is simply revenue, and most of the time it's revenue that is collected from those who can least afford it. Consider Camden, New Jersey, one of the poorest cities in the country—unemployment is double the national rate, and 40 percent of the people live below the poverty line. In Camden, fines for loitering reach upward of $1,000.[7] According to a survey conducted by National Public Radio,[8] forty-three states charge the accused for some of the costs of a public defender. Some states charge for electronic monitoring bracelets; some venues even charge for jury trials, rights guaranteed to be free of cost by the Constitution.

What's worse, people are put in jail for nonpayment of these fines.

NPR tells the story of Steve Papa, who was arrested for "climbing up on the roof of an abandoned building while intoxicated." Later, a judge would sentence Papa to twenty-two days in jail, not for trying to break into the building but because he couldn't pay the fine. Papa was an Iraq War veteran and was homeless.

Fine-collection companies have sprung up all over the country. These companies operate with little oversight and practically no transparency.

Every year, courts in the United States sentence hundreds of thousands of people convicted of misdemeanors to probation that is handled by these firms who then charge fees to the probationers. You don't have the money to pay? Guess what happens? Right, you go to jail.

According to Human Rights Watch, one Georgia man was arrested for shoplifting a $2 can of beer. He was fined $200, and ultimately went to jail for failing to pay the private collection company $1,000 in fees. At the time, the man was homeless and selling his blood twice a week to survive.[9]

In Clanton, Alabama, city officials are running what amounts to a debtor's prison, according to the Feds.[10] Poor people arrested for misdemeanors are jailed for up to a week, or until they can come up with the $500 fine.

These violations of civil liberties do not operate in the shadow but rather in full view of the Feds.

According to an editorial in the *New York Times*, the Justice Department is currently monitoring fourteen police departments around the country "with the aim of making sure that police operations under its guidance obey the Constitution." A recent report released by the DOJ accused Ferguson cops of unfairly targeting African Americans with traffic stops and excessive force. According to statistics compiled by the Ferguson PD, black drivers were twice as likely as whites to be stopped, searched, and arrested, even though statistically less likely to be carrying contraband.[11]

So on one hand, the DOJ condones the practice of offender-funded justice, or at least looks the other way, and on the other hand they investigate it and condemn it—especially when the community is under a media glare.

The hypocrisy is breathtaking.

Government overreach is like Doc Ock from the *Spider-Man* movie.

It has its mechanical tentacles that reach into just about every facet of our lives—and a zealous disregard for the Second Amendment.

Take the case of twenty-seven-year-old Shaneen Allen. A single mom with two kids, she was robbed twice last year. A family member suggested she obtain a gun for self-defense. She just wanted to protect her family. She took the required gun safety course and obtained a concealed carry permit.

Unfortunately, Shaneen's permit was obtained in Pennsylvania, and one day while driving in New Jersey she was pulled over for what the police called an "unsafe lane change" but is commonly referred to in African American communities as a "driving while black" citation.

They asked her if she had a gun and she told the truth. That was a big mistake. Now she's facing a mandatory minimum of three years in jail.

Then there's Edward Young, who received a mandatory fifteen-year prison sentence when cops found that he had seven shotgun shells in a drawer. Never mind that he didn't even have a shotgun to fire the shells or that the shells were only in his house because he was helping a neighbor sell her late husband's possessions. Young had no idea that his felony conviction from twenty years earlier made it illegal for him to own ammunition. The Sixth Circuit just turned down his appeal.

Government tentacles also reach into the pockets of the poor, and I find that despicable and inexcusable. The policy of offender-funded justice is by its definition predatory. Like most predators, it targets the vulnerable. But Doc Ock cares little about the Constitution. All it cares about is feeding its ever-expanding appetite.

Civil Asset Forfeiture

Say your name is James, and one day you're driving to see a dentist. Because you work at a food processing plant that doesn't offer a dental plan you have to pay cash for the procedure. You have $3,900 of hard-earned money in the glove compartment. All of a sudden, you see flashing lights in your rearview mirror. The police officer says he pulled you over for driving too close to the white line. He then asks if you've been smoking marijuana; he says he smells it in your car. The cop asks you to step out so he can search the vehicle. He opens the glove compartment and sees the money. He confiscates your cash, impounds your car, and you get to spend a night in jail.

When you protest, the cop says, "Don't even bother getting a lawyer, the money always stays here."

Each year, federal and local law enforcement agencies team up to confiscate billions of dollars from people they suspect of criminal behavior. You don't have to be convicted of a crime to lose your property. The government can take your truck, your house, and your cash even if they never charge you or even if you are found innocent.

Instead of innocent until proven guilty, you can be treated as though you're guilty even if found innocent. The statute, called "civil asset forfeiture," might be the most egregious government overreach on the books today.

James is a real person. His full name is James Morrow, and the event happened in Tenaha, Texas. It was recounted not too long ago in a long piece about civil asset forfeiture that ran in *The New Yorker* magazine.[12]

James is only one of a countless number of victims of a law whose primary purpose is to collect revenue. The word "forfeiture" here is used in the legal sense, meaning that you're not giving up your property. It's being taken by the government without compensation, and without due process of law. Only the inference of criminal behavior is necessary.

Like much of government's overreach—and the road to hell—good intentions paved the way to today's version of civil asset forfeiture. The idea was to take money from drug dealers and put it directly into the fight against crime. Some of it is applied as the law intended. In Connecticut, for instance, police use the confiscated cash to buy undercover vehicles, laptops for patrol cars, and police dogs.[13] Cops in Tulsa roll up on you in a Cadillac Escalade with the words "This Used to Be a Drug Dealer's Car, Now It's Ours!" pasted on the back window.[14] This policy has gone way too far. Some of the military-style equipment you saw in Ferguson was paid for, at a drastically discounted price, by civil asset forfeiture. The town of Spring Grove, Illinois, population 5,800 last year, purchased a twenty-ton mine-resistant ambush protected (MRAP) vehicle from the government for $4,000 with civil asset forfeiture funds.

There is little oversight of civil asset forfeiture, and much of the confiscated cash and property finds its way into places and pockets where it should not reside.

Here's a little history of the law. The statute can be traced back to English common law, which stated that the Crown had the right to confiscate an object that caused a death. That object, called a deodand, the Latin word for "given to God," could then be sold and the proceeds given to the needy or some other good cause.[15]

After the American Revolution, the fledgling U.S. Congress authorized something that was akin to a deodand but was even more expansive. It gave the government power to appropriate vessels and cargo that were *suspected* of being used by smugglers or pirates. The legal term is *in rem*, and it refers to the power a court may exercise over property. This way, it didn't matter if the pirate who owned the ship was on board or not. If the vessel was being used for illegal activity, or was thought to be, the government had the right to take it.

In time, the practice of pirating, at least that of the Captain Kidd variety, faded to lore and literature.

But the forfeiture law stayed on the books.

Civil asset forfeiture was resurrected in the 1970s and retooled for the war on drugs. The subtle shift in the law from Colonial days was the presumption by the government that the property or cash seized did not belong to the person from whom it was appropriated but were ill-gotten gains. This way, ownership claims did not apply. Still, if the law had any effect on stemming the tide of drugs flowing into the United States, it did so mostly on a public relations level. How many times on television have you seen news stories about high-profile drug busts with police proudly displaying stacks of confiscated cash and bundles of cocaine or heroine? Though they looked pretty impressive, such seizures really did little to stop the proliferation of drug smuggling or use.

In 1984, Congress passed the Comprehensive Crime Control Act, and the practice of civil asset forfeiture changed dramatically. The pumped-up version works like this: local cops determine the illegal activity, then make a quick call to the Department of Justice, which "federalizes" the case. This allows both the Feds and the local cops to sidestep any pesky state laws that might impede them. The local police then seize the money or property, turn it over to the Feds, who take 20 percent off the top (like an agent's fee), and then kick back up to 80 percent to the local police department.

Equitable sharing would change the face of small police departments for the next thirty years.

Here is an example of equitable sharing at work. Russell Caswell was the owner of the Motel Caswell in Tewksbury, Massachusetts. A suburb of Boston, Tewksbury, like most working-class towns with high unemployment, had seen better times. So too had Mr. Caswell's motel, which was built by his father in 1955. Russell remembers sitting on a bulldozer at age eleven helping his dad clear the plot of land on Main Street, just off Interstate 495. Not too long after the motel was completed, Annette Funicello and the Mouseketeers stayed there during an early tour, which was a big thing back then. More recently, however, the motel's patrons consisted of people down on their luck, pensioners, and, no doubt, the occasional lovers' tryst—some of the rooms came with a hot tub, after all.

Still, Russell and his wife showed up each day for work and, in time, were able to pay off the note on the building and have some equity for a retirement that was fast approaching. Though property values in Tewksbury weren't exactly at Manhattan levels, the motel was estimated to be worth $1.5 million.

One day Russell received notice that the Tewksbury Police Department—in concert with the Department of Justice—was seizing his motel for illegal drug-related activity. The government cited fifteen drug busts over a fourteen-year period, during which time Russell had rented rooms to almost 200,000 guests. "A local paper found big-box stores down the road had more drug activity than my motel," Russell wrote in a letter published by the *Washington Times*.[16]

There is little doubt that the motor lodge, being debt-free, was of more interest to law enforcement than any criminal activity that might have occurred there. In fact, according to Russell, a DEA agent would later testify that it was his job to scour the register of deeds looking for unfettered properties.[17]

Though he had not committed a crime, Russell shelled out $100,000 in lawyers' fees in the hope of stopping the federal government from taking his motel. He was fighting a legal battle that most in his situation lose. Many can't afford the legal fees that pile up to fight civil asset forfeitures. Those who do have the money face a law that favors the government.

Around the same time equitable sharing was instituted, the DOJ came up with its own souped-up version of the civil forfeiture law, called substitute assets. Feds could now estimate how much money a drug dealer in their sights made and then confiscate property of equal value.

Not to be outdone, the IRS (what would any scandal be without them?) has its own role in this. In 1970, Congress passed the Bank Secrecy Act, which required financial institutions to report all deposits of $10,000 or more. This includes multiple deposits if the bank suspects the person is trying to circumvent the ten-grand threshold. The practice is called "structuring." Again, the idea of the law was to catch money launderers and drug dealers. So what could possibly go wrong? Well, how about this: the IRS uses the law to target individuals, business owners, and everyday Americans who they suspect of tax evasion. They don't file a criminal complaint. They just seize the money in the bank account and leave the account holder with the burden of proving their innocence. As is the case with asset forfeiture laws, many people just give up. According to the Institute for Justice, a public interest law firm that battles civil forfeitures, the frequency of these raids by the IRS has increased markedly over the past decade or so.[18] Only after an investigative piece appeared in the *New York Times* did the IRS promise to curtail the practice. If your view of governmental overreach is anything like mine, a promise from the IRS does not instill much confidence.

Stacks of cash, unchecked power, and little oversight, what could go wrong?

Well, take Bal Harbour, a town of about 2,500 people in the Miami area. Known for its luxury shopping, Bal Harbour is virtually crime-free.

According to city crime rate data, between 2007 and 2012 Bal Harbour had a total of no murders, no rapes, and no robberies. There were, however, eight cars stolen in those five years.[19]

Yet in one month's time, Bal Harbour cops confiscated $3 million in civil asset forfeitures, which is a record for police departments throughout Florida, including the Miami PD. The tiny force became something of an assets forfeiture road show. Although Bal Harbour officers made few arrests, they traveled around the country infiltrating drug organizations and seizing cash and property. They paid hundreds of thousands of dollars to informants. Bal Harbour cops flew first class to Vegas and to the California wine country on the tail of drug dealers. They spent the confiscated cash as quickly as it came in, including: $100,000 for a thirty-five-foot boat powered by three Mercury outboards, $108,000 for a mobile command truck equipped with satellite and flat-screen TVs, $25,463 for next-generation Taser X-2s. There was $7,000 for a police chiefs' banquet, $45,839 for a Chevy Tahoe, $26,473 for Apple computers, $15,000 for a laser virtual firing range, and $21,000 for an antidrug beach party.[20]

Given all that crime-fighting gear, I feel sorry for the eight Bal Harbour car thieves.

Bal Harbour might be an extreme example, but it's certainly not the only one. The number of police departments that seek to profit from civil asset forfeiture continues to grow, and abuse of the law continues to astound. Throughout its history, civil asset forfeiture has provided police and prosecutors such creature comforts as tanning beds, gold-plated police whistles, and even a weekend home called the Ponderosa.[21] My intention is not to be antipolice here. I am not. What I am against is the policy that allows these abuses to happen.

In 2000, Congress tried to rein things in by passing the Civil Asset Forfeiture Reform Act (CAFRA), which requires that federal prosecutors prove "a substantial connection between the property and the offense." It also allows the people whose property was confiscated a day in court to prove themselves as "innocent owners," which gives them a little leverage, but is still far from the standard of innocent until proven guilty. Many prosecutors, Loretta Lynch prominent among them, continue to abuse civil forfeiture. During her time as U.S. Attorney for the Eastern District in New York, she confiscated $113 million. From one company that sells candy and snack foods, she confiscated $446,000. It took the owners two and a half years to get their money back. Lynch avoided CAFRA reforms by keeping the cash but not ever filing the civil forfeiture action in court.[22]

Luckily for Russell Caswell, his motel had its day in court, and it was, literally, the motel that was on trial. The case was labeled the United States of America v. 434 Main Street, Tewksbury, Massachusetts. In January 2013, a federal magistrate ruled that Russell had met the "innocent owner" standard. "This court finds it significant that neither Mr. Caswell, nor anyone in his family, nor anyone over whose behavior he had any control, was involved in any of the drug-related incidents," wrote Magistrate Judge Judith G. Dein of the U.S. District Court. "There was no reason for Mr. Caswell to suspect that every guest, or even a particular guest, who was coming to the Motel would engage in illegal behavior... Courts do not expect the common landowner to eradicate a problem which our able law enforcement organizations cannot control."

If Russell's case hadn't caught the attention of the press and the Institute for Justice, he would have most likely lost his motor lodge, according to statistics.

The Texas State Legislature has ordered Tenaha police to stop making roadside stops, like the one that involved James Morrow, which resulted in civil asset forfeiture. Finally, this past January, the Justice Department rolled back much of the equitable sharing portion of the civil asset forfeiture law, but did so only after extraordinary pressure by me and many others in Congress. In addition to speaking out repeatedly against civil asset forfeiture, I introduced the FAIR Act, which sought to change federal law by requiring that the government prove its case with clear and convincing evidence before forfeiting seized property. My bill would reform civil forfeiture to restore the presumption of innocence. If my bill passes, the government would not be able to confiscate property without a jury first deciding upon a conviction.

Despite our victory over equitable sharing, civil asset forfeiture abuses continue. Stop one case of abuse and another pops up. Why shouldn't it? There's big money to be made. The FBI's website describes assets forfeiture as a way to take "the profit out of crime."[23] But for law enforcement at the local levels it's a growth industry. In 1985, civil asset forfeitures totaled $27 million. In 2013, they had ballooned to $4.2 billion.

According to the Institute for Justice, the City of Philadelphia alone has seized more than a thousand homes, 3,200 vehicles, and $44 million in cash in the past decade or so. The DAs in Philly pad their budgets with $6 million a year in forfeiture cases.

In a recent case there, a couple's home was forfeited after their twenty-two-year-old son was caught selling $40 worth of heroin to an undercover police officer. The parents had no idea their adult son was even involved in drugs. According to one recent poll, prosecutors estimate that between 50 and 80 percent of the cars they seize belong to a person other than the driver, usually a family member such as a parent or grandparent.[24]

Little of what is forfeited is returned to the people who are innocent of any wrongdoing. In St. Louis County, in which Ferguson is located, authorities seized more than $220,000 in forfeiture raids and returned less than $2,000 in 2012. This despite the fact that only seven of the eighty-eight cases of civil asset forfeiture resulted in criminal charges being filed.[25]

While there is no explicit racial bias in civil forfeiture laws, they result, like everything involved in the war on drugs, in the unfair punishment of a disproportionate number of minorities.

I spend much of my time battling our gargantuan federal government, and still I can't keep up with all the damage it does, everywhere, every day, and in countless ways. As former White House adviser David Axelrod said recently in defending President Obama over one of the many IRS scandals: "Part of being president is there's so much beneath you that you can't know because the government is so vast."

Interestingly, neither Axelrod nor Obama has ever shown much concern in taming the federal beast. In fact, virtually every solution they offer makes government bigger. This often leaves the individual American citizen defenseless against a system so relentless that even its greatest champions can't seem to comprehend or control it.

Here's what I believe. Our criminal justice system is built on the immutable fact that the burden of proof should always be on the government. That statement has no wiggle room, and it applies equally to *all* Americans.

Civil asset forfeiture, offender-funded justice, and other policy-driven law enforcement abuse must be stopped in its tracks. The FAIR Act and other legislation I've introduced goes a long way to doing just that. But more needs to be done, and it needs to be done from the top down. There is a simple answer to government overreach. It is called the Constitution.

10

★ ★ ★

Economic Freedom

When government picks the winners and losers
we usually end up with the losers.

* * *

When I spoke at the Detroit Economic Club a few months back, I opened my talk by telling the story of the little girl who wrote a letter to God asking for a hundred dollars. When the postman saw the letter he thought it was cute and decided to address it to the president. The president's secretary read the letter and told her boss about it. The president, too, thought the letter cute and told his secretary to send the little girl a $5 bill and a note signed by him.

When the girl opened the letter from the White House she looked curiously at the five bucks. Her parents had taught her well. She sat down to write a thank-you note.

"Thanks, God, for the money," the note began. "But next time don't send it through Washington. They stole 95 percent of it."

At the time I spoke there, Detroit had entered into the largest municipal bankruptcy in U.S. history—over $1.3 billion. Once home to nearly 2 million people, only 700,000 remain in Detroit, and unprecedented urban decay surrounds many of them. According to Detroit's Blight Removal Task Force, as of this writing, more than a third of the city's buildings are condemned and headed for demolition.

Since the day I spoke there, Detroit has come through its bankruptcy and, thanks in no short measure to the people who live there, has begun to valiantly fight its way back. Yet too many poor and disadvantaged individuals continue to struggle with little hope of breaking the bonds that keep them marginalized.

I promised the people of Detroit to come up with a plan to help those who have lost hope. My plan will not only help Detroit. It will help depressed areas across the country.

Those are not just empty words.

The answer to the problems Detroit and other places like it face is right in front of our noses, if we only open our eyes.

American cities, towns, and rural communities that are mired in blight and unemployment already possess the best natural resource available: the residents who live there, people who are willing to work, people who are willing to start new businesses, and people unwilling to exist on a free ride.

Lisa Schlossberg is a young intern who works for Quicken Loans. She wrote in a company journal, "Detroit is unstoppable." She's right.

Thanks in large part to Quicken Loans and the company's owner, Dan Gilbert, downtown Detroit has already staged a miraculous turnaround, and the excitement of downtown is starting to spread outward to all reaches of the city. Residents and shop owners aren't waiting for government assistance—they're cleaning up their own neighborhoods.

Detroit Survivors/Entrepreneurs

A few years back, two college students from the University of Michigan started the Michigan Urban Farming Initiative in Detroit's North End. Once home to the Motor City's black elite and Motown stars like Aretha Franklin, Smokey Robinson, and Diana Ross, the North End has suffered some of the worst urban decay in modern American history.

The farming initiative began by clearing the rubble from a one-acre abandoned lot and cultivating the ground. In 2013, the urban farm produced 12,000 pounds of organic Detroit-grown, Detroit-sold, and Detroit-bought vegetables, filling the streets and nearby abandoned buildings with fresh aromas and views of green space.

Then there's Detroit Dirt, a composting company that collects plant-eater manure from the Detroit Zoo and food scraps from local restaurants and recycles them into mineral-rich fertilizer. The company's cofounder is Pashon Murray, who's been featured in a Ford commercial and won Martha Stewart's American Made Award.[1]

In Detroit's Midtown neighborhood, new restaurants, coffeehouses, and clothing stores are opening where illegal drugs and prostitution once flourished. The neighborhood is literally bursting with entrepreneurship.

Our ancestors came here hungry. Their hunger drove their desire to work. Their hunger drove their desire for education. Their hunger drove their desire to freely follow their faith. They came to Detroit from Eastern Europe, from Ireland and England. They came from the Southern states during the Great Migration. The auto industry in Detroit, specifically the Ford Motor Company, was like a beacon for African Americans searching for a better life. They were willing to work and shed blood, sweat, and tears, and they carried the Motor City on their backs.

I believe that ambition is still alive in Detroit. I believe it's still alive in eastern Kentucky—I see it in the faces of the miners. It's alive in Mobile, Rockford, and Toledo. We just haven't given these communities the chance.

Government stimulus packages haven't worked because they insist on picking winners and losers, doling out money to firms that are politically well connected or located in congressional districts that benefit the ruling party. Firms without political connections or the ability to navigate bureaucratic hurdles, or that are deemed unimportant to Washington, will lose out. When government picks the winners and losers we usually end up with the losers—think Solyndra. The president gave a $500-million loan to one of the richest men in the world to manufacture a product nobody wanted. Imagine, instead, those millions left by tax breaks in the pockets of the hardworking people of Detroit. Think of the groceries, clothing, and maybe even tickets to a Lions game that money could have bought. Instead it went up in the smoke of cronyism and government deceit.

What these places need is not more government stimulus or welfare checks. They need the exact opposite: relief from government policies that chain them to poverty.

I have a solution. A similar idea was originated in England by a London School of Economics professor named Peter Hall. In the United States, Jack Kemp, the Republican congressman from Western New York State and Housing Secretary under George H. W. Bush, adopted Professor Hall's idea and adjusted it for American use. Kemp loved to figure out ways to empower people, real people, regardless of race or background. You might remember that he was the quarterback for the Buffalo Bills in the days of the AFL. He was one of the few white members of the league to join a boycott of the 1965 AFL All-Star game, which was being held in then racially segregated New Orleans. Kemp was dedicated to upward mobility for the poor and disenfranchised.

He called his plan "a conservative war on poverty," and Ronald Reagan endorsed it. "Those who view poverty and unemployment as permanent afflictions of our cities fail to understand how rapidly the poor can move up the ladder of success in our economy," Mr. Reagan said. "But to move up the ladder, they must first get on it. And this is the concept behind the enterprise zones."[2]

My Economic Freedom Zones will capture the spirit Kemp championed in his enterprise zones but update it for the twenty-first century. I recently told someone that my plan is like Kemp's on steroids. It will allow blighted and bankrupt areas like Detroit and Eastern Kentucky to remove the shackles of big government by reducing taxes, regulations, and burdensome union work requirements. These zones will give parents and students the flexibility to find better schools, will allow talented immigrants to pursue entrepreneurial and job-creating endeavors, and will provide additional incentives for philanthropy to help those in need.

Most of Detroit, twenty-five counties in Kentucky, and many other poverty-stricken areas across the country will be designated as areas of reduced taxation. Unlike a government stimulus, these zones will encourage businesses and individuals that the market has already selected. You're a hard worker? You're going to make more money because less will be taken out of your check. You're a small business owner, or you want to start a small business? Your profits will be higher because you'll pay less tax.

I propose a stimulus that simply leaves the money in the hands of its rightful owners: those who have earned it.

For those who work or own businesses in designated areas, my plan slashes individual income tax to 5 percent and payroll tax to 2 percent. In Detroit, it would mean over $1 billion in tax revenues staying in the pockets of those who can make the biggest change in their own lives and the life of the city in which they live.

Here's the nuts and bolts of it. Any city, county, or municipality that has officially entered Chapter 9 bankruptcy will be eligible. Any city, county, or municipality that is at risk of entering Chapter 9 will be eligible. And any city, county, or municipality with unemployment 1.5 times the national rate will be eligible. Other criteria will also make you eligible. It's not my intention to exclude people from these tax breaks. If you need it, you'll get it.

What Will It Entail?

As I've mentioned, my plan will reduce the individual income tax to a single flat rate of 5 percent. This includes not only a reduction for individual wage earners but also for small businesses. More than 75 percent of small businesses are organized as pass-through entities, businesses that pass along income directly to the individual and therefore get taxed at the individual income tax rates.

According to the Tax Foundation, small businesses organized as sole proprietorships in states like Kentucky and Michigan have a top marginal tax rate above 45 percent; in California it's as high as 52 percent.

It's as though the current tax rate is structured to discourage business!

Can you imagine the boost a 40 percent reduction of the tax rate would be for small businesses in depressed areas? Not only would it help the businesses in place, it would encourage entrepreneurship and investment.

The plan also includes a reduction in the corporate income tax to a single flat rate of 5 percent for ten years. At 35 percent, the U.S. corporate income tax rate is among the highest in the world. Countries like Spain, Switzerland, and the United Kingdom have tax rates at 30 percent or less. China, one of our largest international competitors, has a corporate tax rate of just 25 percent. Even our neighbor to the north is outcompeting us. Canada's tax rate is only 15 percent.

Brown-Foreman, the distilled spirit giant in Louisville that produces Woodford Reserve and Southern Comfort among other brands, employs a thousand workers. The company pays a corporate tax of 35 percent. Compare that to the corporate tax of 13 percent that Bacardi, which is located in Bermuda, pays, and you have to wonder how long it will take Brown-Foreman's accountants to pressure family ownership to move, lock, stock, and barrel, overseas. Could you blame them?

We need to allow U.S. businesses to better compete internationally, and we need to reduce the corporate rate from the current 35 percent to a low rate of 5 percent for businesses in economically depressed areas to allow these businesses to expand and compete globally, and to keep their businesses here.

We'll also reduce the payroll tax for the employer *and* for the employee to nearly one-third lower than the current rates. There is an oft-cited document by the Congressional Joint Committee on Taxation highlighting the statistic that 47 percent of all U.S. households pay no federal income tax. I want to help those people, too. All workers still pay the federal payroll tax, and for many of these households and individuals the payroll tax is their largest tax liability. Lowering the payroll tax is the best way to help low-income workers.

Allowing low- to middle-income families to keep more of their hard-earned money will increase their standard of living, help the local economy by giving people more to spend, and reduce individual debt. The plan would mean more jobs for everyone. By reducing the amount of payroll taxes employers have to pay, we would encourage them to hire more workers.

Inside these zones, we'll suspend the capital gains tax to stimulate greater investment in business and real estate. We'll allow all small businesses to deduct all they invest in their first year of operation. We'll streamline the National Environmental Policy Act (NEPA) to encourage and speed up road and bridge projects and reduce the regulatory burden on these areas. We'll cut out the red tape that keeps new businesses from starting and old businesses from thriving.

Economic Freedom Zones will expedite visas for those from foreign countries who have $50,000 that they are willing to invest in these areas. Let them come to our country to build their dreams.

We'll also offer a charitable tax credit that would allow all Americans to reduce their tax liability by the amount they donate to any educational institution, religious organization, or homeless shelter that is located within Economic Freedom Zone areas.

The zones are a win all the way around. Instead of raising the minimum wage, which places a burden on small businesses and start-ups and, in study after study, disproportionately limits jobs for blacks and teens, my plan will raise the wages for everyone who lives in these zones by significantly lowering their tax, which will leave more money in their paychecks.

Economic Freedom Zones represent an ambitious plan, but given the opportunity, it will work. It will work because it depends on the individualism that made this country great.

When he was fourteen, my great-grandfather came to America from Germany with nothing more than what he carried. His father died shortly after they arrived in Pennsylvania. Great-grandfather peddled vegetables, saved his money, and eventually came to own a few acres of land where he built a dairy business. When he died, he left the five acres to his five children.

My father worked at a drugstore, for a moving company, and painted houses. He paid his own way through college and medical school. He put his career on hold during Vietnam to join the Air Force as a flight surgeon. As an ob-gyn he has delivered more than 4,000 babies and provided discounted and free care to those who couldn't afford it—he never accepted Medicare or Medicaid. He would tell his patients to put their cards away, but he never refused to help them.

I began working when I was eight. There was no allowance in the Paul house growing up. If you did nothing you got nothing. So I mowed my neighbor's lawn. That job got me about three more lawns.

I continued mowing lawns into my teens. I listened to Paul Simon and The Who on my cassette player while I pushed the mower. For you younger readers, a cassette player is like a prehistoric iPod.

I worked at a putt-putt golf course, cleaned pools, and later gave swimming lessons.

We certainly weren't poor, but we were expected to work. We lived in a nice house, in a nice neighborhood. We also knew the value of a dollar. I was proud of the money I earned. I bought my cassette player with money I earned. I bought my brother's bicycle and later my first car, the Volkswagen Rabbit with the defective roof, with money I earned. I bought my first stereo with money I earned, and thirty-three years later, I still have that stereo—how about that for fiscal conservatism!

I love to work, and, yes, making a buck is the idea of work. But the greatest satisfaction I received was not from the money I earned, but from the pat on the back from the homeowner whose lawn I mowed in straight lines, or the smile from a kid I taught to swim. The satisfaction comes from the feeling I get when I see the joy on the face of a patient who sits up from cataract surgery, smiles, and says, "I can see again."

John Allison, president of the Cato Institute, puts it well. The only kind of self-esteem, he says, is earned self-esteem, and that primarily comes from work.[3] I want every American to work. If you have lost your job, I believe in a temporary safety net, but everyone who can work should work as part of a safety-net program—not as punishment but as a stepping-stone to a real job, independence, and legitimate, earned self-esteem.

I've practiced medicine for twenty years, and after my political career is over I will continue to practice until I physically cannot. I don't know why anyone wouldn't want to work if they could. When our kids were younger I'd make an announcement at the start of each week: "Today is Monday, the best day of the week!" The boys would look up from their cereal and roll their eyes. Whether it was school or work, I always looked forward to Monday. Work for me has never been a punishment but rather a challenge.

I know I'm not alone in this. America is a country of workers, a country that works toward its dreams and doesn't dwell on its limits. In fact, the only thing that limits our dreams, I believe, is our bloated government. In my vision for America I see a job for everyone. After all, no one dreams of a life of dependency on government.

Actually, the goal of a job for everyone is not as farfetched as it sounds. The math is actually pretty simple. It only requires more money for job creation. Money equals jobs.

How do we do that?

By cutting everyone's taxes, and I mean everyone's: middle class, poor, or rich. Some will say the rich are already too rich—why would we cut their taxes? Why? Because their tax cut will leave the most money in the marketplace. I'll say it again: money equals jobs.

I know the liberals will scream. Paul Krugman will write a raft of "how dare he cut taxes on the rich" columns in the *New York Times*. Yet even Paul Krugman would have to agree that you can't have jobs without money. You can't sufficiently stimulate the economy if you only cut taxes on the working class. To really stimulate the economy you must cut everyone's taxes.

In my plan for America, there's a simple, fair, flat tax that is a tax cut for every American, and a tax plan you can understand and live with.

Ever since our older sons could drive, they have worked as lifeguards, in restaurants, and in telemarketing jobs, usually for minimum wage. There is much higher teen unemployment in countries like France that set their minimum wages at a rate above what the market will bear. When our son Duncan was seventeen, he took a job delivering pizza for Mr. B's in Bowling Green. Just before he started working, he asked a friend what kind of money he could expect to make. Though only seventeen himself, Duncan's friend could speak from experience: he worked at a local restaurant.

"With tips, the money's great," the friend said. "But don't expect much out of your check."

"Why's that?" Duncan asked.

"'Cause the taxes will kill ya," he said.

Unfortunately, the conversation Duncan had with his friend is repeated countless times every day in America. Very early on in our American working lives we find out the sad truth of just how much our government costs us.

In my plan, a tax cut for "everyone" means especially the working class—and it will be the largest tax cut in our history. We will create a maximum 17 percent income tax for every taxpayer in America, individuals and businesses with a standard deduction per individual filer. Every single taxpayer in America would see a tax cut under my plan. No one will be left behind. In fact, in addition to the income tax cut, I am creating a special tax cut for lower-wage workers, people who are often left out of tax cuts because they don't pay federal income taxes.

I call this the worker's tax cut, and it can make a big difference for families struggling to get by.

My goal is to eliminate the worker's tax entirely for low-income workers. As your income rises, the worker's tax cut will be lessened or phased out, so that those who earn more won't receive this particular part of the plan. This part is aimed at those who have often been ignored at tax cut time. If you are trying to make ends meet in an hourly wage job, my tax plan will mean $1,000 or more in take-home pay every year.

My plan for America will bring the largest tax cut in our country's history, and it will benefit all Americans.

In my plan, everyone pays their fair share. So what's fair? Well, for starters, we'll eliminate the loopholes that allow the superwealthy to avoid taxes, and that allow some corporations, with armies of lawyers, accountants, and lobbyists, to pay nothing.

The days of big business filing 50,000-page tax returns and getting away without paying tax will be over.

Here is real tax fairness: Make sure no one can lobby for special breaks. End corporate welfare. Stop the system that rewards the biggest businesses versus the mom-and-pop store. Stop the system that lets the superrich have tax shelters everywhere.

Make a tax code every American can both understand and afford.

You will be able to file your taxes on a single sheet of paper, without an accountant or lawyer.

I want the system to be fair to taxpayers, and it just isn't right now. Everyone knows it. But the other side is too busy demagoguing.

I'll say this again: I entered politics because I abhorred a government that took from the middle class to bail out big banks. I hate the concept of legalized privilege. As a Republican, I fight each day to end welfare to big business and to end special breaks that apply only to the rich. With my plan, we will end ALL corporate welfare. According to economist Stephen Moore, direct corporate welfare exceeds $20 billion each year. In the *National Review*, he tells us the average handout for Fortune 100 companies is about $200 million. Of these "corporate-welfare queens," as he calls them, the biggest grant recipients are General Electric ($380 million), followed by General Motors ($370 million), Boeing ($264 million), Archer Daniels Midland ($174 million), and United Technologies ($160 million).[4]

This practice is indefensible and, in my America, there is no place for it.

My plan includes Economic Freedom Zones, which I've already discussed, and which will provide a billion-dollar stimulus for Detroit and a billion-dollar stimulus for Appalachia and other economically depressed areas, with the money staying in the pockets of those who need and deserve it.

In my plan for America the income tax burden on a family making less than $32,000 will be removed.

My design for America will allow you to save for your health care, your childcare, your kids' college, and your retirement in one unlimited tax-free account.

My plan for America will allow you to deduct not only the interest but the principal of student loans. Your student loans should be treated as a business expense, and you should be able to deduct them over a period of time as your career begins. Linking student loan relief to work provides incentives. This is one of my big concerns: how young people are going to pay for college. The Democrats, typically, want relief but no strings attached, which only exacerbates the problem: nearly a quarter of all student loans go into default after three years. There are Democrats, including Senator Kirsten Gillibrand, who are starting to talk with me about my plan.

In the America I envision, there will be a 100 percent tax credit to care for children with special needs and for disabled adults.

Wait a minute. I can hear the naysayers lining up. How will we pay for all of this without exploding the debt?

By doing something not attempted by our government in a century but something that millions of American families accomplish every month, and that's spending no more than what we make. So let's do something extraordinary. Currently some $3 trillion comes in in tax revenue. Let's spend just that.

We will cut spending by no longer sending aid to countries that despise us and burn our flag. We will quit building bridges in foreign countries and instead do something really novel, such as building new bridges at home.

We will audit the Pentagon. We will audit the Fed. Our government is rife with waste and fraud. The America I see will eliminate all duplicate programs. It will send back to the states any and all functions that don't need to be located in Washington, D.C.

Government workers will no longer be paid more than ordinary private sector workers. Government contracts will go to the lowest bidder. We will not rehire federal workers who retire until we seriously shrink the size of government.

The federal government will get smaller so the private sector can grow larger, and we'll grow the economy like never before. We will, like President Reagan before us, create millions of jobs by dramatically lowering taxes and reducing the size and scope of government.

We'll bring back manufacturing jobs that pay well. We will dramatically lower the tax on American companies that wish to bring profits home. More than $2 trillion in American profit sits overseas. In my vision for America, highways, bridges, and other infrastructure projects will be built not by raising your taxes but by bringing back the $2 trillion in tax revenue that U.S. companies have stashed in foreign banks. The idea is to lower the repatriation tax and put that revenue into the highway fund. I'm working on this concept with Democrat senator Barbara Boxer.

Under my plan, we will immediately and responsibly open up new energy exploration in our country. The energy industry employs pipefitters, welders, electricians, and dozens of other skilled workers at good wages. The current administration has blocked permits that would allow these great jobs to be offered. Instead of putting our foot on the brake, let's put it on the gas.

My plan will open the door for American energy independence and hundreds of thousands of new skilled jobs. American jobs have been going overseas because our taxes are too high and our regulations too burdensome. I will put a moratorium on new regulations, sunset old regulations, and require Congress to carefully review and approve any new, expensive regulations.

Is my vision for America too extravagant? I think not. It hurts me deeply that America's work ethic is in question.

My plan for America doesn't mean an end to assistance, but it does mean that every able-bodied person in America is working.

Those who can work and who need temporary assistance will collect assistance by showing a pay stub. What do I mean? All companies with government contracts will be required to have daily job pools for the unemployed. When the taxpayer pays to build roads, the unemployed will show up daily to join the work pool. No new government money will be paid out. Existing programs will pay these workers. What will be new is that government assistance will simply require work either in the private market, in charity work, or in government contractor work. Those who find private jobs will receive more assistance than those who must accept government jobs. Assistance, though, will be temporary. Even *New York Times* columnist Nicholas Kristof admits that America's safety net can "sometimes entangle people in a soul-crushing dependency."

Disability payments have exploded and threaten the solvency of Social Security. Sixteen percent of Social Security payments go to the disabled. Of course, those who are truly disabled with medical problems that preclude them from working should not be forced to work. More money will be available for the truly disabled if we find work for the able bodied who have found their way onto the disability rolls. It is these people who are sending Social Security into bankruptcy.

Under my plan an independent doctor will examine and evaluate every claim, every year. If you're only able to do a desk job, we'll find one for you. For example, instead of getting a machine or a person in a foreign country when you call a government agency, you will get an American who is doing his or her fair share—and is grateful for the opportunity. A work requirement like this will help reform the disability program.

The choice is pretty clear. We can stick with the failed Great Society policies that for too many years have chained the poor to poverty. We can keep the policies that have doubled the unemployment rate of minorities, the policies that feign compassion but are in reality not in the least bit compassionate, or we can do something so exciting, so special, that we will again have a middle class, the class that once made America great. We can be a country that is again driven by, and takes pride in, its work ethic, one that is driven by excellence and driven by the spiritual replenishment and hope that work brings.

Two months before the March on Washington, Martin Luther King Jr. delivered a kind of warm-up in Detroit. Though history remembers his words, which soared over the massive gathering in front of the Lincoln Memorial on August 28, 1963, the speech at Cobo Hall in Detroit electrified the crowd of 25,000. You can watch at least some of it on YouTube. It was in this speech that he first publicly used the phrase, "I have a dream..."

Part of Dr. King's dream was equal employment opportunity. The speech in Detroit focused on this, and so too did the March on

Washington. Both were about jobs: "I have a dream this afternoon that one day, right here in Detroit, Negroes will be able to buy a house or rent a house anywhere that their money will carry them, and they will be able to get a job," Dr. King said that June day.[5]

Dr. King knew, like John Allison after him, that employment was essential to self-worth. That in order for black people to be lifted from the chains of discrimination they first had to be given the opportunity to work. When I read his words, I hear opportunity, not dependency. Yes, there's a place for a safety net in our society. I won't be part of any movement that turns its back on the truly needy. But I think what we really need to give the needy are jobs that pay well, not a life of welfare. The first step to ending the cycle of poverty is simply a job.

Detroit doesn't need a handout, and I don't think it wants a handout. Look at the proud history of Detroit. Look at Henry Ford, who not only produced a car built on an assembly line that people could afford but shortened the workweek and increased wages. Detroit was the industrial giant of the world. Government didn't do that. Detroit did that. Government didn't discover Smokey Robinson or Diana Ross. Motown did. Government didn't turn downtown Detroit around. Detroiters did.

Economic Freedom Zones will remove government obstacles to success. We'll empower a generation with a new bargain that promises government will get out of their way. It will treat everyone equally under the law. It will help parents guide their children's future, it will help job creators create more jobs. It will treat you the same way it treats everyone else, regardless of the color of your skin or your beliefs.

We've tried the other way, the excessive bailouts, regulation, and taxation. It doesn't work.

Let's not rely on our government, let's rely on ourselves—we're much more dependable.

Escaping the poverty trap will require all of us to relearn this basic truth: we are not only our brother's keeper, we are our own keeper. While a hand up can be part of the plan, if the plan doesn't include the self-discovery of education, work, and the self-esteem that comes with work, the cycle of poverty will continue.

It's time for new, fresh ideas.

It's time to take a stand.

11

★ ★ ★

The War on Liberty

To defend minority rights, we must acknowledge that democracy must be restrained by the rule of law, or more specifically by the Bill of Rights.

* * *

I arrived in Ferguson a few months after the shooting of Michael Brown without any particular insight into what had happened that August afternoon. I came to learn what had made so many so angry.

Ferguson community leaders were very receptive and courteous to me. Not only was I the only national Republican to ask them their opinion, I was one of very few members of Congress to seek to learn more about the events and protests. In fact, one community leader, a woman in her seventies, called out during the meeting: "Where the hell is my Democrat congressman? I haven't seen him since this whole thing started."

I told them of the bills I had introduced in Congress to reform criminal justice. The leaders of Ferguson were intrigued, but they want something more, something more immediate.

I suggested that they try to harness the energy of the protests in voter registration drives. More than 60 percent of the population of Ferguson is black, so with any kind of voter registration effort, city government would reflect their concerns, including the lack of African Americans in the police department.

While residents of Ferguson were unhappy with the shooting death of Michael Brown, they didn't want violence that would inevitably damage minority-owned businesses. These leaders were the elders of the community—teachers, lawyers, and doctors. They wanted peace, but they also wanted justice. It seemed to me the discontent they felt was long held and borne out by something that was larger than Ferguson.

Although I was born into the America that experiences and

believes in opportunity, my trips to Ferguson and Detroit and Atlanta and Chicago have revealed to me an undercurrent of unease.

Congressman John Lewis, who heroically marched and was beaten on the Edmund Pettus Bridge in Selma, still sees the two Americas that Martin Luther King Jr. famously talked of. In a recent article in the *Atlantic*, he writes: "One group of people in this country can expect the institutions of government to bend in their favor, no matter that they are supposedly regulated by impartial law. In the other [group], children, fathers, mothers, uncles, grandfathers . . . are swept up like rubbish by the hard, unforgiving hand of the law."

Lewis goes on, "They are offered no lenience, even for petty offenses, in a system that seems hell-bent on warehousing them by the millions . . . while others escape the consequences of pervasive malfeasance scot-free."[1]

Like many of the protesters across America, Ferguson leaders were dismayed that, fifty years after the passage of the Civil Rights Act, these two separate Americas still existed. The legal barriers might have been removed, but social, economic, and criminal justice was still far from color-blind.

Although just a few years earlier we had elected a black president, racial tensions seemed to be worsening. Polls showed that while the public perceived an improvement in race relations for a year or so in the immediate aftermath of President Obama's election, more people than ever felt race relations were souring.

I do not question President Obama's desire to help the poor, or to help people of color. Yet, under his administration, the poor have gotten poorer, and the rich have gotten richer. Income inequality is worse under President Obama than it was under President Bush. Black unemployment is still twice white unemployment. Households headed by a black parent have lost an average of $3,500 in median household income.

I spoke with the president a few months before the 2014 elections about these issues. I reminded him that I had joined forces with Senator Cory Booker on a bill to expunge the records of nonviolent felons to help them find employment. I refreshed his memory about the bill I brought to the floor of the Senate that would make some minor nonviolent drug felonies misdemeanors in order to avoid the employment problems associated with a felony record. I even mentioned the bill I have written with Harry Reid to restore voting rights to people convicted of nonviolent crimes who have served their time. The president offered little in the way of help. Even after the election, the president invited a bipartisan group of representatives and me to the White House to discuss criminal justice reform. Again I was disappointed. Even with bipartisan support, nothing gets done.

The uneasy coexistence of the two Americas was brought to the forefront by the deaths of Michael Brown in Ferguson and Eric Garner in Staten Island. We need to notice and be aware of the injustices imbedded in our criminal justice system, though we shouldn't be misled to believe that excessive force is the norm, not the exception. The vast majority of police are conscientious. Most do their difficult jobs in a just and helpful way, serving and protecting their communities.

Just before Christmas 2014, Helen Johnson was desperate to feed her two daughters and their small children, who had gone two days without food. When she got to the store she discovered that the $1.25 she had was not enough to buy eggs. She was fifty cents short, so she stuffed the eggs in her pocket.

Helen didn't even make it out of the store.

When police officer William Stacy arrived, something special happened. Instead of handcuffing Helen and taking her to jail or writing her a summons, he used discretion and compassion to mete out justice.

He warned Helen not to steal again, and he bought her the eggs himself.

No doubt there are bad cops just as there are bad factory workers and bad taxi drivers and bad politicians, but it's not the people who enforce our criminal justice system who are the main problem. The problem lies in the system itself, a system that fosters the unease felt in poor neighborhoods across the country.

I think peace will come when those of us who have enjoyed the American Dream become aware of those who are missing out on the American Dream. The future of our country will be secure when we break down the wall that separates us from "the other America." I want to be a part of a united America in which every child, rich or poor, black or white, truly believes that they have a chance at the American Dream. We need to address the undercurrent of unease that seeps through our land. The first step in changing this culture is to acknowledge the problem.

Cops in Tanks

For decades, big government policies have kept the poor poor and our jails filled with minorities, while draining any vestige of hope from a class of people government tries to sweep under some tidy rug.

The reaction to protests in Ferguson has two sides. On the one side, protesters burned businesses, burned cars, and terrorized the town. There is no excuse for such violence. On the other side, thousands of peaceful protesters were met with rubber bullets, tear gas, and a police department that showed up at the protest in gear more fitting for Fallujah or Kandahar. While the show of force was impressive, it did little to stop the damage that was done to the town.

In his column, Walter Olson of the Cato Institute asked a question that was on the mind of many:

> Why armored vehicles in a Midwestern inner suburb? Why would cops wear camouflage gear against a terrain patterned by convenience stores and beauty parlors? Why are the authorities in Ferguson, Mo., so given to quasi-martial crowd control methods (such as bans on walking on the street) and, per the reporting of *Riverfront Times*, the firing of tear gas at people in their own yards?[2]

A photograph that ran on front pages of newspapers and websites around the world showed a SWAT team member sitting on top of a BearCat, an armor-protected vehicle that can withstand bullets from a .50 caliber rifle, and holding a military M4 weapon. That gun has a scope accurate up to 500 meters. The rest of his team also had M4s, and side arms with thirty rounds, and body armor, and camouflage battle-dress uniforms (BDUs).

There's nothing wrong with that kind weaponry if it's used where it's supposed to be used and not carried by cops on Main Street. The "surplus" military equipment is to be used in the event of a terrorist attack—in fact, the federal government prohibits its use for riot control. Obviously, someone forgot to tell the Ferguson PD.

As I wrote in an op-ed for *Time* magazine soon after the event, there is a systemic problem with today's law enforcement. Not surprisingly, big government has been at the heart of the problem. Washington has incentivized the militarization of local police by using federal dollars to help municipal governments build what are essentially small armies. The system allows for a culture in which police departments compete to acquire military gear that goes far beyond what most of Americans think of as appropriate for law enforcement.

When you couple this militarization of law enforcement with an erosion of civil liberties and due process of law that allows the police to become judge and jury—national security letters, no-knock searches, preconviction forfeiture, and broad general warrants—we begin to have a very serious problem on our hands. It becomes almost impossible for many Americans not to feel that their government is targeting them.

In the wake of the tragedy in Ferguson, President Obama promised to overhaul the system and stop the flood of surplus military equipment to police departments. The government giving police military weapons has been going on for so long it will take a generation for attrition to deplete the supply that's already out there. Attorney General Eric H. Holder Jr. said the equipment "flowed to local police forces because they were increasingly being asked to assist in counterterrorism."[3] Let me know when the terrorists get to Fargo, or Franklin, Indiana, or Ferguson, or any number of the small towns that receive this equipment. Recently, the Homeland Security Committee had a hearing on the overmilitarization of domestic police forces. I asked a Defense Department official what possible use local police had for the 12,000 bayonets they handed out last year. Were they planning some type of charge?

The constitutional protection against cops acting like soldiers resides mostly in the Third and Fourth Amendments. Often overlooked as archaic, the Third specifically prevents the quartering of military in private homes without the owner's consent. It reads in full: "No Soldier shall, in time of peace be quartered in any house without the consent of the Owner, nor in time of war, but in a manner to be prescribed by law." It was written into the Bill of Rights in response to the British Quartering Act, which allowed British troops to commandeer colonists' homes during the Revolution.

The broader interpretation of the amendment is that the military's purpose is to protect the United States from foreign threats and not to enforce domestic laws.

Sound familiar? The NSA is supposed to operate under the same restrictions. Supposed to.

Radley Balko is the author of *Rise of the Warrior Cop*, perhaps the seminal book on the militarization of America's police. In one of that book's many illuminating passages, Balko poses the question that has bothered me since before the shooting in Ferguson. "How did we evolve from a country whose founding statesmen were adamant about the dangers of armed, standing government forces—a country that enshrined the Fourth Amendment in the Bill of Rights and revered and protected the age-old notion that the home is a place of privacy and sanctuary—to a country where it has become acceptable for armed government agents dressed in battle garb to storm private homes in the middle of the night—not to apprehend violent fugitives or thwart terrorist attacks, but to enforce laws against nonviolent, consensual activities?"

Though you can chart the history of police militarization from Colonial times and the writs of assistance (yes, them again), and Balko does, I'll cut to the more recent chase. The antecedent to the Ferguson military response resided in Los Angeles in the 1960s, where a young, ambitious police commander who had seen sections of his city burned to the ground during the Watts riots came up with an idea of a heavily armed, specially trained police response team. When he approached his superiors with the idea he called the proposed unit a "special weapons attack team." The police chief of Los Angeles at the time, Thomas Reddin, liked the concept but didn't particularly care for the word "attack" in the unit's title. The young commander, whose name was Daryl Gates, was disappointed. He was fond of the name he'd bestowed on his team, particularly because of its snappy abbreviation. Gates suggested "special weapons *and* tactics" and Reddin gave him the go-ahead.

Gates knew a good acronym when he saw one.

Partly by early successes, or at least the involvement in high-profile cases like the raid on the Los Angeles headquarters of the Black Panthers and a shoot-out with the Symbionese Liberation Army of Patty Hearst fame, Gates's SWAT team captured America's imagination.

There are legitimate reasons for local police to employ SWAT teams, but the proliferation of the paramilitary unit is indicative of a fundamental problem in our country. One of the ways big government supports this encroachment on our rights and oversteps its constitutional power is with no-knock warrants.

Essentially, there are three basic reasons a police officer in his or her official capacity is allowed to enter a residence: if permission is granted by the occupant, if the police have a warrant issued by a judge, or if the police officer is in "hot pursuit" or deems that an emergency inside the home necessitates his or her immediate entry.

A no-knock warrant is a kind of hybrid of the second and third reasons. The emergency in the case of a no-knock is usually the belief that occupants are destroying evidence, for instance, the sound of a toilet flushing or a window opening.

If this justification seems vague, it is.

No-knock warrants came into use during the Nixon administration. Though included prominently in President Nixon's anticrime initiatives and overwhelmingly passed into law by Congress, the no-knock aspect of the crime bill was controversial. It gained support because of a pervading fear of drugs and crime at that time. Like most laws passed in the heat of the moment, the bill had more than its share of flaws, not the least of which was that it was unconstitutional.

Senator Sam Ervin, the Democrat from North Carolina who described himself as an "old country lawyer," was one of the early warriors against no-knock warrants. In July 1970, Ervin took to the Senate floor to express his displeasure over the bill, which is a nice way of describing the James Otis–like explosion that happened that day on the Hill. He even evoked Otis's defense of the Castle Doctrine: "I stand on the proposition that every man's home is his castle, and that the Congress should not go on record as allowing Department of Justice officials to break into a home like burglars." For four and a half hours, Ervin railed against the crime bill, and specifically the no-knock provisions. They "ought to be removed from this bill and transferred to the Smithsonian Institution, to manifest some of the greatest legal curiosities that ever have been evolved by the mind of man on the North American Continent," he said.[4]

Nixon's no-knock warrants were initially limited to federal law enforcement agents and cops in Washington, D.C., but were meant to be a model of a nationwide plan. Whatever Nixon's long-term hopes for it were, in the short run the bill unfairly targeted the poor in every possible regard. Then as now, the poor made up the largest percentage of the population of our nation's capital.

The outcome was predictable. Balko writes about the aftermath of the passing of Nixon's crime bill: "[But] then a curious thing happened. A few years later, stories began to emerge about out-of-control federal drug cops ripping down doors and terrorizing people, often without a warrant, and frequently finding no drugs or contraband at all."[5]

Rolling Stone published perhaps the most famous of these "raids gone wrong" stories. It was titled, appropriately for its era, "Death in the Wilderness: The Justice Department's Killer Nark Strike Force," and was written by Joe Eszterhas. It tells the story of Dirk Dickenson, a twenty-four-year-old hippie who was shot fleeing from a heavily armed SWAT team who had stormed his Humboldt County, California, cabin.

A police informant had told federal narcotics agents that Dickenson was running a major drug operation that included a PCP lab. The raid included agents from the ATF, the Bureau of Narcotics and Dangerous Drugs (the BNDD was the DEA of its day), and, of course, the IRS (what would a raid be without them?). Half of the team arrived at Dickenson's cabin in a Huey helicopter, the other half by car. The team in the car hid in the woods surrounding the cabin to provide cover for the assault team in the helicopter. Agents also brought along several reporters to document the event—it would, they thought, be good PR. One reporter wrote that the raid resembled "an assault on an enemy prison camp in Vietnam." Dickenson was not armed. The landing of the helicopter had frightened him so that—imagine a Huey helicopter landing unannounced in your backyard and you get the picture—he took off running. He didn't hear the command to stop and was shot in the back. "They said nothing," Ezsterhas wrote. "Their faces were blank and waxy. They aimed and fired. He heard the gunshots and saw the glop of his own blood. He was dying..."

There was no PCP lab. Cops found two small bags of marijuana, some peyote buttons, and two LSD tablets.

Joe Ezsterhas's article became part of the Congressional Record,[6] and the story of Dirk Dickenson and others like it so disturbed America that when Sam Ervin took to the floor of the Senate again the people listened. In 1975, Gerald Ford signed the law repealing no-knock warrants.

This would be a much better story if that was the end of no-knock warrants. It wasn't.

As in a horror movie, they keep coming back to life.

By the early 1980s, SWAT had inspired a network television show, a magazine, and a hit song. By the mid-1990s, there would be a SWAT video game franchise and a number of reality shows based on SWAT, including one that featured a SWAT team in Detroit that gained national attention for the wrong reason.[7] In May 2010, the Detroit SWAT team in full battle gear entered a ground-floor apartment through an open door. They threw a flash-bang grenade that landed so close to a little girl it singed her blanket. Then they shot and killed seven-year-old Aiyana Mo'nay Stanley-Jones as she slept on a couch. Her grandmother sat a few feet away in a chair watching TV. The police were executing a warrant for a man suspected of murder who lived in the apartment above.

An A&E film crew from the TV show *The First 48* was filming the raid. The show's premise is the need for police to solve a crime in forty-eight hours or the case will go cold. The murder for which the warrant was issued was seventeen hours old. The clock was ticking, the cameras were rolling, and Aiyana was shot in the head because of it. The leader of the SWAT team had been featured on the show before, and the bullet that killed Aiyana came from his gun.

Still, thanks to Madison Avenue and Hollywood spin, America loved and felt safe that SWAT was there to protect us, but SWAT was never about protection. Though the word "attack" might have been dropped from the team's original name, it hadn't been dropped from its mission. SWAT teams are specifically trained as use-of-force specialists.

I don't know about you, but "use-of-force specialists" does not sound like who I want patrolling my street.

In 1981, Congress sprinkled Miracle-Gro on SWAT. That year they passed the Military Cooperation and Law Enforcement Act. In what was to be a mutually beneficial relationship in the war on drugs, the government promised (what could go wrong there?) that the Feds would receive local knowledge and local law enforcement would receive federal intelligence-gathering resources, money, and military equipment.

In the 1990s, the Feds opened the floodgates of military supplies for local police. Bill Clinton's "1033" program authorized the

Department of Defense to allocate to local police Black Hawk and Huey helicopters, grenade launchers, and other military equipment. In 1994, the Justice Department began funding surveillance technology and other military-level security systems for local police. By 1997, 1.2 million pieces of military equipment had been transferred to local police departments. By 1999, that number had jumped to 3.4 million. All of it was in direct opposition to the Third Amendment.

Then came September 11, 2001.

In the aftermath of the terrorist attack, George W. Bush signed the Patriot Act and with a stroke of his pen brought back the no-knock warrant. If Bill Clinton stomped on the Third Amendment, George Bush trampled the Fourth.

The Patriot Act also authorized wide use of "sneak and peek" and "sneak and steal" warrants. Officially called Delayed-Notice Search Warrants, sneak and peek warrants allow law enforcement to enter your home legally without notifying you right away. In other words, agents can sneak into your house or business, root around at will, and not notify you about it until months later. Even worse are sneak and steal warrants, which allow cops or agents to enter your home without your knowledge and remove what they deem as evidence without telling you. Even if they don't physically take anything from your home or place of business or other property, they're allowed to riffle through your mail, search your computer, and even install surveillance devices. There have even been cases in which agents ransacked the premises to make it look like a burglary to cover their tracks.[8]

Sneak and peek and sneak and steal warrants are supposed to be used in the fight against terrorism, but very few are used in that manner. In fact, they are overwhelmingly used to find evidence of illegal drugs, mostly marijuana. According to the latest government report[9] detailing the numbers of sneak and peek warrants issued, out of a total of 6,775 requests, 5,093 were used in drug cases. Only thirty-one were actually used to fight terrorism (the remaining were used in investigations of other crimes, mostly fraud).

Under President Obama, the two-pronged attack on the Third and Fourth Amendments has grown exponentially. In 2013 alone, the 1033 program handed military equipment worth more than half a billion dollars over to local law enforcement. Today sneak and peek warrants make up fully 10 percent of all warrants issued by the federal government.[10]

Last year, the Homeland Security Grant Program instituted after 9/11 gave local police departments almost a billion dollars in "counterterrorism funds," money that was used to buy drones, among other things. It also funds the Suspicious Activity Reporting (SAR) program, which sounds to me like something out of a dystopian novel. Operating in cities around the country, the program compiles "see something, say something" reports into a database. What constitutes suspicious behavior? The answer is fuzzy at best. In my own home state of Kentucky, a list of suspicious behavior the Homeland Security Office published includes people who avoid eye contact, people who are overdressed for the weather, and overloaded vehicles.[11]

My God, you'd have to report every teenager in the state.

Then there's the Edward Byrne Memorial Justice Assistance Grant (JAG) Program, which provides funding to local police departments for, among other things, body armor, helicopters, and joint task force operations. The grant was named after a twenty-two-year-old New York City police officer who was shot and killed by drug dealers while he was protecting a witness to a drug case. I'm all for cops getting the equipment they need to protect themselves: bulletproof vests, the best appropriate firearms, and all the training possible. Money from the Byrne grant also funded a SWAT drug raid in Tulia, Texas, that resulted in the arrest of forty African Americans—10 percent of the town's black population—and produced no drugs and no weapons. But the team did manage to wreck many homes and the lives of far too many people.[12]

The thing about federal money is, once it starts flowing it keeps flowing until it floods any hope of personal liberty. By 1999, 90 percent of the police departments in municipalities of over 50,000 people and 75 percent of the departments in towns under 50,000 had paramilitary police units, according to Peter Kraska, professor and department chair of the School of Justice at Eastern Kentucky University. Today, more than 600 cities have mine-resistant ambush protected vehicles (MRAPs) that weigh over 20 tons. According to a statistic cited in a Cato Institute report, currently there are upward of 150 SWAT raids every day in America.

Every single day.[13]

In his article titled "Militarization and Policing—Its Relevance to 21st Century Police," Professor Kraska, who was one of the first to write on this subject, states that such a proliferation of SWAT raids would have been unthinkable just twenty years ago. "It is critical to recognize that these are not forced reaction situations necessitating use of force specialists; instead they are the result of police departments choosing to use an extreme and highly dangerous tactic, not for terrorists or hostage-takers, but for small-time drug possessors and dealers."

How ridiculously small-time? Well, in 2010 in Florida, a SWAT team engaged in a series of raids on barbershops. They found a few instances of barbering without a license, but little else.[14] Many other raids, however, aren't nearly as harmless.

In spring 2014, a SWAT team executing a no-knock warrant threw a concussion grenade through Alecia Phonesavanh's window in Janesville, Wisconsin. The grenade exploded in the crib of Alecia's nineteen-month-old son, Bounkham Phonesavanh Jr. Part of the infant's nose was destroyed, his face received extensive injuries, and a hole was blown in his chest wall. For weeks Bounkham languished in a coma. Though the boy survived, the family was saddled with $1 million in hospital bills.[15] The police found no drugs.[16]

Police use of flash-bang grenades has gotten so commonplace that cops in Little Rock, Arkansas, used them in over 80 percent of their 112 raids between 2011 and 2013, nearly all of which were conducted in black neighborhoods, according to ProPublica, which cites an ACLU survey.[17]

SWAT raids also kill police. In December 2013, in Sommerville, Texas, a SWAT team executed a no-knock warrant on the trailer home of Henry Goedrich Magee. Magee and his girlfriend were sleeping at the time. The police used flash-bang grenades that startled Magee, so he grabbed a rifle he kept next to his bed, then shot and killed the first intruder through the door. The "intruder" was thirty-one-year-old sheriff's deputy Adam Sowders. A grand jury believed Magee, and the capital murder charge against him was dropped.

This has to stop. The military imagery out of Ferguson and other American towns is not only an affront to the local citizens but a worldwide embarrassment for the United States. How can we pretend to be a country of constitutional law when we allow tanks to roll over our constitution?

We've veered off the constitutional rails, and there's a wreck around the corner. The good news is there's a way to get back on track. With my staff, I am working on legislation that would stop the flow of military equipment to local police. The Stop Militarizing Our Law Enforcement Act would restrict what equipment can be transferred or bought through the 1033 program, the Department of Homeland

Security Preparedness Grant Program, and the DOJ's Byrne Grant Program. It will prohibit the transfer of militarized weaponry that was never designed to be in the hands of law enforcement—including mine-resistant ambush protected vehicles and weaponized drones. If local law enforcement is convinced that these items are necessary to protect their communities, then they should pay for them with local tax dollars and be held accountable for the expense by the people they serve.

If I am elected president of the United States, the Constitution will again be the law of the land. There will be no government overreach by my administration. I will continue to fight every day to restrain government and promote personal freedom. That's my promise.

12

★ ★ ★

The War on Christians

Any country that fosters the war on Christianity or, for that matter, any country that allows an unchecked hatred for the United States should be excluded from receiving foreign aid. They get not one penny. Period.

* * *

When Naghmeh Abedini first came to my Senate office and told me of her husband Saeed's persecution, it reminded me of the Christian martyrs during the Roman Empire. I couldn't help thinking of the extraordinary courage and faith it must take to evangelize in an Islamic country today.

Naghmeh and Saeed's story begins like a fairy tale. Naghmeh was born in Iran but grew up in Boise, Idaho. There she became a Christian. "That's the most beautiful part of America for me," she told a reporter from the website Townhall. "I had the freedom to choose my religion." In 2001, she returned to Iran. She was called there, she says, to minister to Muslim women. At the time, Saeed, who had also converted to Christianity, was preaching in an underground Christian church. "As a young woman I always prayed, 'Lord, I can't marry someone who is mediocre,'" she told Christian Broadcast News.

The happy couple soon married in a ceremony that drew hundreds of Iranian Christians. It also drew the attention of the Iranian Revolutionary Guard.

Undeterred, Saeed carried his message often to Iran, where he helped found scores of underground Christian churches and orphanages. In the summer of 2012, on what he thought was a routine trip, he was arrested and sent to Evin Prison. What had started as a fairy tale for Saeed and Naghmeh became a nightmare.

Naghmeh is young and striking looking, with jet-black hair. I can still see the tears streaming down her face as she told me that Saeed had been beaten so severely in prison that he had to be hospitalized. She told me about the daily threats her husband received from fellow inmates and how he lives in fear for his life. As a father, it was especially heartbreaking to think of Naghmeh and Saeed's two small children who continue to grow as the memory of their father fades.

I promised her then that I would do whatever it took to rally Christians to pray and call for Saeed's release. It is a promise I've kept to this day. I wrote this letter on January 24, 2014, to President Hassan Rouhani of Iran:

> I am writing to you today to urge you to commute the sentence of Pastor Saeed Abedini and release him from prison. I have recently met with his wife, Naghmeh, and she is very concerned for her husband's well-being. His health is deteriorating and he is apparently under constant threat of harm from both prison personnel and other inmates at Rajaei Shahr prison.
>
> I wish to remain cautiously optimistic regarding the recent diplomatic progress between our two nations. However, I must point out that if something were to happen to Pastor Abedini while he is incarcerated, any goodwill forged over the past few months would likely evaporate. Conversely, granting clemency to Pastor Abedini and allowing him to return to the United States would do much to create a positive atmosphere that would reflect well on future discussions.
>
> Cooperation and trust are built one gesture at a time and actions speak louder than words.

Along with the letter, I introduced a resolution in the Senate that calls for the immediate release of this American pastor. As of this writing, Saeed still suffers in an Iranian jail.

Iran is only one of several countries that are complicit in this wrongdoing. Throughout this chapter I will present evidence of a persecution of Christians the likes of which has not been seen since the Roman Empire. The proof is clear, inescapable, and overwhelming: there is a worldwide war on Christianity, and it's a war that's being funded by your tax dollars.

Let's start with Syria.

I have a friend who went to Duke University School of Medicine with me. Though he was born here in America, his family is Syrian Christian. I once asked him how long his people have been Christian. "A lot longer than yours," he said with a friendly smirk. Many Christians of European ancestry forget that Christianity in the Middle East preceded Christianity in northern Europe by several hundred years. In some villages in Syria they still speak Aramaic, the language of Christ.

There have been Christians in Syria since St. Paul converted on the road to Damascus. Just north of Damascus is a town called Maalula, or the "land of martyrs."[1] From there, modern-day stories of persecuted Christians filter out to the world. In September 2012, an armed Islamist group went from house to house, terrorizing the occupants and destroying sacred Christian images. In one of the homes, they came across three Greek Catholics, including Sarkis el Zakhm.

"Convert to Islam or die," the gunmen ordered.

"I am a Christian," Sarkis said, "and if you want to kill me because I am a Christian, do it."

Those were Sarkis's last words.

Not long after Sarkis was killed, a rebel gang in Maalula swept through town forcing Christians to convert at gunpoint and slitting the throat of a Christian man in front of his fiancée.

Then there's the story of Father Frans.

As recently as 2011, the Old City in Homs, Syria, had a Christian population of 60,000. When the civil war began, the city was a rebel stronghold. It was also a city under siege, isolated by Bashar al-Assad's army. As food and other basic supplies grew short, Christians were beaten, robbed, and finally driven from their homes—according to conservative estimates there are a half million Syrian Christian war refugees. But even as their numbers dwindled in their home country, hatred grew toward the ones who remained.

By April 2014, only a few more than a hundred Christians remained in the Old City. Father Frans was one of them. He lived in a small brick monastery. The seventy-five-year-old priest's face was friendly but war worn. A Dutch-born Jesuit, Father Frans van der Lugt had for thirty-five years ministered to the sick and disabled in the Christian and Muslim communities in Homs.

He insisted to all who would listen that he was neutral, and he tried to bring the Christians and Muslims together, arranging meetings in a farmhouse outside the city. When his own food supply grew short, the priest subsisted on a soup made primarily of grass. He helped smuggle medical supplies into the city, and he bartered food from the rebels for elderly Christians. Father Frans also had a coveted talent. He made alcohol out of grape leaves.[2]

One day Father Frans heard his housekeeper in conversation and went to the gate to see what the commotion was about. There he saw a soldier, a cloth wrapped around his head cloaking his identity, holding an AK-47 in his hand.

The soldier ordered the priest to come with him.

"Why would I go with you?" Father Frans asked. "I can't even see your face."

When Father Frans wouldn't go willingly, the rebel pulled him through the gateway. Outside the monastery was a plastic chair. Father Frans liked to sit there and watch the children from the area, some of them war orphans, splash in the small plastic pool he filled for them. Now he sat there with a gun pointed at his head, a gun that could very well have been paid for by American tax dollars.

The Syrian rebel didn't care how many Muslims the priest had helped. He didn't care that Father Frans was a man of peace. He was Christian, and that was reason enough for him to die.

The soldier pulled the trigger.

A hateful ideology drives this violence against Christians. By definition, it owns no empathy, tolerance, or compassion. It simply seeks to destroy what it opposes, and what it opposes is the Christian faith. Much has been written about the destruction of mosques, but little of the razing of Christian churches. Christians are an endangered species in Syria, just as they are in Iraq, Afghanistan, and Somalia. Make no mistake, the war against Christianity crosses the globe, from Egypt to Nigeria to Zanzibar, and even to our own shores. Yes, the war against Christians has reached America.

Yet, unbelievably, it is a war that the mainstream media ignores. If you want proof of this, look no further than the Boko Haram kidnapping in Nigeria. The two hundred schoolgirls who were taken were mostly Christians, a detail that most recognized news organizations decided wasn't important enough to report—not even when the terrorists released a video showing the girls dressed in Islamic garb and praying to Allah.[3]

Last year I had the opportunity to meet a young girl who was kidnapped by Boko Haram. My friend the author Doug Wead, a former special assistant to President George H. W. Bush, together with his wife, Myriam, brought the young woman to my office. Her name is Mercy Paul, a fact that led to some good-natured speculation about our being distantly related.

She told Kelley and me that when Boko Haram came to her school they rounded up all of the girls and put them in trucks. They were told that they were to be "married," and if they tried to flee or jump from the truck they would be shot. This brave girl decided that not being "married" to one of these thugs was worth risking a bullet, and so she jumped. She hid in the roadside brush, frozen in fear, for hours. Miraculously, she survived. The Weads helped her to come to America and are paying for her to go to school. Everyone in my office that day was moved by the courage of this remarkable young girl, and the hopefulness in her eyes as she talked about going to school here in America. When it came time for Mercy to leave, I told her that I would not forget her story, and that if she ever needed my help all she had to do was call.

Mercy Paul is one of the lucky ones. The leader of Boko Haram warned that he would sell off the two hundred kidnapped Christian schoolgirls as sex slaves. As of this writing, their whereabouts are still unknown. Some of the girls are as young as nine. The Nigerian group has ties to al-Qaeda, and the kidnapping is not the worst of their crimes. Many schools were attacked before the girls were kidnapped, including one where fifty-nine students were murdered while they slept in a dormitory. Boko Haram soldiers snuck in and shot them with machine guns. Over the last four years, thousands of Christians have been murdered in northern Nigeria.[4]

Around the world, the bodies of martyred Christians pile higher by the day.

In Kenya, motorcycle assailants hurled bombs at a Christian ministry. In Indonesia, three girls were abducted on their way to their Christian school and later beheaded. In Guinea, a Muslim mob attacked and killed ninety-five Christians and injured one hundred and thirty.

In Egypt, eighty-two churches were attacked, with hundreds killed and wounded. In Cameroon, two Christians who converted from Islam were murdered. In Libya—the country we supposedly freed from oppression—Benghazi militias tortured and killed Christians.

Last year in Pakistan, our "ally" to which we continue to send foreign aid, seventy-five Christians were killed and several hundred were injured in a church bombing. Christians in Pakistan are routinely falsely charged with blasphemy, a charge that can bring a sentence of public execution.

Such is the case of Asia Bibi, a Pakistani Christian who sits on death row. In her memoir, *Blasphemy* (her husband relayed her words from the tiny jail cell to a French journalist), she tells the story of picking fruit with other women on a blistering hot day. She drew some water from a well that was supposed to be used by Muslims only. A Muslim woman approached her. There was a heated exchange and threats. Fortunately, Bibi was able to leave unharmed.

Five days later, however, as she was again picking fruit in a field, she wasn't as lucky.

The angry crowd approached her, shouting, "Death! Death to the Christian!"

She pleaded for her life.

They pelted her with stones, punched her in the face, and dragged her through the streets. The local imam finally intervened, but only to say, "If you don't want to die, you must convert to Islam."

"I'm not going to convert," she said. "I believe in my religion and in Jesus Christ, who died on the cross for the sins of mankind."

The crowd descended on her again, this time with sticks. Finally, the police stopped the attackers, but then arrested her.

For several years now, Asia Bibi has been on death row for her alleged crime. As of this writing, the Pakistani government has moved her to a jail in a remote part of the country, perhaps in the hope she will quietly die far from public scrutiny.

Most times, the accusation of blasphemy arises out of personal grudges or petty disputes—or as a cover of outright theft of property. Christians have no legal recourse in such matters. They're sent to jail, lose their homes, and often lose their lives without a single word uttered on their behalf. In the first three centuries A.D., the crime of following Christ's teachings was punishable by death. Pardons were offered to Christians who renounced their faith and offered sacrifices to the Roman gods. Too many Christians now live in the same ancient fear.

Christian women in particular are targets of radical Islam.

In Sudan, Meriam Yahia Ibrahim, who is married to an American Christian, was sentenced to death for converting from Islam to her husband's religion. Pregnant, she was released from death row in a woman's prison only to give birth and nurse her child, which is Sudanese law. Luckily, Meriam was granted asylum, and in August she was allowed to come to the United States.

In Saudi Arabia, one of the most intolerant and oppressive countries in the world when it comes to treatment of Christians, thirty-five Ethiopian Christians were jailed for eight months simply for holding a service in a private home. Most of them were women who were subjected to invasive strip searches.[5]

It breaks my heart to hear the stories of this persecution. Protecting Christians should be a priority of the next administration. It would be for mine. We need a president who will ensure that our country, our policies, and our tax dollars are on the side of ending this violence.

In January 2014, Open Doors, a nonprofit Christian organization, released its world rankings of the most oppressive countries for Christians. Nine of the top ten are Muslim-majority states. The tenth is North Korea. According to Open Doors, there are more than a hundred million oppressed Christians in the world today.[6]

Maybe the worst of all radical Islam groups is ISIS, which carries out the systematic beheading of Christians, including women and children.[7] When ISIS overran Mosul, in northern Iraq, they went from Christian home and business to Christian home and business and marked each with the letter *N*, which stood for Nazarene, Arabic for Christian. The mark came with the warning to convert or be killed. Most of the Christians fled. Then, last February, in maybe their most heinous display of barbarity, ISIS videotaped the beheading of at least thirteen Coptic Christians in Libya and then streamed it to the world.

We cannot turn a blind eye to the plight of our Christian brothers and sisters around the world anymore. We can begin by putting a stop to foreign policies that put innocent Christians at risk. Any country that fosters the war on Christianity or, for that matter, any country that allows an unchecked hatred for the United States should be excluded from receiving foreign aid. They get not one penny. Period.

At the start of the Iraq War, Christians in Iraq numbered around 1.5 million. Estimates today have that number at fewer than 450,000. As recently as 2010, the Islamic State in Iraq specifically targeted Christians. A mission statement posted on their website read: "all Christian centres, organizations and institutions, leaders and followers, are legitimate targets for the muhajedeen [holy warriors] wherever they can reach them."

Since we deposed of Saddam Hussein, leadership in Iraq has been a revolving door, but the persecution of Christians has remained a constant. Still, we continue to give billions of dollars and military support to a government that allows the purge of Christians.

Just months before the final withdrawal of U.S. troops from Afghanistan, members of the Afghanistan parliament called for the extermination of any Afghans who converted to Christianity—a provision for executing Christian converts is in the country's constitution.[8] We have spent over $100 billion rebuilding the Afghan infrastructure. If their government insists on laws that unjustly jail and persecute Christians, then they can rebuild their own country!

Egyptians climbed to the roof of our embassy in Cairo and burned the American flag on the anniversary of the 9/11 attacks. According to a Pew poll taken in early 2013, just 16 percent of Egyptians had a favorable view of America.[9] Yet we send Egypt $1.55 billion in aid every year.[10] Although the Muslim Brotherhood was forced from power, new elections are unlikely. The Egyptians have traded one despot for another. Coptic Egyptians are still persecuted and live under the threat of Islamic fundamentalists. Copts have been in Egypt since St. Mark the Evangelist wrote his gospels. Before the Arab Spring, Christianity flourished in small outposts, like those of the Coptic Christians in Egypt. I had hoped that the Arab Spring would bring freedom to long-oppressed people throughout the Middle East, but I fear the Arab Spring is becoming an Arab winter—especially for Christians in the Middle East.

Until the persecution of Christians stops, these countries should not get one penny from us.

I know withholding aid will work. I have already used the tactic when Americans were detained in Egypt for running democratic organizations. At the time, Hillary Clinton was the secretary of state and had repeatedly ignored the abuses of countries receiving our aid and certified them as "democratic." Even as they arrested the sixteen American democracy workers, including the Transportation Secretary's son, Egypt received certification from Mrs. Clinton.

When asked why, Mrs. Clinton responded that Egypt was democratic and still warranted our endless foreign aid.

Likewise, when the Muslim Brotherhood took over in Egypt, Mrs. Clinton continued to certify them as worthy of our aid. Even when the generals prevailed in a military coup, Mrs. Clinton continued to certify Egypt as behaving in a democratic way worthy of American tax dollars.

Only when I brought a bill to the floor that sought to end ALL foreign aid to Egypt—economic aid, military aid, all aid—in thirty days unless our citizens were set free did Egypt finally back down and release the Americans. The threat alone was enough. Imagine how compliant they would be if we shut off the money completely?

Even if Christians weren't being subjected to persecution in these countries, we simply don't have the money to engage in this foolishness. We borrow the money that we send to Pakistan from China. The countries we send money to are not our true allies, and no amount of money will make them so. They are certainly not allies of Israel, and I fear that one day the money and military arms we have paid for will be used against Israel.

In fact, the leader of the Syrian Muslim Brotherhood, Muhammad Riyadh Al-Shaqfa, has already declared his intention to take back the Golan Heights. "It is our right. Are we supposed to acquiesce to the occupation of our land?" he said on Dubai television. If and when he tries, his forces might be carrying American weapons.

I have spoken at conferences and gatherings of pastors and Christians for over a year now on the topic of Christian persecution, trying to get pastors across the country to rally to this cause. We might not be able to force what's left of the Obama administration to change its stripes and stop hiding the inconvenient fact that there is a war on Christians, and, frankly, it will be an uphill battle to get the mainstream media to stop calling the violence "sectarian."

We can start by raising our own voices in protest. As Christians, we understand that the rights to life and freedom of religion exist prior to all government. These rights are not granted to people by other people, these rights are granted to us by our Creator. We need to shout this from the rooftops. We can't let one more innocent person die in silence.

I am certainly not talking about a crusade here. I am not in favor of fighting a conventional war against radical Islam, as some of my colleagues seem to be. It has been proven that massive military deployment does more harm than good in the fight against terror. It would certainly be the same in the war against Christian persecution. Millions of radical Muslims are spread out across the globe. The Iraq War only fostered more Islamic extremism. The same is true after a decade in Afghanistan. Conventional war will continue to prove ineffective and too costly against an unconventional enemy that numbers in the tens of millions. According to a recent Pew Research poll, 21 percent of Egyptians, 13 percent of Pakistani Muslims, and 15 percent of Jordanians find terrorism acceptable if not laudable. Some of these people are supposed to be our friends.

As Christians we should prepare for war but actively seek peace. Ronald Reagan said we should strive for peace through strength, and I agree.

But we should not be naïve about our enemy's motives.

Two days after the attack on the World Trade Center, Frank Silecchia, a tough Brooklyn construction worker with a Fu Manchu mustache, was assisting firefighters in a search for survivors in the wreckage. No one who remained in what was left of the buildings, however, had survived. In the smoldering pit littered with the giant broken shards that was once World Trade Center 6, Frank came upon what he considered a miracle. Overcome with emotion, Frank dropped to his knees. Not too far from Frank, Father Brian Jordan stood in the rubble, consecrating remains.

"Come, Father," Frank yelled. "You have to see this."

It took a few moments for Father Brian to see what Frank saw. In the middle of what looked like a grotto made of jagged chunks of cement and wire mesh stood a seventeen-foot-tall cross made of the steel beams. While the fires that smoldered for months at Ground Zero burned, the cross became a sanctum where firefighters, steelworkers, and volunteers brought their battered faith and found solace.

Father Brian blessed it on October 4, 2001.

You can believe that what came to be called the World Trade Center cross was a sign from God or not—I'd like to think that it was. Yes, you can believe, and certainly won't be alone in your belief, that the attack on the World Trade Center had nothing to do with Christianity. You can also believe the bombing of the Boston Marathon had nothing to do with Christianity. If you do, you have to discount the reports that the radical Islamist preacher Feiz Mohammad, who urges young Muslims to kill infidels, was an influence on Tamerlan Tsarnaev. You must also discount the ideological hate that propelled the hijackers into our buildings.

The message of the gospels is not war, but the God I believe in does not condone the persecution of the defenseless. The country I would lead would not either.

Finally, there is something else that can put a stop to the war on Christianity, something over which we have little direct control.

Most Muslims today describe Islam as a peaceful and tolerant religion, and it certainly once prized inquiry over contempt, education over exclusion, and the scientific method over fanaticism. At one time, Arab countries were the cultural and intellectual centers of the world. Islam once carried the light of learning. Math and science flourished in its glow.

The great medieval physician Rhazes identified smallpox and

measles. For centuries, his writings were essential medical texts in European universities. In 1025, the physician and philosopher Ibn Sīnā—Avicenna—produced *The Canon of Medicine*, still one of the most famous medical encyclopedias ever written.[11] As a physician, I know about Islam's early advances in medicine. The Muslim world then understood better than any other culture how disease spreads and how it can be healed, and the medical arena was only part of the faith's contribution to civilization.

The Persian poet and mathematician Omar Khayyám is one of the fathers of modern algebra. He devised a calendar that is more accurate than the Gregorian. He is probably best remembered, however, as the author of *The Rubáiyát*.[12] When translated, his poem became one of the most popular in the English language:

"A jug of wine, a loaf of bread, and thou..."

The library in Alexandria, Egypt, was not only a treasury of literature—it contained 700,000 scrolls, the equivalent of 100,000 books—but also an architectural wonder, towering over the world's most traveled trade route. Greeks, Indians, and Chinese all passed through Egypt, taking the knowledge they found in the library of Alexandria and spreading it wherever they went.[13] It was the Muslims who mastered pens and printing. As late as the 1960s, it was said that books were written in Cairo, printed in Beirut, and read in Baghdad.

Muslims paved the way for Europe's Renaissance and Enlightenment. They invented or helped develop the magnetic compass, coffee, zoology, eyeglasses, the technique of inoculation, the crankshaft (perhaps the biggest mechanical advancement after the wheel), and if not the fiddle, the great-grandfather of the violin, the rebab. Islam was known for its scholarship, its resourcefulness, and its art.[14]

The whole of Islam has seemingly forgotten its tolerant past.

Yes, it is true that most Muslims are not committed to violence against Christians, but that's not the whole truth. The unfortunate whole truth is that far too many Muslims are dedicated to a single and unimaginable objective: to wipe Christianity from the face of the Earth. These are the militants, the suicide bombers, and the terrorists who incinerate churches, kill priests, and murder innocent Christian children. These are the ones who target the defenseless. These are the ones who condone this violence or simply look the other way.

These are the ones Islam must stop.

The war on Christianity will cease only when Islam gets its own house in order and condemns the element of hate that is distorting it. The war will end only when civilized Islam steps up and destroys the aberrant barbaric offshoot that condones the murder of innocents.

Sometimes poetry can make sense out of a world that defies logic. Parveen Shakir, a Persian poet in the Urdu tradition, wrote, "they insist on examining the firefly in the daylight. The children of our age have grown clever." Radical Islam will end only when Islam has had enough of its extremists. Until Muslims stop tolerating their own intolerance the war will continue. Only when Islam allows her children, like Malala Yousafzai, the Pakistani girl who was shot by the Taliban for promoting education for girls and survived to accept the Nobel Peace Price, to examine the firefly in the daylight will things begin to change. Only then will knowledge and enlightenment begin to grow. Only then will violence recede.

I pray for that moment to come sooner rather than later.

In 1903, my great-great-grandmother wrote to her son who was working a few hours away from their home in Youngstown, Ohio. "Our Sabbath was lovely which I spent at home as usual," she penned. "But the dear Lord willing I hope I can soon go to his house again. Anyway His grace is sufficient for me. There is a song in my soul today, a blessed sunshine that no outward circumstances can take away. The

Lord is a sun and a shield to all that trust in Him. May He always be your guide."

My faith has never been easy for me. Never been easy to talk about and never without its obstacles. Fyodor Dostoyevsky wrote, "I did not arrive at my hosanna through childlike faith but through a fiery furnace of doubt." I don't wear my religion on my sleeve. I'm a Christian and proud to be one, but maybe not always a good one. Like Dostoyevsky, one of my literary heroes, I have had my doubts. As a medical student and then as a physician, I have struggled with understanding God's role in inexplicable diseases like terminal tumors in children. My first patient as a medical student on the surgical service was a beautiful young woman about my age with metastatic melanoma to her ovaries. Though I still had much to learn then about medicine, I knew enough to know her time left on Earth was very short. How could a tragedy like this occur in a world that was supposed to have purpose and design?

I struggle, too, to understand the misery and pain that war inflicts on our young men and women. I struggle to understand man's inhumanity to man.

I pray for understanding, and the Bible says that if you act as if you have faith it will be given to you.

There's an old story about the man whose neighborhood begins to flood. He climbs to his roof and prays to God to save him from the rising waters. Rescuers come in a boat and then a helicopter. But the man tells them that his faith in God will save him. Eventually, the man drowns and goes to heaven, where he meets St. Peter at the Pearly Gates. "Why didn't my faith in God save me?" the man asks. "He sent you a boat and a helicopter," St. Peter says. "What more did you want?"

Prayer is a great start, but prayer without action won't stop the onslaught of atrocities against Christians.

We need to shout down the silence. We need to stem the flow of American taxpayer cash that funds this war on America and Christianity, and we need to use our military wisely.

We need someone to take a stand.

As William Lloyd Garrison stated, "I do not wish to think, or to speak, or write, with moderation... I am in earnest—I will not equivocate—I will not excuse—I will not retreat a single inch—and I will be heard."[15]

13

★ ★ ★

Defending America

If we destroy our enemy but lose, what defines our freedom in the process? Have we really won?

★ ★ ★

There is no greater priority for the federal government than national defense. When I deliberate on spending, and when I consider what rises to the greatest of importance under the Constitution, I unequivocally conclude it is absolutely necessary to defend our freedom.

Dwight D. Eisenhower once said that America's foreign policy is simple: "We're for peace, first, last and always." I believe, even in today's complicated world, that America should still hold fast to Eisenhower's belief as the root of our foreign policy. In an ever-changing world, though, foreign policy must understand and see the world as it is, not at we wish it to be.

I believe a strong foreign policy should consist of fundamental beliefs—for example, that war should be the last resort. No matter the events of the day, our foreign policy should reflect who we are as a people. We can and should adapt to a fast-changing world, but guided by the principle that we are a nation that does not seek new territory, that we are a nation that acts in self-defense, and that we are also a nation that will react with overwhelming force to defend our nation and our liberty.

So how do you assemble a foreign policy for today's world while holding on to what defines us? Well, maybe the first thing to do is not repeat the mistakes of those who came before you.

From George W. Bush's rush to war to Barack Obama's *just don't do anything stupid,* stance,[1] our foreign policy can be categorized by its extremes. Obama's handling of the Middle East—from his misuse of troops in Afghanistan, to his bungled withdrawal from Iraq, to his arming of rebels, his heated proclamations and red lines (which turned out to be so much hot air), and his active role in regime change, which, in my opinion, produced the volatile environment that reigns in the Middle East today—has not only been inept but has put America and Americans in further danger. Obama's approach to Syria alone is so convoluted that his own ambassador to Syria, Robert Ford, told CNN's Christiane Amanpour that he quit because he could no longer "defend America's policy."[2]

Regime Change

If there is one theme that connects the dots in the Middle East, it's that terrorism is a direct result of chaos, and chaos is a direct result of toppling secular dictators. The removal, or attempted removal, of Saddam, Gaddafi, and Assad can be directly tied to the emergence of radical jihadists. The pattern has been repeated time after time after time, and yet, still today, those who steer our foreign policy either refuse to understand or are incapable of understanding the indisputable fact that the same actions produce the same results.

This pattern began with the war in Iraq. Just about every false assumption imaginable about the cost, challenge, and purpose of the Iraq War occurred. Perhaps most disturbing of all was the utter lack of consideration of what an Iraq without Saddam would look like. In the Iraq War, over four thousand American soldiers were killed, and over thirty thousand were injured. Taxpayers spent trillions of dollars on a war that removed the balance of power and destabilized the region. With Saddam gone, Iran is stronger. Where Saddam once counterbalanced Iran, a vacuum now exists, and into that vacuum has poured radical Islam.

Then there is Hillary's war in Libya. In March 2011, Obama ordered airstrikes at Hillary's request, including Tomahawk missiles, to support rebel fighters who overthrew Colonel Muammar el-Gaddafi. He did so in direct contradiction to the Constitution, which explicitly reserves the power to declare war to the legislature. In going to war in Libya, President Obama not only overruled top Pentagon lawyers but his own Justice Department.[3] After Gaddafi fell, Libya became a sanctuary and training ground for terrorists from Northern Africa to Syria. Today, Libya is awash in American guns, rockets, and ammunition, much of which has found its way to all sides of fighting in Syria. It's not only America who is arming the rebels, but our supposed allies: Qatar, Saudi Arabia, Kuwait. Militants control our deserted embassy in Tripoli.

Libya now is a jihadist's wonderland. Extremists swim in the pool of our embassy. Our ambassador was assassinated in the attack on Benghazi, and the remaining embassy staff ultimately was forced to flee overland to Tunisia. Hillary's war may well have ramifications that make the whole world less safe.

A few years before this, the U.S. government had sent a message to Gaddafi: give up your weapons of mass destruction and help us with the war on terror—or else. Interestingly, this seemed to be the whole point of the Bush Doctrine in the Middle East: you are either with us, or you're with the terrorists. In Libya, the Bush administration had what could have been considered a resounding success for this doctrine. Except we grasped defeat from the jaws of victory.

Both parties are to blame for this. Just a year before Hillary's war in Libya, Senators McCain and Graham were there, celebrating Gaddafi's newfound cooperation with America, and taking a victory lap with him over ridding his country of weapons of mass destruction. In other words, he did what we told him to do, clearly and verifiably.

Then just a year later, Senators Graham and McCain were stridently joining Hillary Clinton and Barack Obama in a chorus clamoring for a war to take out Gaddafi. It made no sense. While a dictator and not a good man, Gaddafi had done exactly what we ordered him to do.

Gaddafi gave up his nuclear ambitions voluntarily, and yet we toppled him anyway.

Now we sit in negotiations with Iran, another troublesome country in the region, and we tell them to rid themselves of their desire for weapons of mass destruction. The problem is, we've already sent the wrong message: the last time a leader gave up his desire for weapons of mass destruction, we bombed his country and took him out.

In September 2013, Obama sought the same strategy in Syria. I opposed bombing Assad because there was no clear, discernible American interest, and I feared that toppling another secular dictator would once again embolden the radical Islamists. I thought it would increase the safe haven for terrorists that had already begun to develop, and I said so. Repeatedly. I thought it would put Christians in further peril. On the Foreign Relations Committee, I made it clear we would rue the day we sent arms to Islamic rebels in Syria. The ultimate irony is that someday our own weapons will be used against us or Israel.

The president backed down only because he knew that Congress was not going to support him and that his plan wasn't popular with the American people. If he hadn't, who do you think would be the ruling faction in Damascus? With little doubt, ISIS. Despite our air assaults on the terror group, ISIS still remains a threat.

As it turned out, under diplomatic pressure, Syria agreed to turn its chemical stockpile over to be destroyed. That option was always open, but Obama had to be forced into taking it. Some would argue that the threat of force convinced Assad to take the deal. Perhaps, but the extended debate that others and I forced the country to have also gave time for diplomacy to work.

As I said in a speech in front of the Senate, "Intervention when both choices are bad is a mistake. Intervention when both sides are evil is a mistake. Intervention that destabilizes the region is a mistake."

As Glenn Greenwald and Murtaza Hussain wrote on *The Intercept*, "anyone paying even casual attention now knows that killing the Bad Dictator of the Moment (usually one the U.S. spent years supporting) achieves nothing good for the people of that country..."

Unfortunately, Obama's decisions, disengaging diplomatically in Iraq and the region and fomenting chaos in Libya and Syria, leave few good options and many more terrorists. Since 2010, jihadist groups worldwide have increased by 58 percent, with twice as many jihadist fighters, according to a 2014 Rand study written by Seth Jones.[4] Al-Qaeda affiliate attacks have tripled in that time. There's a greater threat of radical Islam attacking the U.S. now than there was before these policies were enacted.

Arming Rebel Soldiers

Two years ago in Syria, Hillary Clinton's desire was to arm and aid al-Qaeda and ISIS-affiliated rebels against Assad. President Obama requested $500 million to arm some three thousand "moderate" Syrian rebels with varied loyalties to fight ISIS. How ridiculous is that? We didn't even see the Arab Spring coming, and now all of a sudden we're experts on who is a moderate rebel or who is not?

One of the so-called "moderates" in Libya, hailed by Republican and Democrat interventionists alike, is Abdel Belhadj, who is linked to terrorism and al-Qaeda in four different countries.

Our past performance in picking the moderates in civil war hasn't exactly been stellar. We spent billions to arm and train the Iraqi army only to see them strip out of their uniforms, drop their weapons, and head for the hills at the first sight of ISIS.

Back in 2013, the chairman of the Joint Chiefs of Staff, Martin Dempsey, had this to say about arming rebels in Syria: "Risks include extremists gaining access to additional capabilities, retaliatory cross-border attacks, and insider attacks or inadvertent association with war-crimes due to vetting difficulties."[5] He further admitted that telling friend from foe in Syria was increasingly difficult. In other words, weapons stamped "Made in the USA" could be used against innocent civilians or used against our own soldiers. In voicing his country's reluctance to go along with Obama's plan to arm Syrian rebels, the German ambassador to the United States said in the *New York Times*, "We can't really control the final destination of these arms."[6]

I'm as vehemently opposed to sending aid to the rebels in Syria today as I was in 2013 when I told my colleagues on the Senate Committee on Foreign Relations that they would be funding allies of al-Qaeda. Even Ambassador Ford admitted as much when he said it was inevitable that the "moderate" rebels would at times fight alongside al-Qaeda or al-Nusra. If that is true, we shouldn't send weapons and aid to allies of al-Qaeda. Haven't we learned our lesson? Our aid money should not be sent to enemies of America. With Syria, we were promised that rebels who received our help would be "vetted." We're now years into the conflict and years into sending aid and arms, and still no one really knows to whom we're giving the guns and money. I warned the Senate committee that giving aid to the Syrian rebels could come back to haunt the United States.

Some rebels are indeed stronger because of our aid. Some rebels gained territory and accumulated U.S. weapons, and those rebels belong to the ISIS terrorist group. So the group that is now perhaps the largest threat to U.S. interests and citizens is stronger simply because we and our allies pumped weapons into this civil war. Still, the neocons and hawks complain that we didn't send enough weapons into Syria.

One former CIA agent had it right when he wrote that the only thing "moderate" about the Islamic rebels we are arming is their ability to fight! How did President Obama respond? By sending more weapons into that cesspool of a civil war.

Mrs. Clinton often talks about America not having "skin in the game" in Syria. I wonder just whose skin she's talking about. Is it the skin of our brave men and women in the armed forces? The truth is, we had "skin" in the game for months before Obama ordered airstrikes in Syria. The CIA has been arming Syrian rebels since at least the spring of 2014. It hasn't exactly been a secret mission. *Frontline* and *PBS* filmed a documentary that included footage of an American-run "moderate rebel" training camp in Qatar. One rebel who was interviewed was disappointed that he wasn't being trained in antiaircraft weapons.

It's a wonder he hadn't been. The amount and type of weaponry making its way into Syria is staggering. Here's a short list of it.

Reports show that the CIA, Saudi Arabia, and Jordan supplied roughly six hundred tons of weapons to the militants in Syria in 2013 alone.

According to U.N. records, Turkey sent forty-seven tons of weaponry to the Syrian Rebels over a period of a few months—sending twenty-nine tons in just one month in late 2014.[7]

Videos appear online of Free Syrian Army rebels with downed M-8 helicopters and MANPAD surface-to-air missiles.

An American-made TOW antitank system was shown in the hands of Harakat Hazm, a group of so-called moderate rebels. According to the *Wall Street Journal,* Saudi Arabia, in partnership with the United States, provided these weapons to the rebels as part of a "pilot program" that would test the rebels' trustworthiness. The report also detailed millions of dollars in direct U.S. aid to rebels.[8]

The *New York Times* reports that Qatar used "a shadowy arms network to move shoulder-fired missiles" into the hands of Syrian rebels.[9]

According to Gulfnews.com, Saudi Arabia has also partnered with

Pakistan to provide a Pakistani-made version of Chinese shoulder-launched missiles to the rebels.[10]

Iraqi officials publicly accused Saudi Arabia and Qatar of also funding and arming ISIS at the same time. The *New York Times* has also reported huge arms and financial transfers from Qatar to the Syrian rebels, beginning as early as 2011.[11]

Sunni Kuwaitis have funneled hundreds of millions of dollars to a wide range of opposition forces both in Iraq and Syria, according to reports by the Brookings Institution.

According to the *New York Times*, Sudan has provided antitank missiles and other arms.

No one really knows whose finger is on the trigger of all of these weapons. It is said there are 1,500 different factions fighting in the Syrian civil war.

What we do know is that since the Syrian civil war started, 140,000 people are dead, including 50,000 civilians. We must ask the question—how many were killed with American weapons?

As Jane's Terrorism Center noted, the transfer of Qatari arms to targeted groups has the same practical effect as shipping them to al-Nusra, a violent jihadist force. As I've said, the so-called "moderate" rebels are merely a pit stop for the weapons. The radical jihadists scarf up American weapons shortly after their arrival by either buying them, killing the person to whom we gave them, or by simply picking them up off the ground after the person we gave them to dropped them and ran.

This is insanity, pure and simple. It has to stop.

We Need to Stop Saying Things that Aren't True

There's a movie from the late 1990s called *Wag the Dog*. A political satire, it was about a campaign spin doctor who represents a president embroiled in a sex scandal. Seeing that it was released in the nineties, the premise wasn't a big stretch. With the election approaching, the spin doctor, played by Robert De Niro, hires a movie producer to stage a war to take the voters' minds off the scandal. Dustin Hoffman plays the producer. The "war" is shot on a Hollywood set. While watching the filming of a scene of a hero soldier left behind enemy lines, Hoffman—the producer—turns to De Niro—the spin doctor—and says, "It's the best work I've ever done in my life, because it's so honest."

Our foreign policy is not a Hollywood movie. Dramatic music does not swell when the president steps in front of the television cameras to tell the world how we're going to handle a threat or crisis, nor should credits roll when those actions are carried out. In fact, much of the problem we have in the war on terror is that we think about it in finite terms, with a final act. But while we think of it in movie time, our enemies think of it in biblical terms. Sunnis have hated Shias since at least the Massacre of Karbala in A.D. 680. When we think it's over, terrorists are just getting started. You have to look no further than Saddam Hussein's generals who now lead the ISIS forces for proof.

It makes sense, therefore, that the rhetoric that comes out of the Oval Office should be carefully considered. Statements like "that's a red line," or "ISIS is a JV team,"[12] or "mission accomplished" make us look foolish and embolden our enemies.

Instead, we should take our cue from the masters of the bully pulpit.

In 1901, Vice President Teddy Roosevelt stood on a stage at the Minnesota State Fair and said seven words that would become his legacy and would also become the most definitive sentence ever uttered about American foreign policy. Those words, of course, were "Speak softly and carry a big stick."

Eighty years later, in his first inaugural address, President Reagan warned our adversaries not to misjudge our reluctance for conflict as a failure of will. "When action is required to preserve our national security, we will act," he said.

Reagan knew more about Hollywood than any president. He also knew as much about substance as any of them. We're the strongest country in the world, his brevity proclaimed. We will act like it.

Eisenhower, George H. W. Bush, and Reagan all occupied the space in between the extremes of foreign policy. Their foreign policies took into account the world as it was and reacted to it by making us stronger and self-reliant. This foreign policy realism rejects the Wilsonian vision of re-creating the world in our image or the utopian vision of nation building. Our government has trouble running the post office. What makes it think it can be somehow successful building nations abroad? Foreign policy realism also rejects the idea that we are the world's policemen.

So do I.

I don't believe that either George W. Bush or Barack Obama set out to make the world more chaotic and unsafe. In some ways both were caught up in 9/11 and its aftermath. I think they both believed they were acting in America's best interest, but the undeniable truth is that their policies did not act in America's interest. In fact, there is now a swath of the world—from Russia and the Ukraine through the Middle East and into China—that is a flint strike away from eruption. The mistakes of our near past have put us in a difficult place. That's the bad news. The good news is, I believe it's fixable.

A Worldview

Having learned from the mistakes of the past, I believe an unshakable foreign policy, one that can withstand any violent eruption, has to be set on a bedrock of fundamentals. Here are the four stones on which my policy would be built.

1. It is essential that we have the might and threat of force to defend our country. As I said at the beginning of this chapter, I believe that the primary function of the federal government is a strong national defense. No purpose has more importance than the defense of our country, none. War is necessary when America is attacked or threatened or when we have exhausted all measures short of war. In times of peace, we should always be prepared militarily to defend our freedom.

2. When war is necessary, the Constitution dictates that Congress initiates war. When we go to war we should do so only as instructed by the Constitution, with an adherence to our core values and with one primary objective in mind: the safety and sovereignty of the United States. Congress, the people's representative, must always authorize the decision to intervene.

3. I believe that peace and security require a commitment to leadership and diplomacy. President Obama never invested in a relationship with Congress, and the same is true of his foreign policy. To have friends, you have to be a friend. In the run-up to the Gulf War in 1991, Arab nations believed that once George H. W. Bush drew a line, he wouldn't let Iraq cross it. Bush didn't "dance on the Berlin Wall" when it crumbled; instead he worked behind the scenes to help the Cold War end calmly. Action is the currency of leadership. Words are the small change of politicians.

4. We're only as strong as our economy. This might be the most important of all the fundamentals. Admiral Mike Mullen, then the chairman of the Joint Chiefs of Staff, put it succinctly: the biggest threat to our national security is our debt. A bankrupt nation

doesn't project power but rather weakness. Our national power is a function of the national economy. During the Reagan renaissance, our strength in the world reflected our successful economy. Today low growth, high unemployment, and big deficits have undercut our influence in the world.

While my predisposition is to less intervention, I do support intervention when our vital interests are threatened. That doesn't necessarily mean a direct invasion or attack. There have been, and will be, situations in which some force is warranted to prevent the escalation of events that could put America at risk.

For instance, America must protect the five thousand people serving at the largest American consulate in the world, the one in northern Iraq. The consulate in Erbil is a day's march away from ISIS-held territory. We must not make the same mistake Hillary Clinton made in leaving the consulate in Benghazi undefended. Some pundits are surprised that I support destroying ISIS militarily. They shouldn't be. I've said since I began public life that I am neither an isolationist nor an interventionist but a legislator who looks at the world realistically and acknowledges the Constitution as the arbiter in America's involvement in war.

Our anger at ISIS's barbarity is warranted, but their barbarity need not dictate our response. Nor should the president dictate our answer to it. Anger might start the debate of whether to go to war, but it should have little to do with the actual decision, something Washington leaders can't seem to understand. Colin Powell knows a thing or two about war. He wrote in his autobiography, "War should be the politics of last resort. And when we go to war, we should have a purpose that our people understand and support."

I agree.

When we have decided that we have an enemy that requires us to intervene, we must have a comprehensive strategy—a realistic policy applying military power and adroit diplomacy to protect our national interests. In Iraq currently, our strategy should include defending our embassy and consulate and aiding the Iraqi government in defeating ISIS. Some say ground troops will be necessary. I agree. I just want those ground troops to be Iraqis, Kuwaitis, Qataris, Saudis—the people who live there.

As I've stated, only civilized Islam rising up and saying this aberrancy does not represent Islam can fully defeat ISIS. We can and should help, but ultimately the people who live there must fight.

If our history of military intervention has taught us anything it's that might doesn't necessarily equal victory in fights against insurgency. This has held true since at least the Vietnam War. The onus of defeating ISIS is squarely on the shoulders of the Iraqis and Kurds, and victory for them should begin by cutting off ISIS's ability to fund its military and terrorist operations.

According to a report[13] by the RAND Corporation, ISIS funding comes almost entirely through extortion and plunder. Make no mistake: ISIS is a criminal organization with a very lucrative business model. "We believe that ISIS will remain financially solvent for the foreseeable future," write Patrick B. Johnston and Benjamin Bahney from the RAND Corporation in a recent op-ed in the *New York Times*. "A conservative calculation suggests that ISIS may generate a surplus of $100 million to $200 million this year that it could reinvest in state-building."

A path to victory over ISIS can begin with the Iraqis and Kurds cutting off the flow of ISIS-controlled oil from Northern Iraq to eastern Syrian refineries. It can continue by Baghdad decentralizing power and spreading its wealth to Sunni-majority areas.

"Baghdad should also work to strike deals with local Sunni Tribes...[to coordinate] in squeezing ISIS out of local markets," write Johnston and Bahney. The United States can and must help the Iraqis and Kurds stop the flow of cash to ISIS. But, as Johnston and Bahney contend, ultimately our role should come from the margins.

A comprehensive strategy must also take into consideration the history of those we intend to fight. That means not only knowing the footing of these relationships in ancient terms but having a firm grasp of the recent history. If the Arab Spring showed us anything, it's that change in the Middle East begins not at the government level but at the level of the street. We were caught flat-footed simply because we didn't bother to notice the social change that swept through neighborhoods and mosques, nor did we comprehend the reasons behind that social change.

Congress Decides

The Constitution is very clear about who holds the power to send this country to war. In writing about the role of Congress in this regard, James Madison came right to the point: "The power to declare war, including the power of judging the causes of war, is fully and exclusively vested in the legislature...the executive has no right, in any case, to decide the question, whether there is or is not cause for declaring war." You'd have to agree, there is not a lot of wiggle room in that statement.

The Framers also gave Congress the power to provide a common defense, the responsibility to fund that defense, and the power to define and punish "Offences against the Law of Nations," the customary rules governing the interaction of civilized countries around the world (for instance, an attack on one of our ambassadors would be considered an Offence against the Law of Nations).

On the other hand, our Founding Fathers gave the president the job to make tactical decisions once Congress has decided to go to war.

As commander in chief, the president's sworn duty is to keep America and Americans safe. His charge is defensive in nature, not offensive. In making a case in the *New York Times* for this constitutional principle, my colleague Tim Kaine evoked our third president: "More than two centuries ago, when President Thomas Jefferson decided to take offensive action to eliminate the threat on American ships from pirates off the Barbary Coast, he sought Congress's approval, arguing that 'without the sanction of Congress,' he could not 'go beyond the line of defense.'"

When Obama ordered airstrikes against ISIS to protect Americans in Iraq, it was arguably within his power, though only for a short time, not for a sustained campaign against ISIS. Even then, it would have been better to come to Congress. As I've said, I think he should have engaged Congress in these decisions—with a congressional debate and vote, a more strategic vision, a better plan for victory, and a proposal for extricating ourselves.

Had I been president, I would have called for a joint session of Congress, laid out the threat ISIS poses to American interests, and asked Congress to vote on a declaration of war. In my role as senator, I was the only one to introduce legislation to go to war against ISIS, and the first to try to declare war since World War II.

There was a time when Barack Obama knew that congressional authority was necessary for war. In 2007, then Senator Obama stated that no president should unilaterally go to war without congressional authority unless there was an actual or imminent threat to our nation. "I take the Constitution very seriously," Senator Obama told a Pennsylvania town hall in 2008. "The biggest problems that we're facing right now have to do with George Bush trying to bring more and more power into the Executive Branch and not go through Congress at all, and that's what I intend to reverse when I'm President of the United States of America."[14] I would like President Obama to reread some of the stands that candidate Obama took.

Congress, too, must realize its constitutional duty. Unfortunately, too many times recently my congressional colleagues have shirked that responsibility. In *The Daily Beast*, Deborah Pearlstein writes how the Framers expected the people's representatives to be fully engaged in the debate about war. James Madison for one expected Congress to be ambitious and willing to assert their views. "But ours has become a Congress that continues to hide in the shadows of presidents whose own political courage sometimes fails," Pearlstein writes.

If there were ever a reason to be fully engaged in the constitutional process it's when the lives of American soldiers are at risk. Last year, when the Senate debated whether to authorize sending arms to Syrian rebels I stood before a nearly empty chamber. Before I came to the Senate, I'd imagined that when war was discussed, everybody would be at their desks, but there I was, with a handful of other senators. Have we become that inured?

Does political fortune now trump the blood of our youth?

I chastised the Senate's failure to debate the great question of war. I admonished them for deferring any debate until after the 2014 election, and I blasted them for slipping war funds into a 2,000-page spending bill that no one would have time to read.

It was our Founders' intention to set up an adversarial relationship between the branches so that ambition would be pitted against ambition and so that, by separation of the powers, a sense of equilibrium would result.

Much has been said and written about the distance between the White House and Capitol Hill during the Obama presidency. The president contends that it was the recalcitrant politics of Congress, particularly the Republican Congress, that was at fault for the dysfunctional relationship between the Hill and him. On a political level, there is little question that the Republicans played hardball. But, in my estimation, what Obama would not grasp was the line of communication that exists outside of politics. I don't care what part of the political spectrum you are from, whether it's hard right, hard left, or right in the middle, all elected officials share one common trait. This motivation might vary in size and strength, but all of us have it to one degree or another—and that's a desire to help the people we represent.

One time, when journalists were questioning his cool aloofness, Obama was asked why he never went out and had a beer with Mitch McConnell. "You have a beer with Mitch McConnell," the president shot back derisively. I truly believe that had Barack Obama worked as hard at building a rapport with us on the Hill as he did at getting elected, his relationship with Congress would have been much more successful and we would have been a better country because of it.

It's really not that hard to do. Last year, a senator from New York, Democrat Kirsten Gillibrand, asked for my support of a bill that would take sexual assault cases in the military out of the chain of command. It was Senator Gillibrand's belief, and I agreed, that victims of sexual assault shouldn't have to report it to their boss, that they should be able to go to someone outside of the chain of command. At the time the senator approached me, my staff and I were focused in other directions. Once she presented her views, however, I jumped on board.

The point is, Senator Gillibrand sought me out because I'm known in the Senate as someone who puts partisanship aside to get things done that need to be done. In fact, rather than dogmatically stick to her original bill, when I brought Senator Gillibrand some suggested changes to her bill, she happily accepted them. That's how you get things done here. The working relationship between the executive branch and Congress should be the same, especially when it comes to foreign policy.

Throughout history, the foreign policy of dictators has been ruinous. For all intents and purposes, Obama's foreign policy has been a one-man show. Instead of executive war orders, we need vigorous debate and a working relationship between the executive and legislative branches. Divisiveness at home projects vulnerability to our enemies abroad. If I were president I would not stand for it.

The Middle East Today

How would the foreign policy I envision look in today's Middle East?

Well, first of all, this foreign policy would understand that hatred toward us exists, and would acknowledge that interference in elections or the administrations of foreign countries may well exacerbate this hatred. We must realize that a good part of the answer to terrorism will come when Islam polices Islam.

In *The Art of War*, Sun Tzu writes: "If you know the enemy and know yourself, you need not fear the result of a hundred battles. If you know yourself but not the enemy, for every victory gained you will also suffer a defeat. If you know neither the enemy nor yourself, you will succumb in every battle." We see the wars we fight in the Middle East, even our excruciatingly long ones, on an American timetable. It's the Mission Accomplished syndrome. The Sunnis and Shiites have been fighting for centuries. As I have already mentioned, when we think the war is over, they're just getting started. That's the mindset we have been fighting against. Does that mean we have to fight in the Middle East forever? No. I think we have to take care and not be forced into reacting to the volatility of the region.

Knee-jerk reactions by the barnacled boots-on-the-ground crowd who fill the halls of Congress with angry rants seldom solve long-term problems. We can defeat ISIS militarily, but the threat from radical jihadists will continue. Do future terrorist organizations in the Middle East and elsewhere shake in their boots at the prospect of fighting America? I don't think so. I think the moment we defeat or even "degrade" ISIS, as Obama's fond of saying, the next terrorist movement is already waiting in line. That's because the underlying reason for ISIS—age-old grudges, new grudges, economics, and religious extremism—will still exist and, for the most part, exist out of our control. For example, ISIS has built something of a terrorist pipeline between the poor suburbs of Istanbul and the front lines of their so-called caliphate. Many of the young men they persuade to fight for them are vulnerable and angry because of poverty and drug addiction.[15]

With aggressive diplomacy we need to seek out new alliances and solidify the ones we already have to form long-term diplomatic relationships that will help bring structure to the region. Much of the solution, like combating local drug abuse, is out of our hands. Turkish suburbs and other terrorist incubators will remain fertile breeding grounds until Islam takes care of its own house. Until then, organizations like ISIS will continue to thrive.

I hope that by the time you're reading this we will have already kicked ISIS to the gates of hell where they belong, though I don't think it will happen that quickly. Our long-term challenge is to guard ourselves in the future against *any* terrorist organization whose growth poses a significant threat to the United States or our allies.

That said, we would be wise to remember former Secretary of Defense Robert Gates's warning that our foreign policy has become overmilitarized. Yes, we must eliminate all terrorist threats to our freedom and way of life, but to accomplish that we shouldn't throw our might around indiscriminately. All that does is alienate the allies and encouragers among the civilized Islamic nations, the people we will ultimately need to succeed against these threats.

My foreign policy would also include protection of our allies' interests. We should help reinforce Israel's Iron Dome protection against missiles, for instance. A realistic foreign policy would include diplomatic reengagement with Middle East and European allies to recognize the threat that radical Islam poses to world peace and the growing influence of Jihadists.

Important partners such as Turkey, a NATO ally, Israel, and Jordan face an immediate consequence from ISIS and other terrorist groups, and unchecked growth endangers Kuwait, Saudi Arabia, Gulf countries such as Qatar, and even Europe. Several potential partners—notably, the Turks, Qataris, and Saudis—have been reckless in their financial support of ISIS and other organizations, which must cease immediately.

There is no silver bullet to the threat of jihad, which is why I have advocated for a long-term strategy to oppose with vigor the terrorist threat wherever it arises. Part of that strategy would reverse our current trend of toppling governments, a strategy that allows radical jihadists to flourish.

We should also engage with countries we would normally not look to for help to isolate terrorist organizations such as ISIS. Despite our differences and our occasional disputes, China and Russia must be engaged in continuous diplomatic engagement. We must not allow the reckless voices in public discourse to rush us into a war we spent seventy years successfully avoiding.

Some argue we shouldn't negotiate with the Chinese or the Iranians or the Russians. We can't trust them! We take China's money; how can we not negotiate with them? Yes, trust isn't easily achieved with adversaries, but it can be done by finding common ground.

Both China and Russia have radical jihadist threats of varying degrees of their own—an aberrant regime in North Korea is not to China's benefit. We share common interests with countries like China, and those common interests can offset our differences. I have no doubt that diplomacy among the great powers can bring about more stability to the world.

As complicated as the Middle East is, our role should not be that hard to figure out. All we have to do is stay true to who we are: a country with compassion, resolve, and the strength to put fear in the hearts of those who hate us.

At home, my policy would emphasize secure borders and an immigration policy that prevents ISIS and other terrorist infiltration. It would revoke passports from any American or dual citizen who is fighting with ISIS and other terrorist groups, and it would eliminate all student visas from countries with fighters in ISIS until we can thoroughly check the backgrounds of those who wish to enter.

A program that George W. Bush started and Obama ended, the National Security Entry-Exit Registration System (NSEERS), provided extra scrutiny of people traveling to the United States from certain countries that are hosts to radical Islamic movements. I would reinstitute that program.

In fact, I would heighten scrutiny of travel to the U.S. from any nation with known jihadist cells. For the foreseeable future that would mean fewer student visas until we can get a handle on who is visiting, where they are going, and when they leave. It would also mean much more scrutiny of international travelers and much less hassling of domestic travelers. The one good reform that has occurred with regard to travel is the frequent traveler program. We should expand and encourage this program as a way for most Americans to opt out of the excessive frisking at our airports.

Our border is porous, and rather than acting to secure and protect it, the administration uses unconstitutional executive action legalizing millions of illegal immigrants. I oppose and will continue to oppose this unlawful usurpation of power.

The administration's policy of student visas requires a full-scale reexamination. Recently, it was estimated that as many as six thousand foreign students are unaccounted for. Let's not forget that the 9/11 hijackers were here on lapsed Saudi student visas. How can we allow this loophole to remain open? This is outrageous, and I've fought the administration about it for almost as long as I've been in the Senate. I proposed legislation that would pressure the Department of Homeland Security to finally follow through on the broken promise of a secure border and an effective visa tracking system.

Our Heroes in Uniform

If you asked me what I believe is the primary characteristic of America's greatness, I would tell you without hesitation that it is our courage. Nowhere is courage embodied more than in the hearts of the men and women in our armed forces.

Unequivocally, I am for a strong defense. With the right resources and equipment and decision making, our courageous men and women in uniform are unmatched and will remain so. They should be treated as our most precious commodity.

More than 5,000 brave American men and women have made the ultimate sacrifice on the battlefields of Afghanistan and Iraq. Although the VA has stopped releasing this data, at last count nearly a million American soldiers have been injured in wars in the Middle East.[16] Of those, some 50,000 have suffered multiple traumatic injuries, including 15,000 amputations. More than 500 have lost multiple limbs. Here at home, one in five returning veterans suffers from PTSD, and some eighteen commit suicide every day. The cost of caring for these deserving veterans is astronomical. Medical care, disability payments, and other benefits from the long war in the Middle East will cost between $3.2 and $4 trillion, according to the Eisenhower Research Project.[17]

Most of these soldiers are in their twenties and thirties. All of them have families, mothers and fathers and brothers and wives and sisters and children who suffer along with them.

When political opponents try to question my resolve for war, I think of the blood our brave soldiers have spilled on battlefields halfway around the world.

I think of Sgt. J. D. Williams.

The roadside explosive device that he stepped on threw J.D. twenty feet in the air and left a thirty-foot crater. With his body literally blown apart but still conscious, his first reaction was to reach for his weapon. The enemy was shooting at his team—his platoon had walked into an ambush. When he realized how badly he was hurt, his thoughts went to his wife, Ashlee, and his baby daughter, Kaelyn.

The blast took both of J.D.'s legs and one arm. His team was able to move him away from the firefight. They did so in a wheelbarrow. He was airlifted to Kandahar Air Base, where a medical team fought valiantly to save him, although his vital signs held little hope. That's when one of the doctors took J.D.'s heart in his hand and began to massage it.

The doctor had good instincts. As hearts go, J.D. has one of the strongest. The next voice the young hero heard was Ashlee's. J.D. had been airlifted to a hospital in Germany, where the medical staff made the phone call for him. "When I heard my wife on the phone," J.D. said, "it was like speaking to an angel."[18]

J.D. now lives down the road from me just outside of Bowling Green. An organization called Helping a Hero, with funds raised and work donated by hundreds of people in Bowling Green and Warren County, built a fully handicap-accessible house for him and his family. Kelley and I were privileged to be part of the effort, along with the hard work and generosity of builders Bennie and Laura Jones, Larkin Ritter, and businessman Fred Higgins.

He goes bow hunting with friends now and mows his own yard. "I'm just glad it was me who stepped on that IED," he would later say. "Otherwise it would have been one of my buddies."[19] When I talk with J.D., he is hopeful for his future. What might be even more remarkable is he's hopeful for the country for which he has given so much.

Thomas Jefferson wrote, "The most successful war seldom pays for its losses." In human lives, in blood and suffering, the cost of these wars is incalculable. Because we borrowed the money to pay for them, the wars in the Middle East have already cost us $185 billion in interest alone. That number, just the interest mind you, will rise to $1 trillion by 2020, according to a study by Brown University.[20]

War is not a game of geopolitical chess. War involves the hands and fingers and feet and lives of our most precious resource—our young. I will not and cannot see our soldiers as meaningless pawns in a pissing match over power.

Our soldiers fight to defend us, to defend the Constitution, to defend our way of life, but they don't fight for dominance or for control or for some vacuous notion of power.

War is not always the answer, and it is most definitely not always the only answer. Every civil war is not a nail, and America is not a hammer.

Defending America is paramount, but that does not always mean war and does not always mean troops on the ground. American might, peace through strength, is a deterrence to war, not a recipe for war.

Above all other considerations, the well-being of our soldiers should come first. Every decision to go to war should be made as if the legislator was sending his or her own child to the front of the first line of attack.

I am not an isolationist. I will not forget what is at stake.

14

★ ★ ★

Peace Through Diplomacy, Trade, and Financial Solvency

I believe that once enslaved people taste freedom and see the products of capitalism they will become hungry for freedom themselves.

* * *

Last year, I was appointed to the Foreign Affairs Committee. I like being on the committee—I'm especially intrigued by the name-calling. We have neocons, realists, hawks, doves, isolationists, globalists, and idealists. It seems the only thing for certain is this: if you don't label yourself first, your opponents will.

I have been a particular target of the neoconservatives. To this crowd, anyone who doesn't agree with them on every war is the next Neville Chamberlain. To this crowd, diplomacy is a dirty word. To this crowd, anyone who doesn't clamor first for the military option is somehow an isolationist.

The irony is that this crowd wants to project power but does so from inside an echo chamber. Though they proudly call themselves neoconservatives, they actually practice a neoisolationism in which diplomacy is distrusted and war is, if not the first option, the preferred option.

I believe that most problems that confront us around the world can and should be approached by engaging both friend and foe in dialogue. No, I do not naïvely believe that dialogue always works. I do, however, believe we should avoid the trap of saying that dialogue never works.

We should approach diplomacy from the belief that dialogue is nearly always preferable to war and that potential enemies should never underestimate our resolve. The threat of force empowers diplomacy.

Theoretically, diplomacy is similar to a market transaction. As I see it, it's only successful when both parties feel they have won, when each party perceives they have gotten the best possible outcome from the bargain. But the market can also literally mend ties that seemed irreparable.

When I was about ten years old, I used to play chess with an old Ukrainian named Pete Karpenko. Captain Pete, as we called him, told us stories of fighting the Bolsheviks when he was fourteen years old. He and his family were little more than peasants, but they resisted the idea of collective farming. Captain Pete fought with the White Army against the Bolsheviks and fled when the communists won. Fifty-five years later he was still afraid to return to the Soviet Union.

So it's easy to understand that around my house we had little use for communists or their sympathizers.

Like many conservative middle-class families, our inclination was to resist anything to do with Red China. In that black-and-white world, you were either for us or against us. Trade with China was thought to be trade with the enemy.

A funny thing happened, though, along the way. Many conservatives came to understand a larger truth. Trade with China not only improved our economic well-being, it made us less likely to fight. Recently, we've had this same debate over Cuba.

My family not only despised communism but collectivism, socialism, and any ism that deprives the individual of his or her natural rights.

I have great sympathy for those who fled Castro's iron fist. More times than I can remember, I've heard horror stories of those who escaped Castro's Cuba. I ran for office to fight for the individual and against statism of any kind anywhere and yet...I think a policy of isolationism toward Cuba is misplaced and has not worked.

I support engagement, diplomacy, and trade with Cuba, China, Vietnam, and many countries with less than stellar human rights records because I believe that once enslaved people taste freedom and see the products of capitalism they will become hungry for freedom themselves.

President George W. Bush wrote that "trade creates the habits of freedom," and trade provides the seeds of freedom that begin "to create the expectations of democracy." I agree. Once trade begins it is hard to hide the amazing products of capitalism. The Soviets used to produce documentaries depicting poverty in America but their plan backfired when Russian viewers noticed that even in the poorest of circumstances they could still see televisions flickering in the windows, something the majority of them didn't enjoy. Once trade is enhanced with Cuba, it will be impossible to hide the bounty that freedom provides.

The supporters of the embargo against Cuba speak with heated passion but fall strangely silent when asked how trade with Cuba is so different than trade with Russia or China or Vietnam.

It is an inconsistent and incoherent position to support trade with other communist countries but not with communist Cuba.

Even the supporters of the embargo agree that it has not worked. A policy of isolationism with Cuba and engagement with China and Vietnam does not make any sense. Communism can't survive the captivating allure of capitalism. Let's overwhelm the Castro regime with iPhones, iPads, American cars, and American ingenuity.

While China's human rights record leaves much to be desired, our engagement and trade has without question helped to open Chinese society. Trade with China and Vietnam has not made either a freedom-loving paradise, but most would argue that the people of those nations are less oppressed than they once were.

Do those who wish to continue to isolate us from Cuba propose we also isolate ourselves from China, Vietnam, Laos, Russia, and dozens of other less than savory nations? Has such isolationism ever worked?

Over the years, many conservatives have come to believe that trade with China and Vietnam is the best way to overcome and defeat communism. Trade and relations also make it less likely that we will ever go to war with China, because the two countries have become economically intertwined.

That being said, it is ultimately Congress, not the president, who will debate and decide whether the embargo will end. Congress, not the executive branch, has dominion over many aspects of the trade and travel embargo. I doubt Congress will vote to end the embargo at this time, but my hope is that restoring diplomatic ties will induce Cubans to rise up and empower them to demand more freedom and more trade with the United States.

Those who love freedom and want to see a free Cuba should continue to demand nothing less than a democratic republic that defends the rights of the individual. After fifty years of embargo and no evidence of tyranny losing its grip, maybe it's time for a new approach.

Public opinion is changing on this issue. Young Cuban Americans have shifted their position on the embargo, and many young people support a change in policy. American farmers and other exporters would benefit by being able to sell more products to a country off the coast of Florida.

Doug Bandow of the Cato Institute writes that proponents of the embargo have it all wrong when they make the fear-mongering claim that diplomacy with Cuba will make America less safe. For seventy years we had diplomatic relations with Russia, despite the gulags, despite the atrocities of Stalin and others. President Reagan himself engaged and negotiated with Communist Russia.

The fifty-year embargo against Cuba has simply not worked. If the goal was regime change, then it sure does not seem to be working. It also hurts the Cuban people more than the regime, because the regime can blame the embargo for hardship.

Emotions understandably run high for those whose parents and grandparents had their land and their lives taken from them. But if we allow the passions to cool, maybe, just maybe, we might conclude that trade is better than war and that capitalism wins every time people get a chance to see its products.

Let's hope cooler heads will ultimately prevail and we unleash a trade tsunami that washes the Castros once and for all into the sea.

Trade with the Middle East is also in our best interest. Trade helps to alleviate poverty and enriches both sides. If the long war in the Middle East is ever to end we must realize that poverty and lack of freedom are part of what incites the Arab street. In order to understand the frustrations of the Arab street, we must come face-to-face with Mohamed Bouazizi and understand the origins of the Arab Spring.

Contrary to accepted wisdom, terrorists often come from people frustrated by a government's heavy hand in preventing entrepreneurship. It isn't always abject poverty or religion that motivates recruits for terrorism. Often it is the despair that comes from overbearing government. The rule of law is not only a route to prosperity, it is a path away from terrorism.

Mohamed Bouazizi was not just a street merchant who set himself afire. He was an aspiring entrepreneur foiled by an overbearing government. Hounded by government inspectors, his dreams dashed by bribe-seeking bureaucrats, he saw suicide as his only recourse.

His family recalled that he had wanted to buy a truck to expand his business but cronyism and corrupt government stifled his dream.

My great-grandfather was little more than a street merchant like Bouazizi until he saved enough to purchase a truck, which elevated him economically to a level that allowed him to purchase a home and small bit of land.

The difference between America in the late nineteenth century and the Arab world today is that bribes and cronyism were not necessary to get a license to purchase a truck or sell vegetables here.

At least part of the answer to winning the long war against terrorism is stopping the pipeline for terrorists by instituting laws that let capitalism grow.

According to Peruvian economist Hernando de Soto, who writes about poverty and property rights, Bouazizi's motive for suicide was not theistic or civic. "Bouazizi and the others [there were some sixty-three other immolations that preceded the Arab Spring] who burned themselves were extralegal entrepreneurs: builders, contractors, caterers, small vendors and the like," de Soto writes. "In their dying statements, none referred to religion or politics. Their great objective was '*ras el mel*' (Arabic for 'capital'), and their despair and indignation sprang from the arbitrary expropriation of what little capital they had."[1]

Bouazizi's brother Salem told de Soto that his brother's legacy was that "he believed the poor had the right to buy and sell."

De Soto investigated the black market in Egypt and discovered that the poor in Egypt owned a hundred times more "off the books capital" than Egypt receives in foreign aid each year.

Informal working assets, this off the books capital, according to de Soto, amounts to $360 billion, which is "eight times more than the value of all foreign direct investment in Egypt since Napoleon invaded more than 200 years ago." But off the books capital does not go back into the free market. It is not invested or saved. It just sits there in the shadows.

Instead of sending foreign aid to corrupt leaders in foreign countries, we should be helping these countries create the rule of law to take advantage of the capital that already exists but is confined to "off the books" because of byzantine rules and poor protection to title.

The money we send does the exact opposite of what we intend it to do—it foments anger toward us and helps our enemies.

"Policy makers are missing the real stakes," de Soto writes. "If ordinary people in the Middle East and North Africa cannot play the game legally—despite their heroic sacrifices—they will be far less able to resist a terrorist offensive, and the most desperate among them may even be recruited to the jihadist cause."

What we've failed to understand is that when the crowd burns the American flag in Tahrir Square they are protesting our monetary support for autocracy, for a regime that allows for indefinite detention and mass trials and stifles their ability to make a living. Our enemies are not so different than us. They want a roof over their head and food on the table. America should be on whatever side allows that to happen for them.

To have a strong national defense we must also have a strong economy at home.

If we keep going in the direction we're headed, in less than five years the interest we pay on our debt will equal what we spend on defense. If we do nothing, by the year 2030, or when your three-year-old daughter or son graduates from high school, entitlement spending will exceed tax revenue. What does that mean? It means we will have to borrow money to pay for everything, including our defense budget.

Right now, the Pentagon cannot balance its books. It can't be audited because it recently admitted it's too big to be audited. The defense budget accounts for one-fifth of federal spending. National defense is the most important thing we spend money on. I believe that it is the primary constitutional function of the federal government. But that does not mean it should get a blank check. We need to know how and where our defense dollars are being spent to know whether they are being spent wisely.

As our debt continues to expand, our ability to spend on defense becomes more and more precarious. We should be very concerned. We are not bulletproof. History is rife with examples—the British Empire, the Soviet bloc—of the havoc debt can wreak.

We need to reduce areas of government that are beyond the scope of what was intended by our Constitution. When the size of government is scaled back through reform and devolution to the states, resources can be more efficiently prioritized. In other words, reducing the overall weight of government allows more resources to be available during times of crisis, such as war or natural disasters. My plan to balance the budget in only five years will draw down the debt and our dependency on China and other countries to which we would rather not be financially beholden. It will also ensure that we can wisely fund our national defense to keep America safe.

15

★ ★ ★

Libya: A Jihadist's Wonderland

As commander in chief, I would not allow our enemies to kill our citizens or our ambassadors. Peace through strength only works if you have and show strength.

* * *

Somewhere around 3 A.M. on the morning of February 14, 1979, a phone rang in the White House. Jimmy Carter was then the president. The voice on the line informed him that his embassy in Tehran was under attack. Armed Islamic fundamentalists had breached the walls and opened fire. The ambassador, William H. Sullivan, had ordered his staff to retreat to the communications vault, the embassy's safe haven. The small attachment of Marines valiantly turned back the attackers, but the event in February was just a prelude to worse things to come.

Leading up to that first attack, Tehran was the center of the civil unrest in Iran. By then the shah was the leader of his country in name only. He had ceded much of his power to the Iranian military. In January 1979, terminally ill from non-Hodgkin's lymphoma, the shah fled Iran and Ayatollah Khomeini returned, triumphantly, from exile.

Yet, as the political turbulence roiled in Tehran, little was done to improve the security for our diplomats. According to the State Department's own report,[1] Victor Tomseth, one of the American hostages, remarked that our government showed an "absence of will and capacity" to protect the embassy.

According to another State Department report,[2] terrorism directed at our foreign missions changed fundamentally during the Carter administration. During the previous two decades, attacks against our embassies were primarily carried out by individuals and small groups and involved mostly kidnapping of diplomats who were held for ransom or for the release of prisoners. By the late 1970s, however, attacks were violent, meant to be symbolic, and were sponsored by states that hated what America stood for.

Countries, movements, and organizations that despised America were nothing new. What had not been seen before was the mindset these anti-American groups brandished. They had little respect for us and no belief that we had the resolve to retaliate for attacks against us.

Ten months after Carter received the 3 A.M. phone call, the embassy was attacked again. This time, radical Islamic students took hostages and kept them for 444 days. Nightly, the embarrassment of the hostage crisis was broadcast on televisions around the world. A rescue attempt ended in disaster. To be fair, Jimmy Carter negotiated tirelessly for their release, but it would not be until Ronald Reagan's inauguration and his promise to restore America to its once proud strength that the hostages would come home.

Nearly thirty years later, Hillary Clinton's campaign office ran one of the most provocative ads of the 2008 Democrat primary. I'm sure you remember it.

> It's 3 A.M., and your children are safe and asleep, but there's a phone in the White House and it's ringing. Something's happening in the world. Your vote will decide who'll answer that call. Whether it's somebody who knows the world's leaders, knows the military, someone tested and ready to lead in the dangerous world.
>
> It's 3 A.M.

A concerned male voice delivers the words over images of children sound asleep in their beds, shadows fall on their peaceful faces, a phone rings and rings in the background. Finally, the commercial cuts to Mrs. Clinton picking up a receiver while the narrator asks, "Who do you want answering the phone?" The spot was meant to portray Mrs. Clinton as a leader who could keep the American people safe. At the time the ad was released, her primary campaign was running behind the junior senator from Illinois, a position that surprised most political observers. Mrs. Clinton was supposed to win that primary, at least according to those who are supposed to know what they're talking about. But what was once thought to be a coronation began to slip away, and the ad was something of a Hail Mary pass. Mrs. Clinton's campaign believed that it represented the most important thing that their candidate had and Barack Obama didn't: the experience to protect the American people from threats unfolding around the world.

Playing on people's fears is a formidable tool in politics, and the ad was effective. It was timed to run prior to the important Texas and Ohio Democratic primaries, both of which Mrs. Clinton won. As we all know, however, the ad wasn't enough to carry her to victory in the overall primary.

But the commercial did raise a very important question. Who do you want answering the phone in the White House?

Apparently, the answer isn't Hillary Clinton.

I wish Hillary Clinton had paid more attention to Ambassador Chris Stevens's cry for help. I wish she'd been more responsible in providing adequate security, and I wish she had acted more decisively in Benghazi.

But she didn't answer the call, and half a world away Americans were murdered.

Because of Mrs. Clinton's inability to secure the safety of her employees, a message was sent to those who hate us around the world: you can murder our diplomats and get away with it. President Obama can say all he wants about bringing those responsible to justice; the people who murdered Ambassador Stevens don't care whether they're caught. Just months before the attack, an America hater posted on

Facebook a death threat to Ambassador Stevens along with the route he jogged each morning. On Facebook.[3]

In January 2013, when Mrs. Clinton testified in front of the Senate's Foreign Relations Committee, I told her that had I been president at the time I would have relieved her of her post.

Pundits and politicians alike took me to task. They said I was grandstanding and using the moment for my own political motivation. The truth is, I decided what I would say to her on the walk over from my office to the hearing. It was not some orchestrated political moment. And, in any event, if calling attention to the preventable death of an American ambassador and the failure to heed clear warnings and respond to requests for security for an American embassy, and then covering up the tragedy to save political capital, is grandstanding, then you bet I was.

For me, the debate about the Benghazi attack has never been political. I know that statement will be met with derision by the hard left, but it's true. In fact, I think the politicized rhetoric surrounding the White House's original contention that an anti-Islamic movie had riled fundamentalists who then stormed the compound drowned out the more important discussion that should have been had, one I will go into below. I will never understand how politicians can give so little credence to the intelligence of the American people.

I knew, like most of us knew, that the talking points and the heated shouting on both sides that followed them were the antics of politics. That I could put behind me.

Here's what I can't put behind me and why the discussion about Benghazi remains as important today as it was in September 2012: I believe that our commander in chief has no greater responsibility than to defend the homeland, defend vital American interests, and defend our personnel abroad. I also believe that anyone who seeks the office of the presidency cannot have been derelict in that duty. If they were, it should preclude them from holding the office.

So let's look at Mrs. Clinton's record on Benghazi.

In the six weeks prior to the attack in Libya, Ambassador Chris Stevens sent cable after cable to the State Department describing the deteriorating political climate surrounding the Libyan diplomatic compound and the need for additional guards. The missives had titles such as: "Libya's Fragile Security Deteriorates as Tribal Rivalries, Power Plays and Extremism Intensify"; and "The Guns of August; security in eastern Libya." His diary, found on the floor of his living quarters by a reporter days after the attack, told of the ambassador's concerns about the buildup of al-Qaeda in Benghazi and even expressed fear that he was on an al-Qaeda hit list.[4] Except for a small complement of Diplomatic Security (DS), protection of the embassy and Ambassador Stevens mostly fell to a local Libyan militia called the 17th of February Martyrs Brigade. Made up of shopkeepers with ties to al-Qaeda, brigade members hadn't been paid for months prior to the attack.

Eric Nordstrom, the Regional Security Officer at the U.S. embassy in Tripoli, twice wrote to the State Department requesting additional security for the Benghazi embassy. Nordstrom told congressional investigators that he thought the security for the compound was "inappropriately low."[5] In one report, he cited fifty security incidents in Benghazi over the three months prior to the attack.[6] Nordstrom had also verbally requested twelve additional agents for the Benghazi mission, but that request, too, was denied.

"For me and my staff, it was abundantly clear that we were not going to get resources until the aftermath of an incident," Nordstrom would later say.

Three months before the attack on the diplomatic compound in

Benghazi, Mrs. Clinton's State Department denied a request from the U.S. embassy in Tripoli to keep an old DC-3 that was used to shuttle weapons and Special Forces around Libya to protect embassy personnel. An elite sixteen-member Special Forces security team assigned to the Libyan mission used the plane. Lieutenant Colonel Andrew Wood led the team. His request to extend his team's assignment in Libya was also denied. The last vestige of the elite squad was pulled in the weeks before the diplomatic compound was stormed. Colonel Wood still believes that his team might have been able to save the lives of the four Americans who died in Benghazi. "I think about that," he told a reporter from CBS.[7] "I spend a lot of time thinking about that."

On August 15, less than a month before the Benghazi assault, embassy personal held an emergency meeting to discuss the ten Islamist militias and their training camps in the area, among them al-Qaeda and Ansar al-Sharia.

The following day, August 16, the embassy sent a cable to the State Department with the warning that the compound couldn't defend itself against a "coordinated attack."[8]

Ambassador Chris Stevens signed the cable. It was addressed to Hillary Clinton.

Time and time again, the State Department denied requests for security at the Benghazi compound.

Time and time again the cables arrived at the State Department.

Time and time again those calls went unanswered.

Given the coordination and scale of the attack—a force consisting of 150 Islamic militants armed with automatic rifles, grenades, and shoulder-held rocket-propelled grenade launchers—there is little doubt that it had been planned for months or even longer. One can only wonder what those who watched the compound over those months reported back to their superiors. Did they think we didn't care about the safety of our diplomats? Did they believe we were too busy with other, more important things? Or did they think we were just plain stupid?

They were so confident in the success of their plan that they picked the anniversary of the worst terrorist attack to ever befall America to execute it.

The Benghazi terrorist assault lasted throughout the night of September 11, 2012, and into the early morning hours the next day. It also had two targets: the diplomatic compound where Ambassador Stevens lived and conducted business, the security of which was broached at about 9:40 P.M., and an annex that the CIA ran a little over a mile away, which began taking fire after midnight.

Almost as soon as it began, a diplomatic security officer led Ambassador Stevens and U.S. Foreign Service Information Management Officer Sean Smith to a gated room called the "safe haven." When the attackers overwhelmed security and breached the walls of the compound, they lit kerosene fires around the gate of the panic room. Both the ambassador and Smith died of smoke inhalation. In would be a full six hours later when mortar fire at the annex killed Glen Doherty and Tyrone S. Woods, the former Navy SEALs who were attached to the CIA security detail.

Six hours of deadly silence.

The quiet of those hours has since been filled with much controversy.

It was reported that a military unit, a counterassault team of Special Forces, was about to board a plane in Tripoli 600 miles away when they were told to stand down. The State Department and military leaders have denied the report. Although the ARB, the Accountability Review Board put in place by the State Department to assess the attack, also discounts the stand down order, it says that there was a great deal of confusion in how those series of events were reported.[9]

One response was that it was not a stand down order but a don't go order. Try explaining that to the families of the victims.

A story in *Forbes* magazine said that President Obama, Defense Secretary Leon Panetta, and other high-ranking officials watched a live video feed of the attack from a drone that hovered overhead, and did nothing.

The White House denied that gathering ever happened.

Another report stated that the embassy made three urgent requests for military backup during those hours and were denied.

The administration refuted that report also.

Here's what we know for sure: the Special Forces and other diplomatic security (DS) that were left in Tripoli couldn't find a plane for hours. Had the DC-3 been on site they might have made it in time to help save Glen Doherty and Tyrone Woods, but the State Department pulled the funding for the plane. What makes this even harder to take is that three days after the State Department turned down the request for the DC-3, the agency authorized $100,000 for the embassy in Vienna to buy an electrical charging station. The charger was for ten Chevy Volts they'd previously purchased at a cost to the American people of over $200,000.

"I still don't quite understand why they couldn't fly aircraft over to Benghazi," said Ambassador Stevens's deputy, Gregory Hicks. "When I was a kid, I grew up watching Western movies, the cavalry always came. I just thought that they would come."

The cavalry didn't come. The State Department's own Accountability Review Board headed by Ambassador Thomas Pickering and Admiral Mike Mullen (appointed by the Secretary of State) gave Mrs. Clinton a scathing review of her State Department's handling of Benghazi. One of the many blistering sections of the report reads: "Systemic failures and leadership and management deficiencies at senior levels within two bureaus of the State Department (the

"Department") resulted in a Special Mission security posture that was inadequate for Benghazi and grossly inadequate to deal with the attack that took place."

There is another historical example that I believe puts the Benghazi fiasco into perspective. Not too long after Mrs. Clinton's husband started his first term as president, U.S. Delta Force soldiers, Navy SEALs, and Army Rangers staged a high-risk military operation in Somalia. The objective of the raid was to arrest two lieutenants of a local warlord who was stealing humanitarian supplies—the civil war in Somalia had caused a man-made famine.

The military operation went terribly wrong. What was supposed to be a quick extraction became a two-day battle in which Somali fighters with rocket-propelled grenade launchers shot down two Army Black Hawk helicopters, killing eighteen Army Rangers and capturing one.

The most lasting images of the event were the photographs and video that showed Somali militia dragging the bodies of U.S. soldiers through the streets of Mogadishu. Those images filled America's front pages and television screens.[10]

The Battle of Mogadishu, more popularly known as Black Hawk Down after the bestselling book and Hollywood movie, was perhaps the biggest military blight on Bill Clinton's presidential record.[11] Most of the criticism he garnered was because of his response, or lack thereof, to the incident. There was no counterattack. Clinton pulled the army out of Somalia afterward, leaving the warlord and his gang of pirates to publicly celebrate their victory over the great United States Army. Soldiers from the Somalia militia involved in the attack did television interviews bragging of their conquest and showed a video that included a close-up of the battered face of the captured Black Hawk helicopter pilot.[12]

But it was the events that preceded the attack that were perhaps Clinton's biggest mistake. In the months leading up to the assault, commanders in Somalia repeatedly asked Clinton's Secretary of Defense, Les Aspin, for soldiers, tanks, and armor-plated vehicles to reinforce their mission. As was the case in Tehran and Benghazi, tensions in Somalia had risen markedly. The commanders' requests were turned down.[13]

Aspin was grilled by Congress but refused to take responsibility. It would be months before Bill Clinton forced the Secretary of Defense to resign (I've often wondered if he had been president during the Benghazi tragedy, would he have fired Hillary?).[14]

Almost twenty years after Les Aspin's resignation, Secretary of State Clinton faced similar questions.

The day she testified in front of the Foreign Relations Committee, Mrs. Clinton seemed annoyed, tired, or both. In answering my questions, her voice had an affected ring to it. Some of her words, however, were nothing less than callous. There is the now famous exchange she had with Senator Ron Johnson from Wisconsin, who pressed her about the reason behind the attack.

"What difference, at this point, does it make?" she said to him dismissively.

Our committee repeatedly asked Mrs. Clinton if she had read the cables from Ambassador Stevens asking for increased security. "I have made it very clear that the security cables did not come to my attention or above the assistant secretary level," she said. She receives 1.43 million cables a year, she insisted.

I wonder how many of those came from a war zone?

I realize that the Secretary of State receives lots of cables from diplomats, that she might not need to personally read every cable from Switzerland or Bulgaria, but Libya was one of the most dangerous spots on the planet. It is inexcusable that while security was denied to our Libyan embassy, the State Department spent $100,000 for three comedians to travel to India on a promotional tour called Make Chai, Not War. The summer they brought home the last vestiges of security from Libya, the State Department spent $650,000 on Facebook ads. Hillary Clinton's State Department found $5 million to buy crystal glassware that summer, but she repeatedly turned down requests for diplomatic security in Benghazi.

After the fall of Gaddafi, Libya was unstable, to say the least. It was, and still is, filled with guns both from Western sources and from Gaddafi's own arsenal, including Gaddafi's stockpile of 15,000 or so man-portable air defense systems or MANPADS. Many of Gaddafi's missiles are still missing. A terrorist attack on an American outpost in post-Gaddafi Libya shouldn't have come as a surprise. According to a 2007 West Point Combating Terrorism Center report,[15] Benghazi was a primary staging ground for al-Qaeda militia being sent into Iraq. In 2011, Gaddafi was going to invade Benghazi for the purpose of wiping out al-Qaeda headquarters there.

"The security in Benghazi was a struggle and remained a struggle throughout my time there," Colonel Wood said in a statement to a congressional oversight committee. "The situation remained uncertain and reports from some Libyans indicated it was getting worse," he wrote.

How could Hillary Clinton ignore cables from her chief diplomat in such a situation?

The State Department's fault in the handling of Benghazi goes much further than just not reading cables.

The State Department could send clowns to India, but they wouldn't authorize a sixteen-person security team in Libya or provide the funds for an airplane to transport security teams around the country.

Why, all of a sudden, was Mrs. Clinton so conscious of budgetary concerns?

In 2009, her State Department signed a ten-year lease and spent some $80 million of American taxpayer money to renovate a hotel in northern Afghanistan, only to abandon the idea because of security concerns.[16] So an empty building warrants attention, but one that houses American diplomats does not?

"I am the Secretary of State," she said defiantly in front of my committee, "and the ARB made it very clear that the level of responsibility for the failures that they outlined sat at the level of Assistant Secretary and below."

In spite of the fact that the investigation was headed up by people handpicked by Mrs. Clinton—who never interviewed her for the report—State Department negligence litters the ARB account of the Benghazi attack, and eyewitness accounts provide a narrative of blunders and indifference. Those mistakes began long before the attack.

The Benghazi mission should have never been allowed to operate in the first place without a significant military guard. If the government wasn't going to give it a military guard, they shouldn't have opened it. And if they decided to open it, as they did, it should have been given adequate security, like the consulate in Baghdad, as if it were in a war zone, with a guard under Department of Defense command.

Instead, Mrs. Clinton ran the Benghazi mission like it was the embassy in Paris.

The question still remains: why?

Well, there is the suggestion, a topic that I broached with Mrs. Clinton, that there was more to the relationship between the diplomatic compound and the CIA annex than what met the eye.

News stories, including one written by Pulitzer Prize winner Seymour Hersh, reported that the CIA ran an operation out of the annex that shipped guns through Turkey to Syria for the purpose of arming Syrian rebels, some of whom were al-Qaeda–aligned fighters.

The details of the story read like something out of a Nelson DeMille novel and include front companies in Libya, secret funds, and retired American soldiers.

According to these sources, the operation was huge, big enough to move a cargo ship filled with guns and other military equipment that once belonged to Gaddafi—including SA-7 surface-to-air missile systems that could bring down airliners.

The operation was said to also include the British MI6, which allowed it to sidestep a U.S. law that would have required its disclosure to senior leadership of Congress. Instead, it operated under a blanket of secrecy, and with impunity. In his article,[17] Hersh quotes a senior intelligence official with knowledge of documents that substantiate his claim: "The consulate's only mission was to provide cover for the moving of arms. It had no real political role," the source told Hersh.[18]

At the Senate hearing, I asked Mrs. Clinton about the CIA annex and reports that it was being used for a secret gunrunning operation. As I've mentioned, she seemed annoyed by the question and suggested I talk to the CIA, as if she hadn't any knowledge of what I was talking about.

It's hard to imagine, should there be any legitimacy to the reports, that the Secretary of State would be kept out of such a loop. If the gunrunning operation in Benghazi existed, then Mrs. Clinton and the very upper reaches of our government had to be aware and perhaps even complicit.

Even if the gunrunning theory can't be proven, a very dark cloud still hangs over the Benghazi issue. American blood was unnecessarily spilled, and I for one won't let it be forgotten.

Mrs. Clinton denies any wrongdoing in her handling of Benghazi, and she boasts of her record as Secretary of State. It seems the bigger the mistake you make, the more outrageous your negligence, the better chance you have to get away with it.

Let's take for example the war in Iraq. Unlike Mrs. Clinton, had I been a senator at the time of the Iraq War, I would have never voted for it, and it troubles me that we were sold that war on false pretenses. It's also bothersome that the mainstream media continues to invite the architects of the Iraq invasion to share their opinions on Sunday morning shows. History has already begun to harshly judge those who made this country's decisions after 9/11.

I believe judgment day for Benghazi is also at hand.

When the Secretary of State answers a question concerning the murders of four Americans, including an American ambassador, by saying, "What difference, at this point, does it make?" I think that's a pretty clear indication that it's time for that person to go.

It's 3 A.M., Mrs. Clinton. The phone is ringing. The American people deserve to know why you never bothered to answer it.

16

★ ★ ★

Tree Hugger

The fact is, big government, democratic and totalitarian alike, has often failed to protect the environment.

★ ★ ★

When we moved into our house on a steep hillside in Bowling Green I began planting trees. That was nearly twenty years ago. I had the most success with native trees, which I'd dug up from various parts of the yard and transplanted. Some of the maple trees I transplanted are now forty feet tall. One of them has never been trimmed and drapes to the ground with a great forty-foot circumference of limbs.

Hickory trees, too, grow everywhere on my property. I have red, white, and chestnut oaks, some of which are two hundred years old. I also have plenty of trees that are just getting started.

I have a cherry tree that is grown from seeds of the Tidal Basin trees in Washington, D.C. Those cherry tree saplings were a gift to the United States from the emperor of Japan in 1912. The First Lady, Helen Herron Taft, and the wife of the Japanese ambassador, Viscountess Chinda, planted the first two of the 3,200 trees. After the planting, Mrs. Taft handed the viscountess a bouquet of American Beauty roses. From that simple gesture the Cherry Blossom Festival was born. In April, when the cherry trees blossom, tourists from across the nation gather near the Jefferson Memorial. The blossoms are so plentiful that they give the appearance of snow.

Democrats think somehow they're the only ones allowed to like the environment. I'm a crunchy conservative and tree hugger and proud of it, maybe because the streets in the town I grew up in, Lake Jackson, Texas, are named after trees and flowers. We lived on Blossom Street. I even have trouble letting my trees go when the time has come. A two-hundred-year-old beech tree guarded the entrance to my house for a decade. Like many beeches, it was mostly hollow and, more ominously, had a spiraling, twenty-foot-long crack that nearly dissected the trunk. By all rational calculation, I should have taken the tree down years before it fell, but I loved its stately charm. Fortunately, the storm blew it toward the street and not toward the house. My boys whooped it up and played in its fallen, hollow trunk for days.

I grew a giant sequoia for about fifteen years. It was affected by a blight that allowed growth at its crown but caused persistent browning of the lower limbs. Finally, the tree succumbed to its disease. I announced to my mostly skeptical family that I would cut it down, bring it inside, and make furniture out of it.

"Sure, Dad," my kids said. They were right to be skeptical, because of course I had never actually made a piece of furniture, and with my crazy travel schedule it was unlikely I was going to acquire the skills to do so. The not so giant sequoia cluttered my workspace, straddling our bench press and poking into the ceiling for a year. Finally, after several months of pointed barbs from Kelley and the kids, I took my table saw, cut it up into "legs," which is a generous description, then wedged them under my workbench. Voilà! Furniture.

In my yard, I also have lilacs, peonies, hydrangeas, dwarf crab apples, nandinas, and ivy, some of which are poisonous and not planted but rather defended against.

Maybe the most prized attraction in my yard isn't growing but soaring over it: a mating pair of bald eagles built a nest near a neighborhood pond across from me and often alight in my old oaks. Our eagles have been here for three seasons now. This year my kids spotted the first baby bald eagle.

Teddy Roosevelt once said, "We have fallen heirs to the most glorious heritage a people ever received, and each one must do his part if we wish to show that the nation is worthy of its good fortune."

Sometimes I think of that quote when I look out at the greenery and flowers of my backyard or the cherry tree whose roots reach back to the Tidal Basin that fronts the Jefferson Monument or the bald eagles that soar to heights this country can reach again.

It boggles my mind to think that somehow Republicans have been branded as a party that doesn't like the environment. It was Abraham Lincoln who laid the groundwork for the first national park in California's Yosemite Valley; it was Teddy Roosevelt who protected 230 million acres of forests, and though his brainchild has become bloated and misguided, Republicans were instrumental in helping our country rise from the industrial mess that occurred in the first part of the past century.

The New GOP, the GOP that I believe in, will fight for a clean environment. We believe that clean and prosperous are not mutually exclusive; in fact they can be, must be, mutually beneficial.

To protect the environment, we must marry sustainability to the cause. To me that often means marrying profit with projects to preserve the environment. To have sustainable environmentalism it must be profitable. Just think of all the businesses that profitably recycle.

The left often forgets that the profits of capitalism have performed some of the greatest acts of conservation. The profits of capitalism have bought and put aside hundreds of thousands of acres to leave undeveloped. Many great capitalists have done this through history.

The Rockefeller family donated the land that became Acadia National Park, Great Smoky Mountains National Park, Yosemite National Park, Grand Teton National Park at Jackson Hole, and Shenandoah National Park.

Many more are doing it today.

Ted Turner is said to be the largest landowner in the United States, with 2 million acres of land.[1] He has placed much of it under conservation easements to prevent future development.[2] Among other missions, his Turner Foundation expansively works to protect natural habitats in South Carolina, Georgia, Florida, Montana, New Mexico, and Alaska.

Then there's the local boy from Franklin, Kentucky. Brad Kelley is now said to be one of the largest landowners in the U.S.—he owns about a million acres. Very little of the land is developed. Instead he uses some of his acreage, a large parcel on the west coast of Florida known as Rum Creek Ranch, to raise endangered species, including tapirs, anoas (small buffalos), hippos, rhinos, bongos (antelopes), bentang (wild cattle), and a host of others, according to an interview he gave to the *Wall Street Journal*.[3] He works with zoos and conservation groups with the ultimate goal of reintroducing the animals back to their native habitat, the article states.

Capitalism is not the enemy of the environment. Capitalism shouldn't be confused with materialism or consumerism.

Capitalists are often the greatest and most innovative advocates for the environment.

Think Bill Gates. It's estimated that Gates has saved 6 million lives through health-care initiatives in Africa. His "reinvent the toilet" campaign seeks to bring sustainable sanitation to two and a half billion of the world's poor. Also remember that Gates's environmentalism, his amazing vaccination crusade in Africa, never happens without capitalism. Think of a world with only the tepid sputtering engine of socialism unable to provide the vast wealth that commonly goes back into protecting the environment. I'm reminded of this quote from Winston Churchill: "The inherent vice of capitalism is the unequal sharing of blessing. The inherent vice of socialism is the equal sharing of misery."

Think of Donald Trump.

* * *

Wollman Rink is an ice-skating rink that is an iconic fixture and has been the backdrop of movies such as *Love Story* for well over half a century in Central Park. By 1980 it had fallen into the disrepair of urban blight. The City of New York and its then mayor, Ed Koch, promised to renovate the rink. Six years after the mayor made his promise, in an entanglement of bureaucracy and big government lethargy, the reclamation project was in shambles, with little hope for completion. Enter Donald Trump. Though not quite the household name he is today, Mr. Trump then ran one of New York City's biggest apartment construction and management companies. He was also just as brash then as he is now. He challenged Mayor Koch to let him take over the project. At first Koch said no, but public pressure forced the mayor to give the private builder a chance. Three months later, New Yorkers and tourists alike were skating in a beautifully renovated Wollman Rink, and nearly thirty years later it's still one of the most popular and well-run destinations in Central Park.

I know what you're thinking: "Rand, Wollman Rink isn't exactly saving the Amazon rain forest!" You're right. Nevertheless, Trump's efforts with Wollman Rink improved the surrounding natural area of the park. Some of the profit the rink turned—the first time it had done so—was given to the New York City Department of Parks and Recreation, which helps keep Central Park and other New York City parks beautiful. Trump's rescue of Wollman Rink also exposed the ineptitude of government-run construction projects and the dominion over private enterprise it holds.

The fact is, big government, democratic and totalitarian alike, has often failed to protect the environment. Think of the threat that is coming from totalitarian regimes in Russia and China who partner with industry to allow state-sanctioned destruction of the environment.

Think of the recent history of rank and putrid rivers and bays in cities throughout the United States that became that way through government-issued permits that allowed vast dumping into our waters. A strict understanding of property rights would never have allowed such incredible pollution. Even a cursory understanding of how profit can sustain the environment can help keep the planet clean.

Here's what I mean: some nine billion pounds of litter end up in the oceans every year, and litter costs $11.5 billion each year to clean up.[4] You need look no further than the sides of our highways and along the trails of our parks if you need a reminder. Look at the junk bobbing in our streams and lakes. If someone owned the lake, the beach, or the stretch of highway, or, even better, if you could determine the price of the lake or highway and what it's worth to business, you could be absolutely sure that pollution would be kept to a minimum.

Big companies are already doing this. Dow Chemical, in cooperation with the Nature Conservancy, the biggest nongovernmental environment organization in the world, is developing software that determines the monetary value of nature. So what's the price of the honeybees that are disappearing, or the price of a polluted stream, or of a depleted forest? Well, software developed by Dow and the Nature Conservancy might be able to give you the answer. So a business that uses honey in its product would likely be willing to invest in ways to protect the honeybee. Connecting profit to environmentalism helps make protection of the environment sustainable.

The idea is, if we can figure out a way for environmental concerns to be good for business, which this software seems to do, then bigger and more influential players will have a stake in keeping our land, water, and air clean. Take a guess what will happen. Our land, water, and air will be cleaner.

A Role for the Feds?

"A lake is the landscape's most beautiful and expressive feature," Henry David Thoreau wrote. "It's the earth's eye; looking into which the beholder measures the depth of his own nature."

Without question, there is a federal role in protecting the navigable streams that flow between the states, and a federal responsibility to keep our lakes, bayous, and oceans clean. No one should favor policies that allow anyone to dump chemicals in the Ohio River, for instance.

But in spite of the Clean Water Act and an ever-enlarging EPA, industry dumped 206 million pounds of toxic chemicals into America's waterways in 2012 alone.[5] I have argued that the EPA and the Army Corps of Engineers have turned too much of their energy toward harassing private property owners and spent too little time policing our rivers.

I support the Clean Water Act that says no one can dump pollutants in a navigable body of water. But bureaucrats went crazy in the last forty years, defining dirt as a pollutant and your backyard as a river. As a consequence, $100 million dollars is diverted from pollution control to people control, to harassing law-abiding citizens.

A man in Michigan was given three years in prison for moving dirt on his own land because the government decreed it a wetland. Meanwhile, tanks alongside the Ohio River in West Virginia that hadn't been inspected in decades dumped toxic chemicals into the river that contaminated the drinking water for months.

The bureaucracy of the EPA keeps expanding, and as it does it squeezes our economy and limits our freedom, all the while allowing extraordinary pollution abuse to occur. You know where I stand on this. Protecting the environment should not be in the exclusive charge of the EPA. The states and localities should be first in line in defending the environment, and the courts should intervene immediately, if necessary, if anyone is polluting their neighbor's property. Protecting the environment should not be a partisan issue.

Common ground is possible. The intentions of many of the environmental protection measures of forty or fifty years ago were often good, and the initial outcomes helped to correct some problems that needed addressing. Our nation's open spaces, waterways, and air need to be protected. We need to keep America beautiful, but we also need to keep America free and Americans working. This is the balance we must seek.

Common ground is not only possible, it's been done before. Republicans and Democrats worked together on legislation in the early 1980s that not only helped to protect 1.3 million miles of beautiful Southeastern American coastline but did so without impeding the free market. How did they do it? By taking away any federal protection for people who wanted to build on the coast. You want to put up a beachfront mansion? Be our guest. You want to construct an oceanfront tiki bar or T-shirt stand? Go right ahead. But don't expect any storm disaster relief or flood insurance from the federal government.

What happened?

Some people went ahead and built. But for the most part the law kept hundreds of miles of barrier coastline pristine.

It's worth noting, for all the partisan extremists out there who roll their eyes at the mere mention of our fortieth president's name, that

Ronald Reagan signed the bill into law. He also protected our forests by approving forty-three wilderness bills during his presidency. The number the current administration has?

Two.

While I'm at it, I find it ironic that there are some who think that people who live in eastern Kentucky don't care about their drinking water, a sentiment that made the rounds on the left. Reminds me of one of the first elected officials I met in Hazard, a friendly Kentucky town of about five thousand or so. Within the first thirty minutes of our tour, the official reached into a creek downstream from a coal holding pond, scooped up some water with his hands, and drank it. (I declined, more concerned about amoebas than pollution.) "People from around here care more about their water than anyone living in Hollywood or Washington, D.C.," he explained. "But we also care about our jobs."

Unemployment in Harlan County, Kentucky, is about 18 percent, so you might understand the ire of Kentuckians when they are told that a crevice in the mountain is an "ephemeral" stream or that dirt is a pollutant and therefore the job must be terminated.

Which really gets to the crux of the problem: distant partisans in faraway places and in exalted positions telling folks in eastern Kentucky what's best for them. Most of these one-size-fits-all environment rules and regulations they promote do more overall harm than good. The impact they have on the environment is debatable. What's not is the crippling effect they have on the economy.

What's more, the deck is stacked in favor of those companies that can afford teams of lawyers whose only purpose is to circumnavigate the byzantine regulations, leaving the biggest companies to survive the pesky rules while thousands of smaller companies are bankrupted by the compliance costs.

There is an honest debate about what regulations are necessary, how they are applied, and by whom. There is an honest debate over whether dirt is a pollutant and whether your backyard is a navigable river.

There is no debate about wanting to protect the environment.

The Christian martyr and Nazi dissident Dietrich Bonhoeffer once said, "The ultimate test of a moral society is the kind of world that it leaves to its children."

In my opinion, the most important development of the past decade, and the one that holds the most promise to keep our environment clean over the next few decades, is how we recycle and how we maximize our ability to use resources with the least amount of waste.

A friend of mine, Nate Morris, started a company called Rubicon Global that is like an Angie's List for waste and recycling. This virtual marketplace draws carters and recyclers big and small. This way local companies can compete with the larger waste-removal firms like Waste Management and Republic Services. In the past, large chains, like 7-Eleven, Home Depot, and Wegmans grocery stores, hired a local company to remove waste. With Rubicon Global's virtual marketplace, recycling now often outcompetes the local landfill business and recycles instead of buries much of the waste. The result is competitive prices and more comprehensive service.

Rubicon also provides consulting services that help clients reduce their waste through logistics advice and recycling suggestions and opportunities. For instance, instead of taking up space in a landfill, discarded Wegmans uniforms are shredded and used as filler for pet beds, and unused pizza dough is turned into biofuel.[6]

Another friend, Charles Price, takes coal ash, a waste by-product, and makes it into concrete. Coal ash, or "fly ash," is the noncombustible portion of coal. The coal ash business, a profitable business that recycles, is threatened by leftists who wish to designate coal ash as hazardous waste, which would put the coal ash recyclers out of business.

Coal ash has the same chemical makeup as volcanic ash, and it has been used as an ingredient in good cement since ancient Rome. Ever wonder why the Parthenon is still standing? Volcanic ash is one of the answers. Concrete with coal ash is strong, reduces greenhouse emissions, and slows the depletion of a natural resource because you don't have to replace it as often.

Charles didn't stop there. He recently started a million-dollar facility that turns sulfur removed from coal-burning smokestacks into fertilizer for a profit. It amazes me to see pollution turned into fertilizer—a human version of photosynthesis.

Coal production is a big point for me. Environmentalists on the left are unified and highly vocal in their opposition, leaving no room for compromise or debate. They talk about coal companies "blowing the tops off of the mountains"[7] of Kentucky. I challenge them to go out to eastern Kentucky and look at the pristine beauty of its countless rolling hills. They make it sound as if miners are laying waste to the land. What the miners are doing is working to put food on the table and roofs over the heads of their families. And they're doing it in a section of this country where it's hard to find any job, let alone a good one. We have to stop destroying families and lives by destroying jobs in the name of environmental protection that is based more in politics than in reality. The coal industry is not destroying the natural beauty of Kentucky. What it is doing is providing jobs, working within tight federal regulations, and looking for ways of cleaner production. Some extremists and alarmists forget the enormous benefits of electricity.

People who live in the top ten electricity-producing countries live twenty-five years longer than people who live in countries that produce the least amount of electricity. While no one wants to excuse pollution, we should be conscious of the great advances that come with electricity.

As our population grows we will need all forms of energy: coal, nuclear, hydroelectric, wind, and solar. Mark my words, it is a mistake for government to unilaterally bankrupt and essentially ban an entire segment of energy production.

Likewise, we will need all approaches in farming to feed our growing population. I am fascinated by the successes of small farms that grow and distribute their products locally. My wife and I visit the local farmers markets in Bowling Green.

Last year, my youngest son, Robert, and I traveled to the Shenandoah Valley to visit a sustainable farm owned and operated by Joel Salatin. Salatin is an author and a lover of liberty and the environment.

Joel likes to say he was "planted" in the Shenandoah Valley. When he was just ten, he tended a flock of hens and would ride his bicycle to church and sell the eggs to the families there.[8]

Today, he raises cattle, hogs, and rabbits without vaccines or antibiotics and uses only manure as fertilizer.

He utilizes grass feeding to supplement his chickens and hogs. His cattle are entirely grass fed—he was at the forefront of this and local farming, too. He has mobile chicken coops that he designed, which he repositions daily. The process goes something like this: Joel moves the cows from pasture to pasture every day—they graze, mow the lawn, and move on. The chickens, in their mobile coops, are right behind them. The chickens gobble up the cow poop, then fertilize the grass to help keep the cycle going. The hogs have a beautiful home in the forest alongside the pasture where they feast on hickory nuts.

Salatin has a dozen or so interns to whom he teaches the art of sustainable farming. Being an intern for Salatin is a sought-after position.

He preaches what he practices, and his words have a soundness that comes from knowledge and experience. In his eighth book, *Folks, This Ain't Normal: A Farmer's Advice for Happier Hens, Healthier People, and a Better World*, Salatin writes:

> Most modern Americans can't conceive of living like this... The United States has too few farmers to merit counting on the national census form. As a culture, we don't cook at home. We don't have a larder. We're tuned in, plugged in, addicted to electronic gadgetry to the exclusion of a whippoorwill's midsummer song or a herd of cows lying down contentedly on the leeward side of a slope, indicating a thunderstorm in the offing.

Like many libertarians, Salatin sees government regulation as written to benefit the large corporate farmer but nearly impossible for the small farmer to follow. He writes and lectures about the inequity of many of the government's agricultural regulations.

I hear the same stories from small banks, small medical practices, and small retailers. If there is one overwhelming truth in Washington, it is that regulatory costs are more difficult to bear for small businesses and often lead to big business gobbling them up. In fact, a dirty little secret in Washington is that big business often lobbies for environmental protections and regulations knowing their smaller competitors will not survive.

Down the road a bit, Barbara Kingsolver wrote of her experience growing and living on local produce for a year. In *Animal, Vegetable, Miracle: A Year of Food Life*, she describes the laborious process of planting and harvesting her garden. Her descriptions remind me of Ada Monroe, the heroine in *Cold Mountain*, and how hard she had to work in her garden to survive the Civil War.

Both Salatin on the right and Kingsolver on the left lament the loss of locally grown markets and the community ties that come with local trade.

While I'm not quite ready to survive on my own garden, Kingsolver did motivate me to dismantle my kids' old tree fort and turn it into a compost bin.

When I paddle across the pond in my kayak or hike in the bottomland by the river, I think to myself that anyone, or any group, who thinks that the protection of the environment is their provenance alone is narrow-minded and is as dangerous to our world as any polluter.

The GOP I see will take a backseat to no one in defending the environment. The New GOP isn't going to let the left mischaracterize us. In fact, the case can be made that the New GOP, the GOP that I belong to, cares as much or more about the environment than any professed environmental activist. Instead of heated rhetoric, the New GOP will face the challenge with a cool-headed understanding that to spread environmentalism, to make it sustainable, we must look for ways to make it profitable.

Government-directed environmental subsidies to solar panel companies or electric cars are not sustainable if those enterprises are not profitable, especially when campaign donations are one of the biggest predictors of who gets the cash. Maybe someday they will be. If you're a company that's devoting time and money to research and development, then Godspeed. But it's not the government's place to fund these endeavors.

Our economy is replete with examples of profitable, environmentally friendly industries. Just look at aluminum recycling. More than 119,000 cans are recycled every minute in the United States. In 2012, recycled aluminum reached $90 billion in sales. The industry employs over a million workers.

Next door to me in Bowling Green, Logan Aluminum employs a thousand people and produces aluminum from recycled cans that are made into new cans for the beverage industry. Aluminum from Logan accounts for 45 percent of beverage cans in America. The energy used to create a new can is reduced by 95 percent with recycled aluminum. From an environmental point of view this is great, but it's even better because it's done to maximize profit. When profit is at stake, things tend to move very quickly.[9]

Or look at Joe Bessler, a friend of mine from northern Kentucky, who makes a living recycling cars and helps the environment one old broken-down heap at a time, so they don't end up in landfills or rust out in some field or woods. Of course, Joe is only a small part of an industry that recycles this "junk" for a profit of $22 billion a year. The Automotive Recycling Association (ARA) says that recycled vehicles provide enough steel to produce almost 13 million new vehicles, which saves an estimated 85 million barrels of oil a year that would have been used in the manufacturing of new or replacement parts.

The car recycling businesses also employ some 103,108 people, according to the ARA, and it's important to remember that government didn't create this industry. Private industry did, because there's a profit to be had, jobs to be had, and money to be made.

Let me tell you how that happened. In 1969, an estimated 20 million discarded motor vehicles littered America. Adam Ozimek, a business writer for *Forbes*, called it "an environmental crisis of abandoned cars." The labor involved in scrapping cars, and the steel industry's refusal to take the inferior metal that cars then consisted of, took the profit out of auto recycling. Then someone invented the car shredder, and the whole industry changed until, as Ozimek wrote, "the last abandoned cars were finally dragged out of the woods."

Like a kid with his first Tonka truck, I am fascinated by these giant shredders that can put a car in one side and shred it into thousands of pieces and then automatically sort the pieces.

From Joe Bessler to Big Auto, recycling profits abound. In 2012, Ford generated $225 million by recycling 586,000 tons of scrap metal in North America, according to the *New York Times.* General Motors sees a profit of $1 billion annually from their recycling and reuse efforts. Meanwhile, automakers are dumping less and less material into our landfills.

In his wonderful book *Junkyard Planet: Travels in the Billion-Dollar Trash Trade*, Adam Minter writes about the recyclable value of the insides of smartphones, computers, and tablets that Americans throw away "like candy wrappers." "The global recycling business, no matter how sustainable or green, is 100 percent dependent upon consumers consuming goods made from other goods," Minter writes.

Let me say it again: having sustainable waste management and recycling requires profitability. To protect the environment we must favor solutions that allow pro-environment companies to thrive. Our concern should be directed to long-term solutions, not quick fixes that require subsidies to persist.

To that end I support state legislation to allow businesses to incorporate as B corps that are not bound by always seeking the lowest-cost item but may take into account the well-being of the environment.

To support alternative fuels like ethanol, methanol, butane, and natural gas, I've introduced legislation to remove regulatory hurdles that inhibit the production and sale of fuels that pollute less.

In the New GOP, we will proclaim from the highest mountaintops that Republicans do care about the environment and about jobs. That jobs and the environment aren't mutually exclusive, but that we cannot blindly keep adding regulations without considering the consequences to the economy and jobs. To give you an example, since President Obama has taken office the EPA has added 2,827 new final regulations, which amount to 24,915 pages in the Federal Register. I'd list the regulations for you, but it would take a couple of more books to do so. One intrepid reporter did a word count on them and came to an approximate total of 24,915,000 words. That's more words than are contained in the seven Harry Potter books—twenty-two times over.[10]

To me, it makes absolute sense that the party that extols individual liberty and property rights should steadfastly stand against any entity that attempts to pollute your land or air space.

In the New GOP, you will find a balanced solution to the age-old question of how humans can tame the Earth and still preserve its beauty and treasures. I hope those who love the environment, those who care about our planet, those who treasure nature's beauty, will look again to the party that led the way on conservation, that led the way in creating our national parks. The New GOP has a place for those who want to preserve and protect and provide for a cleaner, brighter future for our planet.

In the New GOP, it will be okay to watch Jon Stewart or read Barbara Kingsolver, perhaps just not both in the same day. In the New GOP, it will be just as admirable to defend the Fourth Amendment as the Second Amendment.

In the New GOP it is cool to compost, shop at the farmers market, and maybe, just maybe, okay to commit civil disobedience and drink raw milk transported across state lines.

Together in the New GOP we'll find a way to preserve the glorious heritage that Teddy Roosevelt spoke of, and we'll be able to pass it along to our children and theirs.

That's the GOP I hope to lead.

17

★ ★ ★

A Look Forward

The next president needs to remember those in Middle America. By that, I mean those of us from small towns, who go to small churches and run small businesses. The part of America that doesn't have all the power, but does so much of the hard work.

★ ★ ★

At the end of my thirteen-hour filibuster, my legs were weak and my voice was raw. I walked away that night unbowed, proud of the stand I had taken. I was proud to have given voice to an America that struggles to be heard. An America that believes its legislators should work for the people and not against each other, an America that believes our rights precede all government and stem from our Creator.

People have asked me if the overwhelming positive reaction to my filibuster was the impetus for my decision to run for president. Actually, a decision like this doesn't come in some single flash of inspiration. At least it didn't for me. I went through a similar experience when I decided to run for the Senate. I have a wonderful wife and three great sons. I was a doctor in a small town, with my own practice. I made a good living, and I lived in a nice neighborhood. I was home for dinner every night unless I was coaching one of my sons' teams. So why did I run? I tell people that I got tired of throwing things at my television, and that is at least partially true.

Mostly, though, I felt helpless. I had watched as our elected officials bailed out big banks and drove deficits into the trillions of dollars. I watched as they passed a health-care law that took away our most basic freedom—the freedom to choose. I watched as a president marched us to war without even a glance at Congress. I ran for the Senate basically because I had had enough—with even my own party. It was Republicans who doubled the debt then and who bailed out the banks. It was Republicans who doubled the size of the Department of Education.

Now I have a different vantage, and now it's the Democrats who are tripling the debt. President Obama is on course to add more debt than all the previous presidents in history—combined. It's the Democrats and their president who now ignore the Constitution and trample those God-given rights I stood for in my filibuster. As a senator I can do more than throw things at the television—and I fight every day against the sellout of America's principles, solvency, and future.

Still, I believe I can do more. Even the great honor and responsibility of being a U.S. senator has its limits, and that is why I am running for president. I don't take this lightly, and I run with all humility that I am not the only person who could help right our ship of state. But I do believe I have something to offer, and I believe in the ideas that have brought me to this point in my life. To right the ship of state, it won't be good enough to just nominate any old Republican. Too often, we settled for Democrat-lite and the inertia of Washington prevents any meaningful change.

I believe in genuine change, not the campaign-button variety.

I believe in making the federal government smaller, balancing the budget, and returning money to the productive sector by dramatically lowering tax rates.

Real change would mean a president who appoints cabinet secretaries who pledge to reduce the size and scope of their departments.

Real change would mean limits on the terms of every single member of Congress.

The next president needs to understand how and where jobs are created. Jobs are created in the private sector. Jobs are created by big and small businesses, but too often the voices of the small mom-and-pop businesses are drowned out by larger voices seeking favors.

The next president needs to remember those in Middle America. By that I mean those of us from small towns, who go to small churches and who run small businesses. The part of America that doesn't have all the power but does so much of the hard work.

The next president shouldn't disparage the builders and creators. The next president should recognize that genius needs freedom as Steve Jobs did when he wrote:

"Here's to the crazy ones, the misfits, the rebels, the troublemakers, the round pegs in the square holes...The ones who see things differently—they're not fond of rules...They push the human race forward, and while some may see them as the crazy ones, we see genius, because the ones who are crazy enough to think they can change the world are the ones who do."

Those of us who are actively pursuing the American Dream simply want one thing: for government to get out of our way.

Pink Floyd understood that genius needs to be left alone. Whether your ideas are politically correct or not, whether you're a painter or a self-proclaimed prophet, the exhortation is to shine, to not let conformity dim your light: "Shine on, you crazy diamond."

For the crazy diamonds to shine, government must get out of the way.

The leave-me-alone generation is a generation that believes they can conquer the world, solve any problem, if left free to follow their dreams.

It isn't about how government will lead us to prosperity. The debate is about getting government out of the way of human ingenuity.

President Obama is leaving office and, as a country, we need to ask ourselves, did we get what was advertised? What direction do we want to see the country move in for the next four years? One big idea is to make sure Washington has less power and less to do.

The next president should not be able to impose his will on us—he should not be allowed to tell us what insurance we can buy, what lightbulbs we can use, and how we generate electricity.

My run for the presidency will be a campaign for people who don't have power—whether they live in a small town or a big city. I will stand for the people who live in places other politicians take for granted.

As president, I will stand for those who feel separated and distant from the American Dream, those who don't want to be perpetually talked down to, forgotten, and left in never-ending poverty.

The War on Poverty is fifty years old, and black unemployment is still twice that of white unemployment. Income inequality has worsened under this administration, and Democrats offer more of the same policies—policies that have allowed the poor to get poorer and the rich to get richer.

Pitting one American against another is not a pathway toward prosperity. The current president is intent on redistributing the pie but not growing it. He misunderstands that the bulk of America wants a bigger pie. They want to work, and they don't want a life of dependency.

Not only do we need new blood in Washington, we need a new way of thinking in Washington.

As a physician, I was taught first to do no harm. To think before you act. To analyze the unintended consequences of your actions.

I think America would be better off if all our politicians took that same approach:

"First, do no harm."

Get out of the way. Do no harm. If we start there, we solve a lot of our problems.

It is self-evident that the president and Congress are unable to do what every family in America must do—balance the budget. So let's try a new way: if Congress cannot—or will not—balance the budget, then we should amend the Constitution to make it mandatory.

The debt is out of control. We borrow a million dollars a minute. Our $18 trillion debt has become an anchor. Some economists argue that the burden of debt costs us a million jobs a year.

I fear that this degree of debt is an imminent threat to our national security.

You cannot project power from bankruptcy court. It does not make us appear stronger when we borrow money from China and then send it to countries that burn our flag. The hollowing out of our national defense comes from the advocates for unlimited spending and perpetual military intervention.

Let me reiterate: Secretary Gates got it right when he said that we've overmilitarized our foreign policy. Should we be engaged in trying to encourage stability in the world? Absolutely. But we must think before we act. We must remember the maxim "First, do no harm."

It's time for a new approach both abroad and here at home.

With our health care, it is a noble aspiration and a moral obligation to make sure our fellow man is provided for, that medical treatment is made available to all.

But compassion cannot be delivered in the form of coercion.

President Obama's fundamental promise that if you like your doctor you can keep him or her—that was a lie. I promise you this: as a doctor, I will make it my mission to reverse the course on which Obamacare has us.

Obamacare at its core takes away a patient's right to choose.

Everyone knows our health-care system needed reforming, but it was the wrong prescription to choose more government instead of more consumer choice and competition.

Obamacare restricts freedom and must be repealed. I was asked recently how we would fix our health-care system. I replied, "Let's try freedom again. It worked for over two hundred years!"

To stimulate the economy, I believe we cut everyone's taxes, from the richest to the poorest, and we cut spending at the same time.

That's why I have proposed the largest tax cut in American history, a tax cut that will include every single American, from richest to poorest.

My tax plan will include a tax code every American can understand. You will be able to file your taxes on a single sheet of paper, no accountant or lawyer necessary.

It will cut taxes, but it will also make sure everyone plays by the rules and pays their fair share. The days of corporations hiring the best lawyers and lobbyists and paying zero taxes must end.

Some will ask, "But what of the safety net?" I promise you this: we will not cut one penny from the safety net until we've cut every penny from corporate welfare!

I will also cut spending. Some so-called conservatives recently voted to borrow $190 billion to fund more defense spending. This proposal is exactly why Republicans and Democrats have created an $18 trillion debt. When I showed these "conservatives" that you could increase defense spending and offset it with cuts to domestic spending, virtually none of them had the courage to vote for the spending cuts. These so-called conservatives are the part of the problem. On the left you have liberals who will borrow for domestic spending but on the right you have a similar problem: conservatives who will continue to borrow money to throw it at the Pentagon.

I propose a third way: all spending must be justified and we must not add more to the debt even for worthwhile expenditures like defense. No other candidate in the presidential race will honestly support this position and that's why the American people must demand something new, someone who will say to the right and to the left that we must stop digging the hole of debt deeper and deeper.

I will continue to advocate for significant reforms to the way we do business in Washington. In addition to balancing the budget, Congress should be required to *read the bills first*.

Congressmen and women should also live under the laws they pass. Congress should pass no law that exempts congressmen and women from the requirements of a bill. We have set up a privileged class in Washington, and Americans are sick and tired of it.

These Beltway elites say, "Trust us, we won't violate your privacy." But when the intelligence director is not punished for lying to Congress, how are we to trust them? Are we to trust them to seize and hold every American's phone records? Remember, these are the same people who have only a 10 percent approval rating!

The Constitution is clear: politicians should *not* collect such information without a warrant. Warrants must be specific to an individual, and there must be probable cause before the government is allowed to search any American's private documents.

The president created this vast dragnet by executive order, without congressional authority. As president, I will immediately end this invasion of our privacy.

We need to return to our founding principles and stand up for the entire Bill of Rights.

To defend the Bill of Rights, we must have a strong national defense. I believe national defense is the single most important constitutional obligation of our federal government. We should have a military that is second to none in the world, one that is ready to defend us from all enemies.

To defend ourselves, we need a lean, mean, fighting machine that doesn't waste money on a bloated civilian bureaucracy. The civilian bureaucracy at the Pentagon has doubled in the past thirty years, gobbling up the money necessary to modernize our defense. That's why I will propose the first-ever audit of the Pentagon and seek ways to make our Department of Defense more modern and efficient.

There is still so much promise for the future of America.

Our future can include a road back to prosperity, back to respect at home and abroad. It can include a balanced budget and a simple, fair tax system. It can include a government that protects your rights *and* your security.

It can include a Congress that is responsive to YOU, the people, and not the special interests. It can include a stronger, better military, in which our troops and our veterans are valued and not forgotten when they return home. It can include a plan to bring prosperity to our inner cities and real justice to all Americans.

The path we are on now does not lead there. But there is time to change course.

For the past six years, this president has had the wrong diagnosis for what ails our country.

It's time for a new way. A new set of ideas.

A plurality of Americans are no longer Republicans or Democrats. These Americans want a new combination of beliefs. These Americans are fiscally conservative and also concerned with personal liberty. A philosophy that joins economic and personal liberty becomes a potent political force. Such a philosophy transcends typical political labels and parties—and crosses all classes.

This philosophy of liberty defends the poor, defends minority rights, and protects the privacy of all of us.

A candidate who champions this philosophy can unify the country. A Republican who defends the entire Bill of Rights, a Republican who demands that justice not disproportionately incarcerate people of color brings a message to the table that could transform electoral politics.

Crowdpac looks at congressional voting records and scores representatives based on several indexes. On economic liberty, I rank as one of the most conservative members of Congress. On personal liberty, on the desire to be free of big-government surveillance, no one in Congress ranks above me.

But what about issues outside of economic and personal liberty, how does a third way handle those?

Simple: by following the instructions that have held us in good stead for 225 years.

The Ninth and Tenth Amendments reserve most rights and privileges to the people. Power not explicitly given to the federal government is left to the states and people respectively, and this is not to be disparaged. Many of the contentious issues of the day can be left up to the states or to individuals themselves.

So how about we take a stand together? America has much greatness left in her. We will thrive when we believe in ourselves again. When we believe in our founding documents. When we believe in economic and personal liberty again.

I see an America where everyone who wants to work will have a job.

I see an America strong enough to deter foreign aggression, yet wise enough to avoid unnecessary intervention.

I see an America where criminal justice is applied equally, and any law that disproportionately incarcerates people of color is repealed.

I see an America that creates millions of jobs by leaving more money in each and every community.

I see our big cities once again shining and beckoning with creativity, and American companies offering Americans jobs.

I have a vision for an America beyond partisan politics, beyond petty divisions, an America that is once again defined by her most cherished founding principles: Liberty and Justice.

Appendix

The following is a list of almost 100 bills that Senator Rand Paul has authored since joining the Senate in 2011:

These bills are available to read at www.congress.gov

In Development—Prohibiting Youth Status Offenders Act

In Development—Smarter Sentencing Act

In Development—TREAT Act

S.889—A bill to provide regulatory relief to alternative fuel producers and consumers, and for other purposes. (03/26/2015)

S.855—A bill to amend the Endangered Species Act of 1973 to permit Governors of States to regulate intrastate endangered species and intrastate threatened species, and for other purposes. (03/24/2015)

S.837—A bill to modify the criteria used by the Corps of Engineers to dredge small ports. (03/23/2015)

S.813—A bill to provide the Secretary of Defense with authority to transfer funds in order to mitigate the effects on the Department of Defense of a sequestration of funds available to the Department of Defense, and for other purposes. (03/19/2015)

S.790—Economic Freedom Zones Act: A bill to provide for the establishment of free-market enterprise zones in order to help facilitate the creation of new jobs, entrepreneurial opportunities, enhanced and renewed educational opportunities, and increase community involvement in bankrupt or economically distressed areas. (03/18/2015)

S.675—REDEEM Act (03/09/2015)

S.663—A bill to repeal the violation of sovereign nations' laws and privacy matters. (03/04/2015)

S.652—Service Members and Communities Count Act of 2014 (03/04/2015)

S.633—Stand with Israel Act of 2015 (03/03/2015)

S.457—Civil Rights Voting Restoration Act of 2015 (02/11/2015)

S.391—National Right-to-Work Act (02/05/2015)

S.353—Justice Safety Valve Act of 2015 (02/03/2015)

S.300—Audit the Pentagon Act of 2015 (01/29/2015)

S.264—Federal Reserve Transparency Act of 2015 (01/27/2015)

S.255—FAIR Act (01/26/2015)

S.226—Regulations From the Executive in Need of Scrutiny Act of 2015 (01/21/2015)

S.34—Defend Israel by Defunding Palestinian Foreign Aid Act of 2015 (01/06/2015)

S.3015—Preventing Executive Overreach on Immigration Act of 2014 (12/12/2014)

S.2657—RESET Act (07/24/2014)

S.2644—FAIR Act (07/23/2014)

S.2567—REDEEM Act (07/08/2014)

S.2550—Civil Rights Voting Restoration Act of 2014 (06/26/2014)

S.2477—Egyptian Military Coup Act of 2014 (06/17/2014)

S.2265—Stand with Israel Act of 2014 (04/29/2014)

S.2216—Protect Small Business Jobs Act of 2014 (04/07/2014)

S.2062—Constitutional Check and Balance Act (02/27/2014)

S.1930—Uphold Our Promise to Veterans Act (01/15/2014)

S.1919—A bill to repeal the Authorization for Use of Military Force Against Iraq Resolution of 2002 (01/14/2014)

S.1852—Economic Freedom Zones Act of 2013 (12/18/2013)

S.1731—Endangered Species Management Self-Determination Act (11/19/2013)

S.1664—One Subject at a Time Act (11/07/2013)

S.1663—Write the Laws Act (11/07/2013)

S.1665—Read the Bills Act (11/07/2013)

S.1469—Congressional Health Care for Seniors Act of 2013 (08/01/2013)

S.1278—Egyptian Military Coup Act of 2013 (07/11/2013)

S.1121—Fourth Amendment Restoration Act of 2013 (06/07/2013)

S.1037—Fourth Amendment Preservation and Protection Act of 2013 (05/23/2013)

S.1016—Preserving Freedom from Unwarranted Surveillance Act of 2013 (05/21/2013)

S.1004—Anti-Trust Freedom Act of 2013 (05/21/2013)

S.956—A bill to permanently suspend application of certain agricultural price support authority. (05/15/2013)

S.911—Emergency Transportation Safety Fund Act (05/09/2013)

S.887—A bill to repeal the violation of sovereign nations' laws and privacy matters. (05/07/2013)

S.890—Defense of Environment and Property Act of 2013 (05/07/2013)

S.785—Federal Employee Accountability Act of 2013 (04/23/2013)

S.732—A bill to modify the criteria used by the Corps of Engineers to dredge small ports. (04/16/2013)

S.643—Bonuses for Cost-Cutters Act of 2013 (03/21/2013)

S.619—Justice Safety Valve Act of 2013 (03/20/2013)

S.583—A bill to implement equal protection under the fourteenth article of amendment to the Constitution for the right to life of each born and preborn human person. (03/14/2013)

S.558—Accountability in Grants Act of 2013 (03/13/2013)

S.530—A bill to make participation in the American Community Survey voluntary, except with respect to certain basic questions, and for other purposes. (03/12/2013)

S.15—REINS Act (02/26/2013)

S.209—Federal Reserve Transparency Act of 2013 (02/04/2013)

S.201—A bill to prohibit the sale, lease, transfer, retransfer, or delivery of F-16 aircraft, M1 tanks, or certain other defense articles or services to the Government of Egypt. (01/31/2013)

S.204—A bill to preserve and protect the free choice of individual employees to form, join, or assist labor organizations, or to refrain from such activities. (01/31/2013)

S.158—A bill for the relief of Dr. Shakil Afridi. (01/28/2013)

S.164—A bill to prohibit the United States from providing financial assistance to Pakistan until Dr. Shakil Afridi is freed. (01/28/2013)

S.83—Government Shutdown Prevention Act of 2013 (01/23/2013)

S.81—Default Prevention Act (01/23/2013)

S.82—Separation of Powers Restoration and Second Amendment Protection Act of 2013 (01/23/2013)

S.3576—A bill to provide limitations on United States assistance, and for other purposes. (09/19/2012)

S.3360—Read the Bills Act (06/28/2012)

S.3361—Write the Laws Act (06/28/2012)

S.3359—One Subject at a Time Act (06/28/2012)

S.3337—Access to Physicians in Medicare Act of 2012 (06/25/2012)

S.3303—A bill to require security screening of passengers at airports to be carried out by private screening companies, and for other purposes. (06/14/2012)

S.3302—Air Travelers' Bill of Rights Act of 2012 (06/14/2012)

S.3287—Preserving Freedom from Unwarranted Surveillance Act of 2012 (06/12/2012)

S.3269—A bill to provide that no United States assistance may be provided to Pakistan until Dr. Shakil Afridi is freed. (06/06/2012)

S.3260—A bill to provide that no United States assistance may be provided to Pakistan until Dr. Shakil Afridi is freed. (06/04/2012)

S.3259—A bill for the relief of Dr. Shakil Afridi. (06/04/2012)

S.3079—A bill to make participation in the American Community Survey voluntary, except with respect to certain basic questions, and for other purposes. (05/10/2012)

S.2470—Service Members and Communities Count Act of 2012 (04/26/2012)

S.2327—A bill to prohibit direct foreign assistance to the Government of Egypt until the President makes certain certifications related to treatment of nongovernmental organization workers, and for other purposes. (04/19/2012)

S.2269—Anti-Trust Freedom Act of 2012 (03/29/2012)

S.2226—A bill to prohibit the Administrator of the Environmental Protection Agency from awarding any grant, contract, cooperative agreement, or other financial assistance under section 103 of the Clean Air Act for any program, project, or activity carried out outside the United States, including the territories and possessions of the United States. (03/22/2012)

S.2196—Congressional Health Care for Seniors Act of 2012 (03/15/2012)

S.2122—Defense of Environment and Property Act of 2012 (02/16/2012)

S.2085—Cost Savings Enhancements Act of 2012 (02/09/2012)

S.2062—Freedom from Over-Criminalization and Unjust Seizures Act of 2012 (02/02/2012)

S.1955—A bill to authorize the interstate traffic of unpasteurized milk and milk products that are packaged for direct human consumption. (12/07/2011)

S.1927—A bill to modify the criteria used by the Corps of Engineers to dredge small ports. (11/30/2011)

S.1800—Parental Consent Act of 2011 (11/03/2011)

S.1648—Emergency Transportation Safety Fund Act (10/04/2011)

S.1326—A bill to implement the President's request to increase the statutory limit on the public debt. (07/05/2011)

S.1070—Fourth Amendment Restoration Act (05/25/2011)

S.1072—A bill to provide for a good faith exemption from suspicious activity reporting requirements, and for other purposes. (05/25/2011)

S.1073—A bill to require the Attorney General to establish minimization and destruction procedures governing the acquisition, retention, and dissemination by the Federal Bureau of Investigation of certain records. (05/25/2011)

S.1076—A bill to modify the roving wiretap authority of the Foreign Intelligence Surveillance Act of 1978. (05/25/2011)

S.1077—A bill to require judicial review of Suspicious Activity Reports. (05/25/2011)

S.1071—A bill to limit suspicious activity reporting requirements to requests from law enforcement agencies, and for other purposes. (05/25/2011)

S.1074—A bill to remove the extension of the sunset date for section 215 of the USA PATRIOT Act. (05/25/2011)

S.1075—A bill to provide judicial review of National Security Letters. (05/25/2011)

S.1050—Fourth Amendment Restoration Act (05/23/2011)

S.768—Government Shutdown Prevention Act of 2011 (04/07/2011)

S.299—REINS Act (02/07/2011)
S.202—Federal Reserve Transparency Act of 2011 (01/26/2011)

In addition, Senator Rand Paul has cosponsored hundreds of bills, including these:

S.877—Police CAMERA Act with Senator Brian Schatz (03/26/2015)
S.683—CARERS Act with Senator Cory Booker and Senator Kirsten Gillibrand (03/10/2015)
S.2567—REDEEM Act (07/08/2014) with Senator Cory Booker
S.1752—Military Justice Improvement Act of 2013 (11/20/2013) with Senator Kirsten Gillibrand

Notes

Chapter 2: A Medical History

1. http://www.newrepublic.com/article/politics/75252/paleo-wacko.

Chapter 3: Health Care: A Doctor's Opinion

1. https://www.osac.gov/pages/ContentReportDetails.aspx?cid=13878
2. http://www.washingtontimes.com/news/2010/mar/26/nepalese-doctor-a-sight-for-sore-eyes/?page=all.
3. http://www.berkeleyhealthtech.org/docs/Vol.3.2.Hospital-Markets.pdf.
4. http://www.nytimes.com/2000/12/09/business/turning-surgery-into-a-commodity-laser-eye-centers-wage-an-all-out-price-war.html.
5. http://www.nytimes.com/2000/12/09/business/turning-surgery-into-a-commodity-laser-eye-centers-wage-an-all-out-price-war.html.
6. http://www.nytimes.com/2014/09/27/health/Ebola-Doctor-Shortage-Eases-as-Volunteers-Begin-to-Step-Forward.html.

Chapter 4: Getting to Work

1. https://www.senate.gov/artandhistory/art/special/Desks/hdetail.cfm?id=2.
2. Details of the fight are disputed in other volumes. According to Cassius M. Clay's own memoir he was stabbed in the side, for example.
3. William H. Turner and Edward J. Cabbell, eds. *Blacks in Appalachia* (The University Press of Kentucky, November 30, 2009).
4. David Gergen, *Ronald Reagan, Eyewitness to Power* (Simon & Schuster), p. 238.
5. http://www.npr.org/2011/06/04/136930966/how-much-is-14-3-trillion-it-s-a-brain-teaser.
6. http://www.thenation.com/blog/159989/rand-pauls-right-about-military-budget-going-have-be-cut.

Chapter 5: A New Kind of Republican

1. http://www.nytimes.com/2010/08/12/us/politics/12rostenkowski.html?pagewanted=all.
2. http://www.gallup.com/poll/159881/americans-call-term-limits-end-electoral-college.aspx.
3. http://www.factcheck.org/2010/01/lawmaker-loopholes.
4. http://www.sanders.senate.gov/newsroom/press-releases/gao-finds-serious-conflicts-at-the-fed;
5. http://www.forbes.com/sites/richardsalsman/2013/04/02/an-overleveraged-fed-punishes-better-capitalized-banks.
6. http://www.royalbounty.com/famous_quotations.htm.

Chapter 6: Can You Hear Me Now?

1. http://www.constitution.org/bor/otis_against_writs.htm.
2. http://www.intelligence.senate.gov/pdfs94th/94intelligence_activities_VI.pdf (p. 617).
3. http://www.washingtonpost.com/blogs/the-switch/wp/2014/01/04/the-nsa-refuses-to-deny-spying-on-members-of-congress.

4. http://www.nbcnews.com/storyline/cia-senate-snooping/cia-accused-spying-senate-intel-committee-breaking-law-n49816.
5. http://www.intelligence.senate.gov/pdfs94th/94intelligence_activities_VI.pdf.
6. http://www.wired.com/2012/07/surveillance-spirit-law.
7. http://www.pbs.org/wgbh/pages/frontline/homefront/preemption/churchfisa.html.
8. http://www.youtube.com/watch?v=9DjJKYYb5-4.
9. http://www.intelligence.senate.gov/pdfs94th/94intelligenceactivitiesV.pdf.
10. The Truong and Humphrey espionage case also played a role in the passage of the intelligence surveillance law and the establishment of the FISA court. http://www.nytimes.com/2014/07/07/us/david-truong-figure-in-us-wiretap-case-dies-at-68.html.
11. https://www.aclu.org/reform-patriot-act.
12. http://www.nationalreview.com/corner/356159/sensenbrenner-nsa-surveillance-abuse-patriot-act-john-fund.
13. https://www.youtube.com/watch?v=8vFhXpfEfQg.
14. http://www.cato.org/policy-report/novemberdecember-2013/decoding-summer-snowden.
15. http://www.nytimes.com/2013/08/18/magazine/laura-poitras-snowden.html?pagewanted=all&_r=0.
16. http://www.theguardian.com/world/video/2013/jul/08/edward-snowden-video-interview.
17. http://abcnews.go.com/blogs/headlines/2014/05/ex-nsa-chief-we-kill-people-based-on-metadata.
18. http://www.nytimes.com/2014/10/28/us/us-secretly-monitoring-mail-of-thousands.html?hp&action=click&pgtype=Homepage&module=first-column-region®ion=top-news&WT.nav=top-news.
19. http://america.aljazeera.com/articles/multimedia/timeline-edward-snowden-revelations.html.
20. http://blogs.wsj.com/washwire/2013/08/23/nsa-officers-sometimes-spy-on-love-interests.
21. http://www.nytimes.com/2014/06/07/technology/internet-giants-erect-barriers-to-spy-agencies.html.
22. http://www.huffingtonpost.com/2014/09/25/james-comey-apple-encryption_n_5882874.html.
23. http://www.wsj.com/video/government-spy-from-the-sky-program-revealed/4CCE1200-0270-4DDC-8157-DC6DF587FAC0.html.
24. http://www.pbs.org/wgbh/pages/frontline/government-elections-politics/united-states-of-secrets/the-frontline-interview-diane-roark.
25. http://www.politifact.com/punditfact/statements/2014/jan/10/jake-tapper/cnns-tapper-obama-has-used-espionage-act-more-all-.

Chapter 7: On the Road

1. http://www.brookings.edu/research/testimony/2012/06/05-poverty-families-haskins.
2. http://www.naacp.org/pages/criminal-justice-fact-sheet.
3. Mark Hendrickson. "President Obama's Wealth-Desroying Goal," *Forbes* (May 31, 2012).
4. http://iroots.org/2013/09/18/african-american-pastors-shocking-comments-on-rand-paul.
5. http://content.time.com/time/magazine/article/0,9171,1720240,00.html.
6. http://www.usnews.com/news/articles/2013/09/16/police-made-one-marijuana-arrest-every-42-seconds-in-2012.
7. http://www.justice.gov/jmd/2014factsheets/prisons-detention.pdf.
8. http://cnsnews.com/news/article/pew-study-prison-recidivism-rates-remain-high.
9. Pennsylvania Department of Corrections, Annual Statistical Report. 2007, 2008.
10. US Department of Education, NCES, Digest of Education Statistics, 2007.
11. http://www.nytimes.com/2004/11/17/national/17sentencing.html.
12. http://www.fredericknewspost.com/news/crime_and_justice/article_27756acf-4a02-5b1e-8ae4-3ca7eb305caa.html.

13. http://www.freep.com/article/20120205/OPINION02/202050442/PUNISHMENT-INSTEAD-OF-TREATMENT-Hundreds-of-Michigan-s-mentally-ill-inmates-languish-in-solitary-confinement-lost-in-a-prison-system-ill-equipped-to-treat-them.
14. http://www.politico.com/magazine/story/2014/01/martin-luther-king-jr-voting-rights-act-102371.html#.U9T3WRZPQds.
15. http://www.sentencingproject.org/doc/publications/fd_State_Level_Estimates_of_Felon_Disen_2010.pdf.
16. http://www.sentencingproject.org/template/page.cfm?id=133.
17. http://kff.org/other/poll-finding/kaiser-family-foundationnew-york-timescbs-news-non-employed-poll.

Chapter 8: Waiting for Superman

1. http://www.aecf.org/resources/early-reading-proficiency-in-the-united-states.
2. http://www.nytimes.com/2014/09/07/magazine/so-bill-gates-has-this-idea-for-a-history-class.html?hp&action=click&pgtype=Homepage&version=HpSumSmallMedia High&module=second-column-region®ion=top-news&WT.nav=top-news.
3. http://www.brookings.edu/research/papers/2011/05/11-class-size-whitehurst-chingos.
4. http://ilpovertyreport.org/sites/default/files/uploads/images/county_pdfs/cook_0.pdf.

Chapter 9: Government Overreach

1. http://www.nytimes.com/2014/04/17/nyregion/suburbs-try-to-hold-onto-young-adults-as-exodus-to-cities-appears-to-grow.html?_r=0.
2. http://www.epi.org/publication/making-ferguson.
3. http://www.newyorker.com/news/news-desk/economics-police-militarism.
4. http://www.nytimes.com/2014/08/25/us/darren-wilsons-unremarkable-past-offers-few-clues-into-ferguson shooting.html?hp&action=click&pgtype=Homepage&version=Hp SumSmallMedia&module=second-column-region®ion=top-news&WT.nav=top-news.
5. http://www.governing.com/topics/public-justice-safety/gov-ferguson-missouri-court-fines-budget.html.
6. http://www.nytimes.com/2015/03/05/opinion/a-chilling-portrait-of-ferguson.html?hp& action=click&pgtype=Homepage&module=c-column-top-span-region®ion=c-column-top-span-region&WT.nav=c-column-top-span-region.
7. https://news.vice.com/article/vice-on-hbo-debriefs-surveillance-city-the-forgotten-war.
8. http://www.npr.org/2014/05/29/316735545/why-your-right-to-a-public-defender-may-come-with-a-fee.
9. http://www.hrw.org/news/2014/02/05/us-profit-probation-tramples-rights-poor.
10. http://www.al.com/news/index.ssf/2015/02/us_department_of_justice_assis.html.
11. http://ago.mo.gov/VehicleStops/2013/reports/161.pdf.
12. http://www.newyorker.com/magazine/2013/08/12/taken.
13. http://www.nhregister.com/general-news/20140628/connecticut-police-use-thousands-in-seized-funds-for-training-trips.
14. http://www.krmg.com/news/news/local/tulsa-police-rolls-cadillac-escalade-seized-drug-d/nRJZN.
15. http://books.google.com/books?id=rOAXAQAAIAAJ&pg=PA672&lpg=PA672&dq=example+of+deodan+in+english+common+law&source=bl&ots=oWIN5roitz&sig=8Es B5YWXSOVa0qZPJGIE9JtpJ6c&hl=en&sa=X&ei=kqkAVJyHI5W9ggS3yYKIBA&ved=0CFQQ6AEwBQ#v=onepage&q=example%20of%20deodan%20in%20english%20common%20law&f=false.
16. http://www.washingtontimes.com/news/2014/feb/9/caswell-the-covetous-cops-of-motel-caswell/?page=all.
17. http://www.washingtontimes.com/news/2014/feb/9/caswell-the-covetous-cops-of-motel-caswell/?page=all.

18. http://www.nytimes.com/2014/10/26/us/law-lets-irs-seize-accounts-on-suspicion-no-crime-required.html?hp&action=click&pgtype=Homepage&version=HpSum&module=first-column-region®ion=top-news&WT.nav=top-news.
19. http://www.city-data.com/crime/crime-Bal-Harbour-Florida.html.
20. http://ivn.us/2012/10/31/floridas-bal-harbour-police-department-epitomizes-the-perverse-nature-of-civil-asset-forfeiture-laws.
21. http://www.npr.org/templates/story/story.php?storyId=91638378.
22. http://www.wsj.com/articles/loretta-lynchs-money-pot-Nov. 21, 2014.
23. http://www.fbi.gov/about-us/investigate/white_collar/asset-forfeiture.
24. http://www.nytimes.com/2014/11/10/us/police-use-department-wish-list-when-deciding-which-assets-to-seize.html?hp&action=click&pgtype=Homepage&module=second-column-region®ion=top-news&WT.nav=top-news&_r=0.
25. http://www.auditor.mo.gov/Press/2013-019.pdf.

Chapter 10: Economic Freedom

1. http://www.detroitnews.com/story/business/2014/10/20/detroit-dirt-martha-stewart-winner/17618947.
2. http://www.nytimes.com/2014/08/07/business/peter-hall-city-planner-who-devised-the-enterprise-zone-dies-at-82.html.
3. The exact quote is: "Do your work the best you can do it, given your level of skill, given your level of knowledge (you cannot do the impossible), and you will raise your self-esteem. And that's more important than getting more money or a promotion because it's about who you are." http://object.cato.org/sites/cato.org/files/serials/files/cato-journal/2012/7/v32n2-4.pdf.
4. http://www.nationalreview.com/article/374321/corporate-welfare-queens-stephen-moore.
5. http://www.democracynow.org/2010/6/23/47_years_ago_in_detroit_rev.

Chapter 11: The War on Liberty

1. http://www.theatlantic.com/politics/archive/2014/12/michael-brown-eric-garner-other-america-john-lewis/383750.
2. http://www.cato.org/blog/police-militarization-ferguson-nationwide.
3. http://www.nytimes.com/2014/08/24/us/in-washington-second-thoughts-on-arming-police.html?hp&action=click&pgtype=Homepage&version=LedeSum&module=first-column-region®ion=top-news&WT.nav=top-news.
4. https://www.aclu.org/blog/criminal-law-reform-free-speech/senator-ervin-no-knock-warrants-and-fight-stop-cops-smashing.
5. https://www.aclu.org/blog/criminal-law-reform-free-speech/senator-ervin-no-knock-warrants-and-fight-stop-cops-smashing.
6. 18480 Congressional Record—House, June 7, 1973.
7. http://billmoyers.com/2014/08/13/not-just-ferguson-11-eye-opening-facts-about-americas-militarized-police-forces.
8. http://www.policestateusa.com/2014/sneak-and-peek-warrants.
9. https://www.eff.org/document/2013-delayed-notice-sneak-and-peek-report.
10. http://www.americanbar.org/content/dam/aba/events/criminal_justice/Fall2012/Roundtable_WitmerRich_Covert_Searches.authcheckdam.pdf.
11. http://homelandsecurity.ky.gov/suspicious.html.
12. http://www.nytimes.com/2005/10/30/books/review/30mosle.html?pagewanted=all.
13. http://www.cato.org/publications/white-paper/overkill-rise-paramilitary-police-raids-america.
14. http://articles.orlandosentinel.com/2013-08-27/news/os-barbershop-raids-lawsuits-sheriff-20130826_1_strictly-skillz-regional-program-administrator-state-licensing-agency.

15. http://abcnews.go.com/US/family-toddler-injured-swat-grenade-faces-1m-medical/story?id=27671521.
16. http://www.theblaze.com/stories/2014/05/30/heartbreaking-photo-of-baby-boy-tells-story-of-late-night-swat-raid-gone-horribly-wrong.
17. https://www.propublica.org/article/flashbangs.

Chapter 12: The War on Christians

1. http://www.news.va/en/news/asiasyria-maalula-land-of-martyrs-death-in-odium-f.
2. http://www.mcclatchydc.com/2014/05/29/228819/for-2-years-the-priest-aided-christians.html.
3. http://blogs.spectator.co.uk/coffeehouse/2014/05/boko-haram-only-kidnapped-the-nigerian-girls-because-they-were-christian.
4. http://www.christianpost.com/news/expert-more-christians-killed-last-year-in-northern-nigeria-than-rest-of-world-combined-108796.
5. http://www.hrw.org/news/2012/01/30/saudi-arabia-christians-arrested-private-prayer.
6. https://www.opendoorsusa.org.
7. http://www.christianpost.com/news/isis-beheads-7-men-and-3-women-in-syria-us-led-airstrikes-hit-stronghold-127367.
8. http://www.state.gov/j/drl/rls/irf/2013/sca/222323.htm.
9. http://www.pewglobal.org/2013/05/16/egyptians-increasingly-glum.
10. http://www.washingtonpost.com/blogs/wonkblog/wp/2013/07/09/the-u-s-gives-egypt-1-5-billion-a-year-in-aid-heres-what-it-does.
11. https://cmes.uchicago.edu/sites/cmes.uchicago.edu/files/uploads/Global/Excerpts%20from%20Ibn%20Sina's%20Canon%20of%20Medicine.pdf.
12. http://www.britannica.com/EBchecked/topic/428267/Omar-Khayyam.
13. http://www.serageldin.com/ancient_Library.htm.
14. http://www.independent.co.uk/news/science/how-islamic-inventors-changed-the-world-469452.html.
15. http://www.u-s-history.com/pages/h2764.html.

Chapter 13: Defending America

1. It was actually "avoids errors. You hit singles, you hit doubles." Either way, he hasn't accomplished his goal.
2. http://amanpour.blogs.cnn.com/2014/06/03/former-u-s-ambassador-to-syria-i-could-no-longer-defend-the-american-policy-robert-ford.
3. http://af.reuters.com/article/topNews/idAFJOE75H01120110618.
4. http://www.rand.org/pubs/research_reports/RR637.html.
5. http://www.npr.org/blogs/thetwo-way/2013/07/23/204793903/no-fly-zone-in-syria-could-cost-1b-a-month-top-general-says.
6. http://www.nytimes.com/2014/09/12/world/middleeast/us-pins-hope-on-syrian-rebels-with-loyalties-all-over-the-map.html?hp&action=click&pgtype=Homepage&version=HpSum&module=first-column-region®ion=top-news&WT.nav=top-news.
7. http://www.worldaffairsjournal.org/content/un-records-show-turkey-shipped-arms-syrian-rebels.
8. http://online.wsj.com/news/articles/SB10001424052702304626304579509401865454762.
9. http://www.nytimes.com/2013/06/30/world/middleeast/sending-missiles-to-syrian-rebels-qatar-muscles-in.html?pagewanted=all.
10. http://gulfnews.com/news/gulf/saudi-arabia/saudi-arabia-seeking-pakistan-arms-for-syrian-rebels-1.1294761.
11. http://www.nytimes.com/2013/06/22/world/africa/in-a-turnabout-syria-rebels-get-libyan-weapons.html?pagewanted=all.

12. The full quote was: "if a jayvee team puts on Lakers uniforms that doesn't make them Kobe Bryant," which was told to *The New Yorker*'s David Remnick for a profile that ran January 27, 2014.
13. http://www.rand.org/pubs/monographs/MG1026.html.
14. http://freebeacon.com/issues/watch-obama-make-the-case-against-his-executive-amnesty.
15. http://www.newsweek.com/2014/09/19/exclusive-how-istanbul-became-recruiting-ground-islamic-state-269247.html.
16. http://www.ibtimes.com/va-stops-releasing-data-injured-vets-total-reaches-grim-milestone-exclusive-1449584.
17. https://news.brown.edu/articles/2011/06/warcosts.
18. http://helpingahero.org/our-heroes/sgt-jd-williams.
19. http://billingsgazette.com/news/state-and-regional/montana/article_10effbe4-0859-59a8-b08f-3a2136e22655.html.
20. https://news.brown.edu/articles/2011/06/warcosts.

Chapter 14: Peace Through Diplomacy, Trade, and Financial Solvency

1. http://www.wsj.com/articles/the-capitalist-cure-for-terrorism-1412973796.

Chapter 15: Libya: A Jihadist's Wonderland

1. http://www.state.gov/documents/organization/176699.pdf.
2. http://www.state.gov/documents/organization/176699.pdf.
3. http://oversight.house.gov/wp-content/uploads/2012/10/Statement-for-Committee-Lt.-Col.-Wood-.pdf.
4. http://oversight.house.gov/wp-content/uploads/2012/10/Statement-for-Committee-Lt.-Col.-Wood-.pdf.
5. http://abcnews.go.com/blogs/politics/2012/10/u-s-security-official-in-libya-tells-congressional-investigators-about-inappropriately-low-security-at-benghazi-post.
6. http://www.collins.senate.gov/public/_cache/files/81d5e2d9-cc8d-45af-aa8b-b937c55c7208/Flashing%20Red-HSGAC%20Special%20Report%20final.pdf.
7. http://www.cbsnews.com/news/security-dwindled-before-deadly-libyan-consulate-attack.
8. http://www.washingtonpost.com/blogs/fact-checker/post/hillary-clinton-and-the-aug-16-cable-on-benghazi-security/2013/04/09/675de8f8-a179-11e2-9c03-6952ff305f35_blog.html.
9. http://www.state.gov/documents/organization/202446.pdf (#2 under subtitle "Findings" and later implicitly stated in report's recount of events).
10. http://ajrarchive.org/article.asp?id=1579.
11. http://online.wsj.com/news/articles/SB1028593490788851400.
12. http://inquirer.philly.com/packages/somalia/dec13/default13.asp.
13. http://www.nytimes.com/1995/10/01/world/study-faults-powell-aides-on-somalia.html.
14. http://www.weeklystandard.com/articles/what-defense-secretary does_703133.html.
15. http://www.scribd.com/doc/111001074/West-Point-CTC-s-Al-Qa-ida-s-Foreign-Fighters-in-Iraq.
16. http://articles.southbendtribune.com/2012-05-06/news/31601004_1_mazar-e-sharif-northern-afghan-city.
17. http://www.lrb.co.uk/v36/n08/seymour-m-hersh/the-red-line-and-the-rat-line.
18. http://www.lrb.co.uk/v36/n08/seymour-m-hersh/the-red-line-and-the-rat-line.

Chapter 16: Tree Hugger

1. http://realestate.msn.com/article.aspx?cp-documentid=24999536.
2. http://www.forbes.com/fdc/welcome_mjx.shtml.
3. http://www.wsj.com/articles/SB10000872396390444799904578050541251702834.
4. http://www.litteritcostsyou.org/9-interesting-facts-and-statistics-about-littering.

5. http://www.environmentillinoiscenter.org/sites/environment/files/reports/IL_wasting waterways_scrn%20061814.pdf.
6. http://www.greenbiz.com/blog/2012/09/20/rubicon-cuts-corporate-costs-waste.
7. http://www.plunderingappalachia.org/theissue.htm.
8 http://www.motherearthnews.com/homesteading-and-livestock/joel-salatin-interview.aspx?PageId=1#ArticleContent.
9. http://www.logan-aluminum.com.
10. http://cnsnews.com/news/article/ali-meyer/new-epa-regs-issued-under-obama-are-38-times-long-bible.

Acknowledgments

I want to thank my family for their love and encouragement: To my wife, Kelley, for reading, rereading, and working to make the book better. I couldn't have done it without you.

To my sons William, Duncan, and Robert—I hope the example I set for you in daily life will help you as you become adults. And I hope things like taking a stand for what you believe in will stay with you, whatever path you choose in life. To my mom and dad, thanks for instilling in me a love of ideas and of writing. This is the third book I've undertaken in public life, but I have spent much of my life writing letters and drafting op-eds and speeches. Your examples and encouragement in those areas are very important to me.

A special thank you also to Doug Stafford and Brian McDonald for their great ideas and for helping to put those ideas into words to bring this book together. Doug and Brian helped me sort through the jumble of a twenty-four-hour nonstop daily legislative and political whirlwind and craft it into the narrative it became.

To my editor at Hachette, Kate Hartson, for her tireless and unflappable help and for remaining my cheerful and dedicated advocate. I'm grateful to publisher Rolf Zettersten for his support, to Patsy Jones for leading the marketing efforts, and to the entire Hachette team, especially production editor Carolyn Kurek—I appreciate your dedication to the book on such a tight schedule.

Index

Abedini, Saeed and Naghmeh, 190–91
Accountability Review Board (ARB), 250–52, 255
Adams, John, 80, 81
Adams, John Quincy, 54
Affordable Care Act. *See* Obamacare
Afghanistan, 198–99, 201, 208, 255
Agricultural Adjustment Act, 136
al-Assad, Bashar, 192–93, 209, 211, 212
Alexander, Keith, 85–86
Alexander, Lamar, 126–27
Alexandria Library, 203
Allen, Lew, 91
Allen, Shaneen, 140
Allison, John, 160, 168
al-Qaeda, 195, 212, 213, 248, 249, 254, 256
al-Shaqfeh, Mohammad Riad, 200
aluminum recycling, 273–74
Amanpour, Christiane, 209
American Board of Ophthalmology, 23–25
American Civil Liberties Union (ACLU), 120–21, 186
American Journal of Ophthalmology, 16
American Medical Association, 42
American Revolution, 80–81, 102, 177
Angelos, Weldon, 117
Animal, Vegetable, Miracle (Kingsolver), 272–73
Apple, 96, 98, 100
Arab Spring, 212, 221, 238–39
Armed Forces Security Agency (AFSA), 90
Art of War (Sun Tzu), 225
Article V conventions, 68
Asia Bibi blasphemy case, 196–97
Aspin, Les, 253
Audit the Fed bill, 71–74
Automotive Recycling Association (ARA), 274
Avicenna's *Canon of Medicine,* 203
Axelrod, David, 149

Bahney, Benjamin, 220–21
Bal Harbour, Florida, civil asset forfeiture in, 145–46
balanced budget, 60, 68, 241, 281, 284
Balko, Radley, 178, 180
Bamford, James, 89–90
Bandow, Doug, 237
Bank Secrecy Act, 99, 145
Barr, Charles, 31
Battle of Mogadishu, 252–53
Baylor University, 3, 12, 13
Bear Stearns, 74
Belhadj, Abdel, 212
Belmont, Sandra, 42
Benghazi attack of 2012, 219, 246–52, 253–57
Berea College, 56
Bessler, Joe, 274
Bibb, Richard, 20
Biden, Joe, 54
Big Stick diplomacy, 216–17
Black Hawk Down, 252–53
Blacks in Appalachia (Turner and Cabbell), 55–56
Boko Haram, 194–95
Bonhoeffer, Dietrich, 269
Booker, Cory, 119, 174
border security, 228–29
Boston Marathon bombings, 202
Boston Tea Party, 103
Bouazizi, Mohamed, 238–39
Bowers, Barbara, 43–45
Bowling Green High School, 26–27, 127
Boxer, Barbara, 165
Boys and Girls Club of D.C., 53

Brandeis, Louis, 94
Brennan, John O., 2, 6
"broken windows" theory of policing, 114–15
Brookings Institution, 129
Brown-Foreman, 157
Brown, Michael, 136, 172, 174
budget deficit, 57, 58, 59
budget proposal, 57–61, 284
Burglary, The (Medsger), 87
Bush, George H. W., 155, 194, 217, 218
Bush, George W., 70, 94, 183, 210, 228, 236
Byrne Grant Program, 184, 187

Cabbell, Edward J., 55–56
California Proposition 47, 116
Camden, New Jersey, offender-funded justice, 138
Canada, Geoffrey, 124, 132
capital gains tax, 158
car recycling, 274
Cardin, Ben, 121
Carter, Jimmy, 13, 91, 244, 245
Castle doctrine, 80–81, 180
Caswell, Russell, 143–45, 147
cataract surgery, 23, 31–36, 39–40, 44–45
Cato Institute, 60, 90, 96, 160, 175–76, 185, 237
Chafee, John H., 267
Chamberlain, Neville, 234
Chang, David, 31
Chapter 9 bankruptcies, 156
charitable tax credits, 159
charity care for the poor, 49–50
charity work, 25–26, 30–38, 45–46
charter schools, 126, 127, 131–32
Children of the Americas, 25
China, 227–28, 235, 236–37
Christian, David, 128
Christian persecution, 190–201
Christian Science Monitor, 94
Church, Frank (Church Committee), 90–91
Churchill, Winston, 263
CIA (Central Intelligence Agency), 86–87, 89, 213–14, 250, 255–56
civil asset forfeiture, 140–49
Civil Asset Forfeiture Reform Act (CAFRA) of 2000, 146–47
civil disobedience, 101, 110
civil fines (civil penalties), 135–39, 148–49
civil liberties, 172–87
civil rights, 106–7, 110–11, 172–73
Civil Rights Act of 1964, 106, 173
Civil Rights Voting Restoration Act of 2014, 122
Clapper, James, 85–86, 97, 100, 102
class sizes, 128–29
Clay, Cassius Marcellus, 55–56
Clay, Henry, 54–55
Clean Water Act, 266
Clinton, Bill, 74, 115, 182–83, 252–53
Clinton, Hillary, 56–57, 214
  Benghazi attack of 2012, 219, 246–52, 253–57
  Democratic presidential primary of 2008, 245–46
  foreign aid to Egypt, 199–200
  Libyan war and regime change, 209–11
coal ash, 269–70
coal industry, 270–71
coin collecting, 17–18
Coleman, Elisabeth A., 72
Comey, James B., 86, 100
Commerce Department, U.S., 58–59
Common Core, 131
Comprehensive Crime Control Act of 1984, 143
compromise, 54, 56–57
Congressional Baseball Game, 52–53
congressional term limits, 65–68
constitutional amendments, 66, 67–68, 70
consumer-directed health care, 38–46
Consumer Financial Protection Bureau, 72
contact lenses, 42
corneal transplant research, 16, 18
corporate income taxes, 157–58
corporate welfare, 58–59, 163, 282
Cosby, Kevin, 112
Crandall, Alan, 31, 34, 39
criminal justice reform, 108, 114–20, 172, 174–75
crony capitalism, 73–74, 76–77
Crowdpac, 285
Cruz, Ted, 7
Cuba, 235–36, 237–38
Cuccinelli, Ken, 85–86
Cunningham, Randall "Duke," 66
curriculum standards, 131

Davis, Jefferson, 53–54
DEA (Drug Enforcement Administration), 117, 144
debt, 12–13, 57, 58, 77, 218–19, 240–41, 279, 281–83
declarations of war, 88–89, 218, 221, 222–23

deficit spending, 57, 58, 59
Dein, Judith G., 147
Delayed-Notice Search Warrants, 183–84
DeMott, Kevin, 119–20
Dempsey, Martin, 212–13
deodand, 142
derivatives, 76–77
de Soto, Hernando, 239–40
Detroit
  death of Aiyana Jones, 181–82
  Economic Freedom Zones, 155–59, 164, 168
  King's speech at Cobo Hall, 167–68
  municipal bankruptcy of, 152–53, 156
  survivors/entrepreneurs, 153–54
Detroit Dirt, 153–54
Detroit Economic Club speech, 152
Dickenson, Dirk, 180–81
diplomacy, 211–12, 218, 220, 226–27, 234–35, 237
"dirtboxes," 101
disability payments, 166–67
Doherty, Glen, 250, 251
domestic surveillance. *See* NSA warrantless surveillance
Dostoyevsky, Fyodor, 205
Douglass, Frederick, 106
Dow Chemical, 265–66
Downing, John, 31
drinking water, 268
drones, 6, 8, 98, 187
Drug Policy Alliance, 115
drug sentencing reform, 114–19
due process, 6, 83, 176
Duke Blue Devils, 21–22
Duke University School of Medicine, 3, 4, 13–14, 16, 18, 21, 22, 23

Economic Freedom Zones, 155–59, 164, 168
economic liberty, 9, 152–69, 281–83
education reform, 124–32
Egypt, 199–200, 239
Eisenhower, Dwight D., 208, 217
Eisenhower Research Project, 230
Elected and Above the Law Bill, 70–71
energy independence, 165–66
environmental concerns, 9, 260–76
EPA (Environmental Protection Agency), 266–67, 275–76
equitable sharing, 143–45, 147–48
Ervin, Sam, 179–80, 181
Estrada, Juli, 34, 36
Eszterhas, Joe, 180–81
Evans, Thomas B., Jr., 267
Exodus (soccer player), 27

FAIR Act, 148, 149
farming, 271–73
Fatal Conceit, The (Hayek), 40–41
FBI (Federal Bureau of Investigation), 86–87, 93, 100–101, 119, 148
Federal Employees Health Benefits Program (FEHB), 47–48
Federal Reserve
  financial crisis of 2008, 74–77
  inflation and, 74, 109
  interest rates and, 74–75
Federal Reserve Transparency Act of 2011, 71–74
federal spending proposals, 57–61
Federalist Papers, 70, 93
Feinstein, Dianne, 86–87
felon voting restoration, 107, 108, 120–22
Ferguson, Missouri, 119, 127, 135–38, 139, 148–49, 172–73, 175–76
Ferrone, Phil and Jeanine, 21
filibuster of Brennan nomination, 2–3, 6–8, 278, 279
financial crisis of 2008, 74–77
First 48, The (TV show), 182
flash-bang grenades, 182, 186
flat tax, 156–57, 161
Folks, This Ain't Normal (Salatin), 272
Ford, Gerald, 181
Ford, Henry, 168
Ford, Robert, 209
Ford Motors, 275
foreign aid, 196, 198, 199–200, 239
Foreign Intelligence Surveillance Act (FISA), 91–93, 95–96, 98, 99, 101–2
foreign policy, 208–31, 234–35
  arming rebel soldiers, 212–15
  Paul's worldview, 217–21
  regime change, 209–12
  role of Congress, 221–25
Fourth Amendment, 81–82, 87, 88, 93, 94, 95, 96, 100, 177, 178, 183, 184, 276
Franken, Al, 64
Franklin, Benjamin, 84
free markets, 38, 76
  in health care, 38–50
free trade, 235–38
FreedomWorks, 60, 85–86
French, Markham, 112–13

Fugitive Slave Act of 1850, 55
Furlong, Roger, 31

Gaddafi, Muammar, 209–11, 254, 256
Garner, Eric, 174
Garrison, William Lloyd, 206
Gates, Bill, 128, 263
Gates, Daryl, 178, 179
Gates, Robert, 226, 282
General Motors, 163, 275
Georgia Baptist Hospital (Atlanta), 18, 134
gerrymandering, 69–70
Gerson, Michael, 50
Gillibrand, Kirsten, 224–25
Google, and NSA surveillance, 96, 98, 100
Gor, Sergio, 32
Government Accounting Office (GAO), 73
government bailouts, 75, 76–77
government contracts, 165, 166
government-fixed interest rates, 74–75
government overreach, 134–49
government regulations, 38, 73, 110, 158, 266–69, 272, 275–76
government stimulus, 154, 155, 156, 164
government subsidies, 16, 136, 273
Graham, Lindsey, 210–11
Gramm, Phil, 12–13
Grayson, Alan, 72
greed, and self-interest, 74
Greenspan, Alan, 74
Greenwald, Glenn, 97–98, 212
Guardian, The (newspaper), 97
Guatemala, medical missions in, 25, 30–38
Gulf War, 218

Hale, Edward Everett, 54
Hall, Peter, 155
Harakat Hazm, 214
Harlem Children's Zone, 132
Harvard Medical School, 39
Hayek, Friedrich, 40–41
health care
  charity care for poor, 49–50
  consumer-directed, 38–46
  new way to look at, 38–50
  Paul's plan for, 46–50, 282
  price controls and rationing of, 14–16, 40–43, 44, 46
  at VA hospitals, 14–16
health savings accounts (HSAs), 49
Heidler, David and Jeanne, 54–55
Helping a Hero, 230–31
Henriein, Robert, 132
Hernandez, Andres and Juan, 34–36
Hersh, Seymour, 255–56
Hicks, Gregory, 251
hidden employment, 77–78
Higgins, Fred, 230
Hippocratic Oath, 26, 50
Holder, Eric H., Jr., 8, 85–86, 88, 177
home and family, 27–28
Homeland Security Grant Program (HSGP), 184, 186–87
Hoover, J. Edgar, 86–87, 90
Hope Alliance, 36–37
hospital mergers, 41
housing crisis of 2008, 74–77
housing projects, 136
Howard University, 106–7, 108
Human Rights Watch, 139
Hussain, Murtaza, 212
Hussein, Saddam, 198, 209, 216
Hyde, Henry, 71

IBM 7950 Harvest, 90
Ibrahim, George and Stacey, 21
Ibrahim, Meriam Yahia, 197
immigration policy, 6, 26–27, 228–29
income inequality, 76, 109, 173, 283
income taxes, 156–58, 162
indefinite detention, 83–85, 240
individual liberty, 10, 284–85
inflation, 74, 109
insider trading, 70
Institute for Justice, 145, 147, 148
interest rates, 74–75
Internet companies, and NSA surveillance, 96, 98, 100
Iran, 190–91, 209, 211
  hostage crisis, 244–45
Iraq, 197–98, 215, 216, 219–21, 225
Iraq War, 198, 201, 209, 229, 257
IRS (Internal Revenue Service), 86, 145, 149, 181
ISIS, 197–98, 211, 213, 215, 219–21, 222, 226
Islamic extremism, 201–4, 210, 212, 227–28
Israel, 200, 211, 227

Jefferson, Thomas, 222, 231
Jefferson, William, 66
job creation, 58, 158, 161, 165–66, 281
Johnson, Helen, 174–75
Johnson, Lyndon B., 121

Johnson, Ron, 253
Johnston, Patrick B., 220–21
Jones, Andrea, 117
Jones, Bennie, 230
Jones, Laura, 230
Jones, Seth, 212
Jordan, Brian, 201–2
Josephinum Academy, 131–32
Junkyard Planet (Minter), 275
Justice Assistance Grant (JAG) Program, 184, 187
Justice Department, U.S. (DOJ), 116, 139, 143, 145, 180–81, 187
Justice Safety Valve Act of 2013, 118

Kaine, Tim, 222
Karpenko, Pete, 235
Keller, Helen, 45
Kelley, Brad, 263
Kemp, Jack, 155
Kentucky Taxpayers United, 5
Kentucky Wildcats, 21–22
Kessler, David, 42
Khan, Salman, 128
Khan Academy, 128
Khayyám, Omar, 203
Khomeini, Ruhollah, 244
Kibbe, Matt, 85–86
Kimbell, Wes, 37
King, Martin Luther, Jr., 87, 101, 110, 121, 167–68
Kingsolver, Barbara, 272–73, 276
Kirk, Mark, 2
Koch, Ed, 264
Kraska, Peter, 185
Kristof, Nicholas, 166
Krugman, Paul, 161
Kuwait, 215, 227
kwashiorkor, 38–39

Land and Water Conservation Fund, 267
LASIK surgery, 41–42
lawn mower trick, 13
Leahy, Patrick, 118
Lee, Mike, 99
Lehman Brothers, 74, 76
Letterman, David, 64
Lewis, John, 173
Liberia, 26–27
Libya
  Benghazi attack of 2012, 219, 246–52, 253–57
  Christian persecution in, 195–96, 198
  regime change, 209–11
Lincoln, Abraham, 112, 262
Lincoln Foundation, 113
Lions Club International, 25, 31, 45
Logan Aluminum, 273–74
Los Angeles riots, 178
Louisville's West End, 108, 111–13, 132
LOVEINT, 99–100
Lucas, Ken, 266
Lynch, Loretta, 147

McCain, John, 64, 84, 210–11
McConnell, Mitch, 54, 66, 224
McCullough, David, 80
McDonald, Larry, 113
McDonald, Susan, 31
Madison, James, 70, 89, 93, 94, 221, 223
Magee, Henry Goedrich, 186
mandatory minimum sentencing, 112, 114–20
Man in Full, A (Wolfe), 137
manufacturing jobs, 165
March on Washington (1963), 167–68
marijuana, 114–15, 116–17, 183–84
Marx, Groucho, 5
medical history, 12–16, 22–26
medical missions, 25, 30–38
Medicare, Paul's plan for, 46–48
Medsger, Betty, 87
Meet the Press (TV show), 69, 90–91
metadata, 97–98
Metaphone, 97–98
Michigan Urban Farming Initiative, 153
Middle East, 225–28. *See also specific countries*
  arming rebel soldiers, 212–15
  Christian persecution in, 190–201
  free trade with, 238–40
  regime change in, 209–12
Midwest Church of Christ (Louisville), 112
militarization of law enforcement, 175–87
Military Cooperation and Law Enforcement Act of 1981, 182
minimum wages, 159, 161
minority rights, 172–87
Minter, Adam, 275
Mises, Ludwig von, 76
Mogadishu, Battle of, 252–53
Mohammad, Feiz, 202
Molina, Otto Pérez, 37
Mondale, Walter, 91
Moore, Stephen, 163
Morris, Nate, 269

Morrow, James, 140–41, 147–48
Mosbacher, Rob, 12–13
Moynihan, Daniel Patrick, 130
Mr. Smith Goes to Washington (movie), 2, 7
Mullen, Mike, 218–19, 251
Munisteri, Stephen, 3
Murphy, Austin John, 66
Murray, Pashon, 154
Muslim Brotherhood, 199–200

Nation, The (magazine), 60
National Affairs, 50
National Board of Ophthalmology (NBO), 23–25
national curriculum standards, 131
national defense, 9–10, 208–31, 240–41, 282, 284. *See also* foreign policy
National Defense Authorization Act, 83–84
National Environmental Policy Act (NEPA), 158
national parks, 262
National Security Entry-Exit Registration System (NSEERS), 228
National Security Letters, 93
Nature Conservancy, 265–66
Nay, Robert, 66
neoconservativism, 234
New GOP, 8, 9, 109–10, 262, 273, 275–76
New York City Police Department, 114–15, 184
New York Times, 42, 100, 137–38, 139, 145, 161, 166, 213, 214, 215, 220, 222, 275
1984 (Orwell), 82–83
Nixon, Richard, 90, 179, 180
No Child Left Behind (NCLB), 125–26
no-knock warrants, 179–81, 185–86
Nordstrom, Eric, 248
Nortel Networks, 3, 4, 21
North Carolina Taxpayers Union (NCTU), 3–5
North Korea, 197, 227–28
NSA warrantless surveillance, 6–7, 81–103, 284
  FISA court's role, 91–93, 95–96, 98, 99, 101–2
  history of NSA, 88–91
  lawsuit against, 85–86, 88
  Patriot Act and, 92–93, 94–95
  Snowden revelations of, 96–99, 101

Obama, Barack
  criminal justice reform and, 173–74
  exploding debt under, 279
  foreign policy, 208, 209–14, 217, 218, 222–23, 226
  income inequality and, 76, 109, 173, 280
  IRS scandal, 149
  lack of relations with Congress, 223–24
  NSA spying and, 91, 97
  police militarization and, 177, 184
  prosecutions of government leakers, 102
  separation of powers, 5–6, 7, 93–94, 223–24
Obamacare, 6, 15–16, 38–39, 46, 69, 282
offender-funded justice, 135–39, 148–49
offshore oil and gas leases, 267
Olmsted, Frederick Law, 111
Olson, Walter, 175–76
1033 Program, 182–83, 184, 186
Open Doors, 197
Orbis Flying Eye Hospital, 25
Orwell, George, 82–83
Otis, James, 80–81, 102, 179–80
Ozaki, Keith, 21
Ozimek, Adam, 274

Pakistan, 196–97, 201, 204, 215
Panetta, Leon, 251
Papa, Steve, 138–39
Parker, Atiba, 117
Parks, Rosa, 110
partisanship, 9, 119
Patient Protection and Affordable Care Act (PPACA). *See* Obamacare
Patriot Act, 92–93, 94–95, 183
Paul, Duncan, 26, 37, 161–62
Paul, Kelley, 3–5, 14, 18–23, 26, 27
Paul, Lisa, 37
Paul, Mercy, 194–95
Paul, Robert, 26, 271
Paul, Ron, 3, 12, 159
  Congressional Baseball Game, 52–53
  jar of pennies story, 16–17
  kwashiorkor, 38–39
  living with, 52–53
  presidential campaign of 1988, 18
  Senate primary of 1984, 12–13
  term limits and, 65, 66
Paul, William, 22–23, 26
payroll taxes, 156, 158, 162
Pearlstein, Deborah, 223
Pelosi, Nancy, 69
personal liberty, 10, 284–85
Pettey, Jeffrey, 31, 37
Phonesavanh, Alecia, 185–86
Pickering, Thomas, 251

Plato, Samuel, 111
Poitras, Laura, 96–97
police militarization, 175–87
Polk, James, 54
pollution, 265–71
Porter, Rob, 37
poverty, 50–51, 109, 120, 122, 127, 136, 155, 168–69, 238–39, 281
Powell, Colin, 219
prayer, 205
presidential run of 2016, 278–81
Price, Charles, 269–70
Priebus, Reince, 109
PRISM (surveillance program), 96
prison sentencing reform, 108, 112, 114–20
Privacy Act of 1974, 70
Project MINARET, 90
Project SHAMROCK, 90
property rights, 265, 276
property taxes, and public school funding, 125
Puzzle Palace, The (Bamford), 89–90

Qatar, 210, 214–15, 227
Quartering Acts, 177
Quicken Loans, 153

Read the Bills Act, 68–69, 283
Reagan, Ronald, 9, 59, 155, 165, 201, 216–17, 219, 245, 268
recycling, 269–70, 273–75
Reddin, Thomas, 178
REDEEM Act, 119
redistricting, 69–70
regime change, 209–12
regulations, 38, 73, 110, 158, 266–69, 272, 275–76, 279
"regulatory capture," 73
Reid, Harry, 2, 5, 9, 71, 122, 174
religious faith, 10, 204–5
Relin, David Oliver, 39–40
repatriation tax, 165
Republican Party, 8, 9, 109–10, 262, 273, 275–76, 279
RESET Act, 118
Rhazes, 202–3
Richmond, Cedric, 53
Rise of the Warrior Cop (Balko), 178, 180
Ritter, Larkin, 230
Roark, Diane, 101–2
Robinson, James C., 41
Rogers, Hal, 66
Rolling Stone (magazine), 117, 180–81
Roosevelt, Franklin D., 88–89, 136
Roosevelt, Theodore "Teddy," 216, 261–62, 276
Rostenkowski, Dan, 65
Rouhani, Hassan, 191
Rubáiyát of Omar Khayyám, 203
Rubicon Global, 269
Ruit, Sanduk, 39–40
Rum Creek Ranch, 263
Russell, William, 20
Ryan, Paul, 60

safety net, 166–67, 283
Salatin, Joel, 271–72
Sanchez, Julian, 90, 96, 99
Sanders, Bernie, 73
Saudi Arabia, 197, 210, 214–15, 227
Schlossberg, Lisa, 153
school choice, 108, 126–28, 131–32
school vouchers, 126, 131
Schumpeter, Joseph, 43
Schwank, Bill and Judy, 25, 34–36
Schweizer, Peter, 70
Second Amendment, 140, 276
Second Suns (Relin), 39–40
self-esteem, 160, 169
Selma to Montgomery marches, 173
Senate Committee on Foreign Relations, 211, 213, 234, 247, 253
Senate Select Committee on Intelligence, 86–87
Sensenbrenner, James, 92–93
Sentencing Project, 121
sentencing reform, 108, 112, 114–20
separation of powers, 5–6, 7, 87, 93–94, 223–24
September 11 attacks, 92, 94, 183, 201–2
Shakir, Parveen, 204
Shinseki, Eric, 44
Silecchia, Frank, 201–2
Silicon Valley, and education reform, 128–29
Simmons College, 111, 112
small businesses, tax rate on, 156–57
Smith, Adam, 40
sneak and peek warrants, 183–84
Snowden, Edward, 96–99, 101
soccer, 26–27, 37
Social Security, 166–67
sole proprietorships, tax rate on, 157
Solyndra, 154
Somalia, Battle of Mogadishu, 252–53
Soviet Union (Russia), 40, 43, 235–36

Sowders, Adam, 186
sports, 26, 52–53
Sprint, 19
Stacy, William, 174–75
Stanford University, 97, 127
Stanley-Jones, Aiyana Mo'nay, 182
StellarWind, 94
Stephenson, Jerry, 112
Stevens, Chris, 246–51, 253
Stewart, Jimmy, 2
Stop Militarizing Our Law Enforcement Act, 186–87
student visas, 229
subsidies, 16, 136, 273
substitute assets, 145
Sudan, 197, 215
Sullivan, William H., 244
Sun Tzu, 225
Suspicious Activity Reporting (SAR) program, 184
sustainable farming, 271–72
Sustainable Growth Rate (SGR), 46
SWAT (Special Weapons And Tactics), 176, 178–79, 180–82, 184, 185–86
Syria, 192–94, 200, 209, 211, 212–15

Tabin, Geoffrey, 39–40
Taft, Helen Herron, 260
tax credits, 159, 164–65
Tax Foundation, 157
tax policy, 156–58, 161, 162–65, 282–83
taxpayer's scorecard, 3–5
Tea Party, 75–77, 77
Tea Party Goes to Washington, The (Paul), 64
teacher pay, 129
temporary assistance, 160, 166
term limits, 65–68
Term Limits Amendment, 67
Third Amendment, 177, 183, 184
Thoreau, Henry David, 266
Throw Them All Out (Schweizer), 70
Tillis, Thom, 4
Title I funding, 125, 126–27
Tolman, Brett, 117
Tomseth, Victor, 244
trade policy, 235–38
Traficant, James, 66
Troubled Assets Relief Program (TARP), 75–77
Truman, Harry, 60
Trump, Donald, 263–64
Tsarnaev, Tamerlan, 202
Turkey, 214, 227
Turner, Squire, 55–56
Turner, Ted, 262–63
Turner, William H., 55–56
Twenty-second Amendment, 66
Tyler, Timothy, 117–18

unemployment, 57, 77–78, 153, 281
Upstream collection, 95–96
U.S. Term Limits (group), 67
USPS surveillance program, 99

van der Lugt, Frans, 192–94
Veterans Administration (VA), 14–16, 44–45, 229
Vietnam, 235, 236
Vietnam War, 87, 159, 220
Volkswagen Rabbit, 134–35, 160
voter ID, 121
voter registration drives, 172
voting rights restoration, 107, 108, 120–22

Wag the Dog (movie), 215–16
Waiting for "Superman" (movie), 116, 124, 131
Wall Street Journal, 58, 127, 214, 263
warrantless NSA spying. *See* NSA warrantless surveillance
Wead, Doug and Myriam, 194–95
Wealth of Nations (Smith), 40
Webster, Daniel, 53
Wegmans, 269
Wehner, Peter, 50
Wells, Carol Creed "Gram," 17–18
wheat pennies, 17
Will, George, 115–16
Williams, J. D., 230–31
Wolfe, Tom, 137
Wollman Rink (New York City), 264
Wood, Andrew, 249, 254
Woods, Tyrone S., 250, 251
work ethic, 14, 159–62
worker's tax cut, 162
writs of assistance, 80–81

Young, Edward, 140
Young Conservatives of Texas (YCT), 3
Yousafzai, Malala, 204

Zakhm, Sarkis el, 192

About the Author

SENATOR RAND PAUL has represented Kentucky in the U.S. Senate since winning the seat in 2010. He has been married to his wife, Kelley, for twenty-five years, and they are the parents of three sons.